"Quiet please, performance in progress."

"A multinational client of ours needed local currency funding in China," says Shirley Ho, Corporate Banking, UBS. "Often the simplest solution is the best. But obtaining Chinese Renminbi at short notice is not always easy. We located a Chinese company in need of U.S. dollars and quickly secured local funding for our client so they could continue growing their business in China."

Union Bank of Switzerland

NEW YORK, LONDON, PARIS, FRANKFURT, ZURICH, GENEVA, SINGAPORE, HONG KONG, TOKYO

Dudley Fishburn: Member of Parliament for Kensington and on the Board of Overseers, Harvard University.

1995 will be a rare, vintage year. All the economies of the world will be growing in unison, and most will be growing rapidly. In the coming 12 months, the world will create more wealth than at any other time in its history; much of it will be made in countries which, under dictatorships or bankrupt, seemed basket cases only a decade ago. Even Russia, which has been in economic free-fall for five years, will turn. Another rarity of 1995 is that the world will be at peace. There will be threats, most certainly: look especially to North Africa for turmoil and at China's growing imperial ambitions for the hint of future troubles. But there will be no major wars to upset the balance of a rapidly improving world. And many of the brushfires in the Middle East, Northern Ireland and the Caribbean will be just smouldering embers before the year is out.

Prosperity and peace will not dispel a general mood of grumpiness. America, Britain, France and Russia will be especially sour as, on May 8th, they celebrate the 50th anniversary of their military victory in Europe. Amid the nostalgia and street dancing will be a twinge of bitterness that those drab days of power and danger have been replaced by these times of wealth, peace and impotence.

In the coming year, the first drafts of the next, post-Maastricht plan for integrating the European Union will be doing the round of Europe's chancelleries. The French elections in April and May will keep the discussion muted until then. (By chance, there are almost no other major elections in the world next year.) After them, the Franco-German alliance will reassert itself and the European argument will begin again, this time with new members chiming in. The nation-state is drawing to an uncomfortable end with the turn of the millennium. In Europe, it is the EU that is taking its place: expect joint foreign-policy statements to become a habit next year. In Africa, the nation-state has fallen to tribalism; in Asia, to the dominance of the Chinese people; in Latin America, to a pervading sameness, now that all are capitalist democracies. Everywhere spheres of economic interest are replacing flags of nationhood. The question will be most intelligently put in Canada next year: that prosperous and happy country will ask whether it should continue as a country at all.

Deregulation, competition, privatisation will be every country's cry next year. Computer-driven telecommunications will be the changing force, whether moving capital across the borders of those countries that resist the new world—or forcing change in the way we live and work. That change will reinforce the Anglo-American pattern of work. Japan's "jobs for life", Europe's huge add-on employment costs and all jobs whose salaries are met by the taxpayer will be knocked sideways. Successful societies will keep educating their citizens throughout their working lives.

The World in 1995 reflects this new world. It is circulated in 80 countries and will appear in 12 different languages. Its predictions will not all be right but they will, I hope, make an interesting and lively read.

Dudley Fishburn
Editor

WHO
WOULD GIVE YOU MORE

OPTIONS

IN EUROPE,
THE MIDDLE EAST AND AFRICA!

Whatever your reasons to travel, you'll find superior quality bedrooms and our renowned warm welcome - no matter which type of Holiday Inn hotel you choose.

Our newest hotels - Holiday Inn Express hotels, offer price-conscious business and leisure travellers top value for money. With a distinctive personality and ambience, Holiday Inn Garden Court hotels offer essential services and facilities for every travel occasion. Holiday Inn hotels provide a full range of facilities and services to meet the needs of today's business and leisure guests. Holiday Inn Resorts offer an extensive choice of great value recreational services, drawing on surrounding locations. Holiday Inn Crowne Plaza hotels, located mainly in the major business areas of cities and at international airports, offer superb rooms, top-of-the-range services and all you could possibly need during your stay.

Yet no matter which option you take, you can be sure of the same warm hospitality and friendly service, at nearly 200 hotels in Europe, the Middle East and Africa.

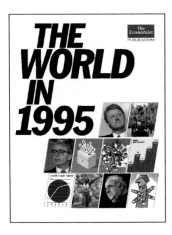

EDITOR: Dudley Fishburn

MANAGING EDITOR: Harriet Ziegler
DEPUTY EDITOR: Daniel Pearl
EDITORIAL ASSISTANT: Samantha Scott

DESIGN AND ART DIRECTION: Bailey and Kenny
DESIGN ASSISTANCE: Tim Carr
CHARTS AND MAPS: Michael Robinson
ILLUSTRATIONS: Derek Cousins
PICTURE RESEARCH: Juliet Brightmore

ADVERTISING DIRECTOR: John Dunn
PRODUCTION: Susie Canitrot
FOREIGN RIGHTS: Hutton-Williams Agency

ASSOCIATE PUBLISHER: David Gill
PUBLISHER: David Hanger

ISBN 0 85058 825 1
© 1994
The Economist Publications Ltd

The Economist Publications Ltd is the specialist publishing arm of The Economist Group. It is editorially independent of *The Economist* Newspaper.

PHOTOGRAPHIC SOURCES: Allsport USA; Associated Press; Contrasto/Katz; Colorific!; Hulton-Deutsch; The Independant; Impact Photos; Katz Pictures; Magnum Photos; Mansell Collection; The National Trust; Photonews/Katz; Rea/Katz; Rex Features; Royal Observatory Edinburgh/Science Photo Library; Saba/Katz; Select Photos; Sipa Press; Frank Spooner Pictures/Gamma; Sunday Times; Sygma.

Printed by BPC Magazines Ltd (Blackpool and Carlisle, England) Reprographics by Rapida Group Plc

THE ECONOMIST GROUP

25 St James's Street, London, SW1A 1HG
Telephone 0171-830 7000

YOU NEED
CASH MANAGEMENT AROUND THE CLOCK, AROUND THE WORLD.

YOU WANT
UP-TO-THE-MINUTE
INFORMATION,
DOWN TO THE LAST DETAIL.

YOU NEED
LOCAL MARKET ACCESS,
AND GLOBAL INTEGRATION.

YOU WANT A BANK THAT
DOES MORE THAN
MEET YOUR EXPECTATIONS.
YOU WANT A BANK THAT
EXCEEDS THEM.

Citibank combines technological innovation and professional expertise to create solutions based on your company's unique cash management needs. In 94 countries, no other bank can maximize your money's productivity like Citibank can.

CITIBANK

POLITICS '95

All eyes on France, **Jean-Marie Colombani**, editor, *Le Monde*, page 40. Why the European Union needs to change, **Leon Brittan**, *European Commission*, page 49. What the Republicans need to do to win in 1996, **William Weld**, Governor of Massachusetts, page 65. Clinton's last chance, **Stacy Mason**, editor, *Roll Call*, page 59. Will Canada fall apart? **William Thorsell**, editor, *Globe and Mail*, page 68. The end of the nation-state, **Nico Colchester**, editorial director, *Economist Intelligence Unit*, page 14. Britain will be grumpy, **Anthony King**, *Essex University*, page 25. The Middle East's chance for peace, **Roland Dallas**, editor, *Foreign Report*, page 82. Pre-election politics in India, **Swaminathan Aiyar**, *India's Economic Times*, page 79.

ECONOMICS '95

A rare year when all the world grows, **Clive Crook**, *The Economist*, page 16. America's boom enters its fifth year, **David Hale**, *Kemper Financial Services*, page 60. Britain's chances get choked off, **Anatole Kaletsky**, *The Times*, page 26. Eastern Europe starts to come right, **Delia Meth-Cohn**, *Business Central Europe*, page 55. Italy's year of learning, **Beppe Severgnini**, *La Voce*, page 42. Learning to live without inflation, **Hamish McRae**, *The Independent*, page 127. Japan adjusts, **Keith Henry**, *Massachusetts Institute of Technology*, page 112. Where the jobs will be, **Graham Mather**, president, *European Policy Forum*, page 124.

MANAGEMENT '95

How to manage your way through life, **Charles Handy**, *London Business School*, page 19. In search of corporate craziness, **Tom Peters**, management guru, page 116. Transparency, the best policy, **Arthur Levitt**, chairman, *Securities and Exchange Commission*, page 137. Managing a world bank, **Peter Middleton**, chairman, *BZW*, page 132. Unfettered competition is the best management of all, **Richard Branson**, *Virgin Group*, page 37. Pharmaceuticals in flux, **Moira Dower**, editor, *Scrip World Pharmaceutical News*, page 111. Airlines manage profit at last, **Paul Betts**, *Financial Times*, page 117.

SCIENCE '95

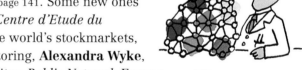

Some very old questions to be answered, **John Maddox**, editor, *Nature*, page 141. Some new ones thrown up by the human genome, **Daniel Cohen**, director, *Centre d'Etude du Polymorphisme Humain*, page 144. Neural networks police the world's stockmarkets, **Matt Ridley**, *Sunday Telegraph*, page 140. Do-it-yourself doctoring, **Alexandra Wyke**, *The Economist*, page 111. Phone for a film, **Jim Chalmers**, editor, *Public Network Europe*, page 107.

PROBLEMS '95

China's new leaders line up, **Dominic Ziegler**, *The Economist*, page 69. And the Asian dragons are spellbound, **John Burton**, *Financial Times*, page 75. A world with too many old people, **Norman Macrae**, *Sunday Times*, page 145. Why they will never get their pensions, **Jonathan Hoffman**, *CSFB*, page 133. Keeping up with America's fashions, **Andrew Sullivan**, editor, *The New Republic*, page 62. How to keep Britain's arts alive, **Martin Vander Weyer**, *The Spectator*, page 31.

MOST AIRLINES WILL FLY YOU TO AMERICA.

You know how it is with some airlines. You fly to the States on whichever flight's available.

You land at terminal one where your airline says 'adios' to you because it doesn't operate domestic routes in the U.S. Now you're on your own.

So you trip over to terminal two (via assorted bus stops) where some other airline flies a plane to where you want to go.

You find yourself one of those concourse seats that are two inches smaller than your backside and wait. And wait. And hope your kids don't grow up before your connecting flight leaves.

Have a nice day.

DELTA WILL FLY YOU TO THE UNITED STATES.

You know how it is with Delta? You fly to the States from just about anywhere you like in Europe on one of the hundreds of flights we run every week.

You land on the other side of the pond, where you're met by a Delta Redcoat who directs you to your departure gate, or our lounge if you have time.

Which you probably won't because we lay on domestic flights more often than anyone else in America.

On average a Delta or the Delta Connection plane will get you on your way within two hours of touching down. To any one of 247 cities.

So when you fly to the States with Delta you fly to the United States. Have a nice day.

▲ DELTA AIR LINES You'll love the way we fly.

"My research makes the roads
safer for millions of drivers.

And a few very special passengers."

Norbert Ehmer

ITT AUTOMOTIVE, FRANKFURT

At ITT Automotive, people like Norbert Ehmer are driven to pioneer important safety innovations like anti-lock brakes and traction control systems.

We also design and manufacture advanced products like ITT Koni® shock absorbers and ITT SWF® Auto-Electric windscreen wiper and washer systems.

ITT Automotive is one of the businesses that make up today's ITT Corporation. This, along with our investment in Alcatel Alsthom, makes us a global, U.S. $23 billion enterprise employing 100,000 people around the

world. In fact, one out of three ITT employees lives and works in Europe. And whether it's ITT Defense & Electronics, ITT Sheraton, or ITT Insurance, these companies and all of our businesses share a common goal. To improve the quality of life. Because helping people is more than just a job, it's our responsibility. Just ask Norbert Ehmer. For more information about ITT phone us on: 0903 273521. Or write to: ITT Europe, The Warren, Worthing, West Sussex BN14 9QD.

THE WORLD IN 1995

New powers, old threats

The West faces three possible adversaries—Russia, China and Islam—in the next century, suggests *Brian Beedham*. Events in 1995 will show how dangerous they might become

The first round of the contest to decide the shape of the post-communist world is now over. It would be an over-simplification to say that the West lost this first round—a loser implies a winner, and nobody has won much in these past five years—but the democracies have plainly not achieved what they could have achieved. Five years ago, as communism began to disintegrate, the West possessed the huge authority of that ideological victory, coupled with great economic power and (as the Gulf war soon showed) unrivalled military strength. If it had used these things skilfully, it could by now have been unmistakably the world's chief mover of events. Instead, because it did not think clearly enough or act boldly enough, it has seen the authority of 1990 trickle humiliatingly through its fingers in Bosnia, Somalia, Rwanda and elsewhere.

The second round of the contest is now beginning, and 1995 should give us some clues about how this one will go. The West has to recognise the main potential challenges to its future security, and put these challenges in their proper order.

The democracies' chief possible competitors for international power in the 21st century are Russia, China and some emerging new centre of power in the Muslim world. The coming year will help to show whether Russia is likely to remain a competitor of the West even if it

Brian Beedham: associate editor, *The Economist*.

does become a free-market democracy; whether China's drive towards great-power rank will continue; whether there is going to be a "clash of civilisations" between Islam and the West; and whether all these dangers could be submerged in a new form of global anarchy.

The ominous events in North Africa (see page 81), and Algeria in particular, make many people assume that the West is heading inexorably for a confrontation with an angry coalition of Muslim states. It is entirely possible that several Arab countries are about to pass into the control of Islamic revolutionaries; that this will send a great wave of refugees into Europe; and that something like a cross-Mediterranean cold war—and maybe not so cold—will break out. But the question to which 1995 should give a hesitant first answer is whether this will be a controllable quarrel or a crisis that could obsess the democracies for a generation.

The phrase "Muslim fundamentalists" covers a wide spectrum of people. Some of these people are indeed furiously anti-western and anti-democratic. Others are much more the Muslim equivalents of men like Jan Hus and John Wycliffe: the precursors of a possible Islamic Reformation which could open Muslims' eyes to a modern democratic future. It matters a great deal that the West, while standing firm against dangerous Muslim reactionaries, should show itself willing to co-operate with Muslim reformers. If the reformers win the inter-Muslim argument, a reconciliation between Islam and the

West is possible. If western mistakes help the reactionaries to win, Europe and America could find themselves entangled in a long and unnecessary fight with Islam at a time when even more serious dangers may be emerging in other parts of the world. How the West handles the unfolding Algerian events will begin to show whether it has its priorities right.

The coming year will also tell us something about Russia's future. By the end of 1995 it should be clearer whether savage cuts in government spending can stabilise the Russian economy without producing so much economic inequality—huge numbers of jobless and almost dole-less people alongside a tiny minority of arrogant new rich—that even the Russians' famous patience snaps. But, even if Russia does in the end peacefully build a free-market democracy, this does not mean that it will necessarily be an easy partner for the West. The idea that only ideology causes clashes between great powers is a fallacy. Great powers also clash when their national aims do not agree.

Russia's aims will not agree with the West's if it continues to say in 1995 that it insists on the right to deploy its troops in ex-Soviet Central Asia for purposes the West does not approve of. If these interventions were designed to help Central Asia move towards democracy (like the American intervention in Haiti), they might be acceptable. If they are done merely to reinsert Russia's influence into the region, as is almost certainly the case, they are not acceptable. It will be equally unacceptable if Russia continues to say that European countries such as Poland and the Czech Republic which pass NATO's membership test—by sharing the same democratic goals—must be excluded from NATO because Russia itself does not yet pass that test. On both these counts, 1995 should produce some telling evidence.

This will also be the year in which China is no longer mesmerised by the authority of Deng Xiaoping. It may therefore be possible to start telling whether the chief aim of Mr Deng's closing years, which was to combine a spectacularly expanding semi-free-market economy with a continuing one-party monopoly of political power, can survive. If it cannot—if a prosperous country necessarily becomes a democratic country, as the optimists believe—China will still get into arguments with the West (and with Russia) when their interests run up against each other. But if Mr Deng is right, and China becomes a great economic power while still pursuing an ideology which claims to be a rival of democracy, the arguments will be even fiercer.

The greatest revelation of 1995, however, will be whether it still makes sense to talk of "great powers" at all, or whether we are heading for a period of nuclear anarchy that will overwhelm any belief in an international order. This is the year of a conference that will decide whether the present Nuclear Non-Proliferation Treaty can be prolonged and reinforced. If it cannot, the 21st century is going to be the century of proliferation. Between a world with its present handful of nuclear powers, and a world in which every country that can lay its hands on nuclear weapons will do so for the same reason that made every medieval baron want his private castle, there is a stupendous difference.

The outcome of that conference depends above all on what happens in North Korea. If when the conference opens it is unmistakably clear that North Korea has no nuclear weapons, the anti-proliferation effort stands a chance. But if by then it seems likely that North Korea has bluffed and prevaricated its way to the possession of even a modest nuclear armoury, it will be very hard to prevent the dam bursting. Several other countries stand ready to tell themselves that, if North Korea can do it, so can they (and most of them, Europeans should uncomfortably note, are within medium-range missile range of Berlin, Paris and Rome). Others will inevitably follow, so as not to be without the protection of a mass-destruction deterrent in a world that has suddenly grown spectacularly more hazardous. So radical a change in the distribution of ultimate military power will be as dangerous for the West as for everybody else.

If, that is, "the West" still exists. The other great question of the 20th century's last years is whether the democracies that won the cold war can manage to hold together as a working alliance. So far they have done so, just. But the steady pressure of economic rivalry, and the mood of political introspection that now grips America, Europe and Japan alike, may yet break them apart. If the West does disintegrate, its victory over communism will have been one of history's briefest-ever triumphs.

The slow death of the nation-state

As sovereign parliaments are demoted, regional, not world, government
will take their place, argues *Nico Colchester*

The threat or promise of government at above the level of the nation-state will be a strong undercurrent in the politics of the rich world in 1995. The dramatic clash between the irresistible needs for such authority and the immovable forces rejecting it is ousting the old left-right divide as the bitterest source of argument within the mature democracies.

The irresistible needs flow mostly from the benevolent economic facts of modern life. Institutionally managed savings now slip across national frontiers like quicksilver, sapping the power of governments to finance themselves through inflation. Great companies now transcend nationality. Elites do the same. So governments are reduced to mere corporate managements,

Nico Colchester: editorial director of the Economist Intelligence Unit.

competing to attract savings, companies and elites to their territories. This is a game that demands a degree of international refereeing.

The chief force against the emergence of supranational government is that My Country remains the main source of most people's sense of identity, and the only cause that they are remotely ready to die for. The paradox is that although people may travel widely abroad and work for international companies and watch foreign television, they nonetheless need, at this stage of history, a sovereign state of their own to cling to as children do to a teddy bear. They are bewildered by the helplessness of elected governments to fend off influences, competition and migrants from abroad. National politicians concur: they detest seeing their hard-won powers overridden in the name of progress. They welcome, in theory, the new open-market consensus across the world. They balk, in practice, at what it means for their own roles.

Consider the GATT. The year 1994 saw those irresistible needs bring its Uruguay round to a conclusion. In 1995 the immovable obstacles will stop it from meaning much. The World Trade Organisation, son of GATT, will not be allowed to do its job. It is supposed to apply more intrusive rules to more of world trade from the start of the year. But the new GATT faces a series of hurdles, of which ratification by the big players, strictly speaking not due until July 1995, is but the first. Will the world's rich governments equip the World Trade Organisation with the manpower and authority it needs to referee trade, rather than just run trade talks? The signs so far are No; they will keep it on a shoe-string. Senator Joseph Biden seemed recently to sum up American instincts: "I don't want to compete; I just want to win."

New institutions please

Next year the Group of Seven, led towards its next summit by Canada, will examine what institutions this changing world needs 50 years on from Bretton Woods. It can scarcely fail to conclude that government-dominated exchange-rate convertibility through the IMF, and government-dominated development-finance through the World Bank, are being superseded by the free market; and that what is now needed are principles that bind national governments—on trade, on direct investment, on cross-border flows of pollution and on cross-border flows of people. As within countries, so between them: government by doing will be replaced by government by rules.

The United Nations, too, is 50 years old next October, and has asked a wise panel to report by the spring of 1995 on how it should evolve. In these post-colonial, post-cold-war times, spheres of national interest have dwindled. The strongest demand for a degree of moral authority over nation-states comes from satellite television and its coverage of selected outrages. But this CNN effect is fickle. It washes unblessed forces up the beach before they are ready, and off the beach before their job is done.

There will be logical talk of Germany and Japan as new permanent members of the Security Council in 1995, but little action, because of countries (such as Italy and India) that would thereby feel miffed. Born out of a mind-concentrating crisis, the United Nations needs another one—perhaps some drama over nuclear proliferation—to refresh it for the aftermath of the cold war. Today's hot peace will not suffice.

The stand-off between the pressures for and against world authority will find its main release in block-building—where governments wrestle with regional rather than global obligations. Encouraged by restored economic growth and by the entry of Austria and the Nordic nations, the European Union will come out of its post-Maastricht inertia in 1995. For any European who detests the idea of this Union there can be nothing more sinister than a committee preparing for another intergovernmental conference on Europe's constitution. The Dooge committee of 1985 pre-ordained the sovereignty-sapping single market. The Delors committee did the same for the push towards monetary union. Next summer a committee will start work on a constitutional conference set for 1996.

Already, influential politicians in France and Germany talk of a new and more determinedly federal core of a wider Union, built around themselves. They underestimate the reticence of their own voters. But it is almost certain that further enlargement of the European Union to embrace up to ten new members soon after 2000 will encroach one degree more on its nation-states' sovereign right of veto. The ambitious single market will become ungovernable otherwise.

Grudging globalists

This sobering prospect will re-emerge as the main political topic in Britain in the new year, given that there is no Left left there; and within the French Right, as France decides on its new president. Watch these French elections in April and May: they will be Europe's most important of the year.

The United States, too, will be increasingly swept up in its own hemisphere. Haiti and Cuba demand its political attention. Its trade pacts are proliferating like a series of hula-hoops, all spinning around Washington—NAFTA, now seen to help American employment and set to reach further into Latin America through a patchwork of linked trade pacts; APEC, stretching across the Pacific basin; the incessant arm-wrestling over trade with Japan, now an unfortunate test of President Clinton's machismo as his next election looms. Why should Washington bow to a Geneva-based Solomon, when it can become the Brussels of its own continent? The smaller ambition is more attainable than the larger ideal. Both, however, are a dagger in the heart of dying national sovereignty.

Neither this introverted United States nor this still-fractious Europe will champion a world order in 1995. They will reinforce the push towards blocks, where groups of nations draw upon cultural affinity to forge regional rules—and grudgingly keep those rules roughly compatible with global principles.

Hurrah for the nouveaux riches

Next year's mistakes in economic policy will come to you dressed in fears about
the growing prosperity of the poor world, predicts *Clive Crook*

Ever since Bill Clinton's campaign for the White House, a new view of the world economy has been guiding popular opinion and western politics. Hitherto, the rich industrial countries had thought themselves challenged mainly by each other. Many a best-seller reflected that view—Lester Thurow's "Head to Head: The Coming Economic Battle Among Japan, Europe and America" is an example of the genre. Now, the focus of rich-country neurosis is switching to what a publisher would want to call "Global Conflagration: The Coming Economic War Between North and South". (If a book with this title has not already been published, expect to see one in 1995.)

This new concern is about as specious as the earlier one—but more dangerous. Why is it false? Because it sees interaction among countries (through trade, technology and finance) as a zero-sum game: one man's gain is another man's loss. Economic history says otherwise. Faster growth in the developing countries will create as many jobs (thanks to bigger markets for western exports) as it destroys (thanks to greater import penetration in the North); the new jobs, on the whole, will be better-paid than the old; and western consumers will benefit from goods and services that are cheaper and better because of expanded economies of scale and stronger international competition.

The past decade has witnessed increasing competition among developed and developing countries—partly because much of the developing and ex-communist world is at last following the North's economic advice. If the zero-summers were right, this would already be making the North worse off. In the aggregate, however, incomes per head are still going up fast. True, particular industries and workers (especially in low-skilled manufacturing) have come under competitive pressure: the pay differentials between skilled and unskilled workers have widened, and unskilled unemployment is a growing problem. But governments can and should address these issues directly (for instance, by improving training and education). There is no need to forgo the benefits of trade.

Moreover, despite the "threat" from the third world, the big industrial countries are looking forward to another year of good growth and low inflation. In Britain and America, well-established recoveries look set to continue, with little sign yet of rising inflation. The worst of Japan's recession is over. The brisk expansion of output elsewhere in continental Europe has confounded earlier predictions of hesitant recovery or worse. Germany, especially, has bounced back vigorously. Its likely growth of more than 2% for the whole of 1994 is about four times faster than seemed likely six months

ago; next year, like the other big economies, Germany will see growth of 3%. Is Europe thriving at the third world's expense? No, on average the developing countries will expand their output by 5-6% in 1995, about the same as in each of the past few years.

If the zero-sum fears are unfounded, why are they a danger? One reason is that they aggravate the present nervousness in the world's financial markets. Another is that they inspire governments (obliged by their electorates to "do something" about competition from the third world) to do growth-reducing things.

The world's financial markets are jittery. Long-term interest rates are high. It is unclear whether this is because the markets are betting on higher inflation to come, or because stiffer competition for global capital is driving up the real (ie, inflation-adjusted) cost of finance.

The remedy for fears of higher inflation is for governments and central banks to follow a cautious monetary policy. But what if the cause of high long-term interest rates is a rise in real yields? This might be a good problem to have, because it could mean that expanding opportunities for profitable investment of capital worldwide has driven up the global rate of return (another name for real interest rates). That would be something to celebrate rather than regret—even though, at the margin, some less profitable investments will be "crowded out". But higher real yields also reflect the heavy demands for credit that overborrowed governments themselves are placing on the markets. That is why sound fiscal policy, as much as sound monetary policy, matters.

The worry is that misconceptions about third-world growth will promote bad supply-side policies in the North. These would not interrupt growth so much as permanently reduce it. One kind of mistake would be to "defend living standards" by carelessly extending regulation that purports to protect workers. Policies such as a minimum-wage and employment-protection laws are a tax on jobs; they burden the aggregate economy and fail even in their immediate aim of helping the unskilled and unlucky. (Subsidies for low-wage employment, financed out of general taxation, would be a far better way to attack poverty.) Another sort of mistake would be to raise import barriers against the third world. These might be overt (tariffs or quotas) or disguised (for example, rules obliging third-world countries to adopt rich-country standards of health and safety in the workplace). They would lower aggregate incomes in the North as surely as an outbreak of new regulation. But they would also (and deliberately) slow the rise of living standards in the world's poorest countries. It is hard to think of another policy that so blends wickedness, stupidity and self-righteousness. Watch out for it in 1995.

Clive Crook: deputy editor of *The Economist*.

Licensed Price-Fighter

N. Sutherland/NPS

Telia is licensed to deliver international calls from the UK.

Telia, the Swedish telecommunications company, is licensed to provide international telephony services in the United Kingdom. Through the new Telia Operations Centre in London, UK business customers are connected to Europe and the world at highly competitive tariffs.

Operating Sweden's national telecom network for more than 140 years, Telia delivers advanced digital network services nationwide. Our service performance is second to none, yet telephony costs are among the lowest in the world.

One of the first operators to face competition on our home turf, Telia is no stranger to international business either. In fact, we are deeply engaged in several major development projects across Europe, east and west.

Together with PTT Telecom Netherlands, Swiss Telecom PTT and, soon, Telefónica of Spain, Telia is a part-owner of Unisource – a leading European supplier of global managed network services for the international business community.

Meanwhile, the Telia Operations Centre in London delivers first rate telephony services at reduced cost for UK based companies with an eye for European opportunities.

For more than a century, Telia has been the leading telecommunications operator in Sweden, the world's most open telecommunications market. Besides the national telephony network, the company successfully operates NMT and GSM mobile networks. Outside Sweden, Telia is directly engaged in operations and development projects around Europe and beyond.

Telia AB
S-123 86 FARSTA, Sweden
Telephone:+46-8-713 10 00. Fax:+46-8-713 33 33.

Telia International UK Ltd
114A Cromwell Road, London SW7 4 ES.
Telephone: +44-71-416 03 06. Fax: +44-71-416 03 05.

Your Swedish Telecom Partner

If you can't make it to the end of the test, your company may not make it to the end of the decade.

This test poses tough questions about customer service. So does the real-world business environment. That's why Unisys is introducing an answer which can transform your customer service into a competitive advantage: CUSTOMERIZE.

When you CUSTOMERIZE, you put the customer at the heart of your world, rather than the periphery. By embedding customer service objectives within your information strategy, Unisys will help you extend the full capabilities of your enterprise to the points of customer contact – the points where business is won or lost. We'll help enhance your ability to receive information from your customers, and communicate information to them, creating an information flow which leads to bottom-line results. As customer service rises to a

cus-tom-er-ize
Align information strategy with your customer service goals – the Unisys Customerize philosophy.

higher level, so will your ability to make new customers, build your relationships with them, and generate revenue.

How to begin? The perfect starting place is our CUSTOMERIZE[SM] assessment. Experienced Unisys business consultants will team with you to evaluate the information flow between you and your customers, identify any barriers to communication, and design technology solutions tied to achievable business goals. We'll commit

---

ARE YOU CUSTOMERIZED?

1. Do you have as many customers as you want?
☐ Yes ☐ No

Can a bottom line be too healthy? Of course not. And neither can a growth-oriented company have too many customers. They're the engine that generates revenue.

2. Are your customers as loyal as you want?
☐ Yes ☐ No

It's one thing to gain customers. It's another to keep them. The strength of your business depends largely upon your ability to sustain a relationship with customers.

3. Do you generate as much business from each customer as you want?
☐ Yes ☐ No

A critical component of business growth is increased sales content. To maximize each business opportunity, you need a way to leverage your entire organisation – to bring it totally to bear at the point of customer contact.

4. Do you really know what your customers want?
☐ Yes ☐ No

Are you alert to *every* product your customers could use? *Every* service that might interest them? *Every* transaction they're prepared to make? *Every* sale they'd allow you to follow through? Are you thoroughly plugged into your market?

5. Does your entire organisation know what your customers want?
☐ Yes ☐ No

A customer orientation has limited value unless it's embedded in the very heart of an enterprise – at all levels, and at every place that directly or indirectly involves the customer.

6. Is your information strategy focused on helping you hear what customers and markets are trying to tell you?
☐ Yes ☐ No

The next best thing to reading your customers' minds is listening to what they're saying. But unless you're constantly tuned in to customers' signals, you're missing messages that could guide you to greater results for your business.

7. Can your organisation respond quickly to what customers and markets are telling you?
☐ Yes ☐ No

When the flow lines of your information system are not within your customers' reach, you won't always sense when opportunity knocks. But even if you do, getting the message is not enough. If you can't reply rapidly to market signals with information, products and services, revenue opportunities are lost.

8. Does your information strategy enable the proactive delivery of information to your customers?
☐ Yes ☐ No

Many business plans underestimate the power of information to build customer relationships. But imagine the advantage of an information technology strategy that transforms information into customer-generating, revenue-generating fuel.

9. Are the full capabilities of your organisation accessible to your customers at all your field locations?
☐ Yes ☐ No

An office. A branch. A retail site. To a customer, that's your company. One small part of the whole. Which is why you need to leverage your entire organisation by extending its capabilities to each point of customer contact.

10. Does your information strategy reflect the bottom-line importance of customer service?
☐ Yes ☐ No

Business is built on customers. Without them, there is no bottom line. Government is also built on customers, the public. And whether you're in the business of commerce or the business of government, no objective of an information strategy is more fundamental than enhanced customer service.

The Bottom Line. *If you answered No to any of these questions, you're not yet customerized. But you might well agree that this simple test suggests the enormous advantages of becoming customerized. And as the leader at customerizing business and government, Unisys will work with you to provide the answers you need.*

---

to adopting a vendor-independent approach to the assignment. And we'll apply our industry-leading expertise at ensuring that an information strategy pays off, not merely shows off.

For more information, fax Graham Roberts on (44) 895 862807. Ask for our CUSTOMERIZE[SM] assessment and discover how we can help your organisation earn high marks in an increasingly customer-driven era.

UNISYS
We make it happen.

Middle-aged school boys

A life of many careers, constantly topped up with further education, will be the way
of the future, claims *Charles Handy*

Our careers used to be something that happened to us; they were developed for us by the organisation for which we worked. In the future it will be very different. A career will be something we do for ourselves, to ourselves, with the help of an organisation, if we want it. It will depend, overwhelmingly, on education—not something learned at school or university but on skills acquired throughout life. The new fashion is to talk of "first and second careers", "a portfolio life" and "lifelong education". In 1995, for the first time, more than half of those in further education in Britain will be "mature" students, mostly part-time career builders.

The new language may not be appealing. But words are the heralds of social change, and these words herald a radical alteration in the contract between individual and organisation. Time was when a person sold his or her working life, or a good part of it, to an organisation to use for its purposes, in return for the promise of work and money for the duration, plus, for the favoured few, increasing power, influence and satisfaction in their work. It was the organisation's responsibility to equip those people whose time it had bought to do the jobs which were and might be needed. Career development and training might benefit the individual but the driving force was the need of the organisation.

That was the old, unspoken, contract. In some countries, like Japan, it will hang on into the next century. But in the West it is being blown away. The people who were the "human resources" that were needed to work the assets are now the assets themselves. This is not a semantic indulgence. It is literally and financially true. Any modern firm, particularly those which deal in services, will have a market value several times the value of its tangible assets. These extra "intangible assets" are its research and development, the value of its brands, the marketing network and, above all, the know-how of its people. As the *New York Times* said, commenting on the rise of the California software giant, Microsoft, "there is nothing there except the factory imagination of its workers." Without those workers there would be nothing at all. There lies the difference. The new assets can walk out of the door at any time. They can also be pushed out if they are not earning their increasingly expensive keep.

Skills for work

A person with an educated skill, or better, many modern skills, finds it easier to take time off for babies, to do that bit of charity work, or put together three or four part-time jobs or to avoid the rigours of retirement at a certain date. These are the people to whom the modern world belongs. Governments may not want to say it but "independents"—those outside the organisation in self-employment, part-time work or unemployed—now amount to over 40% in every country, and the proportion is growing. Politicians will soon have to find a way of articulating these people's interests: so far they have failed dismally. A "proper job" inside a corporate organisation will be a minority occupation by the end of the century. Governments may not say it but far-sighted workers sense that it is true. For them the only ultimate security is in having salable skills, constantly updated, and a portable pension to go with them.

A career then begins to live up to its original meaning of a "swift headlong course" through life, with many stages and phases, some inside, but some, quite possibly, outside any established organisation. Your life is your own and your career is increasingly yours to shape. Education and training at once become essential instruments for personal survival and advancement, no less important to a full life than health itself.

Two jobs better than one

Opportunities for learning have now become individual "rights". Firms advertise them as lures for new recruits: "Join the Army to learn a trade", says the British Army slogan. Some firms offer individual training budgets, to be spent by the individual at his or her discretion; others invest in sabbaticals, scholarships to universities or to business schools, community projects or secondments to other organisations. The best American corporations insist that their senior people sit on outside boards or work in the community. Others, again, practise what one can best call "horizontal promotion"—assignment to increasingly challenging projects and tasks across a variety of disciplines. The firm hopes, of course, to profit from this enrichment of its human assets, but the driving force, increasingly, is the demand of the individual for learning and for change.

What the ambitious executives know, however, the rest of the workforce has yet to discover. Learning, unfortunately, happens only when the learner wants it, and too many still suppose that a job is what it used to be, a guarantee of a livelihood for life. Too many think that the old contract still applies, that if the firm needs them to learn anything the firm will so arrange it. No longer. It is easier and cheaper to find someone else, someone who already has the skills. To change the perceptions of such people remains government's biggest challenge in the modern state. Jobs will always be in short supply, but customers there are in plenty, for goods and services not yet invented. If all people could learn to look for customers, not jobs, and to hunt down the skills and the know-how to get those customers, there would be work

Charles Handy: fellow of the London Business School and author of "The Empty Raincoat" (Arrow).

and wealth for all.

It would, however, be folly to wait for the demand before creating the supply. This has to be a supply-led revolution. Schools need to start it, because everyone goes to school for a time. Everyone could also be promised the chance of further education at some time in their lives. A one-chance society is not an encouraging place for late or slow developers. The trade unions could usefully reflect that a new credential will do more for their members than any strike, once those members face personal contracts wherever they work. But the new supply will happen only when we all realise that the old contract no longer holds, that our destiny is ours alone to shape, that brains not brawn make wealth today and that learning is no longer one of those childish things to be done away with as soon as we may.

Blood sports go boom!

More people will try to kill an animal next year than ever before; and more people will try to stop them, predicts *Matt Ridley*

Blood sports are about to enjoy a boom. This prediction may surprise anti-fox-hunting campaigners in Britain, who are on the brink of getting the sport banned altogether, and conservation and animal-welfare organisations whose membership is booming. But the facts are incontrovertible. More people in rich countries are spending more money and more time trying to kill deer, birds, fish and other creatures. This is not necessarily a bad thing for conservation.

All leisure activities are growing in popularity, and hunting, shooting and fishing have long ago mostly lost their peasant subsistence value and become forms of recreation for the middle-class instead. The number of Britons who fish is rising at 20% a decade; the number who shoot is rising at a similar rate, though mainly because of the growing popularity of clay-pigeon shooting. The number of pheasants reared just to be shot is past 12m and rising. The price of rights to good chalk-stream trout fishing or moorland grouse shooting has relentlessly outpaced inflation. In Italy, France and Spain, it will never have been more popular to go out to try to kill something next year.

Moreover, some conservationists are suddenly changing their tune on hunting. A generation ago, uncontrolled hunting was a prime threat to wildlife in Africa. Today most conservationists admit (though not when raising funds) that controlled hunting is the best hope for much of Africa's wildlife that lives outside national parks. In parts of Zambia, Tanzania and Zimbabwe, for instance, local people now make such handsome profits from the sale to rich westerners of licences to pursue their local buffalo, kudu and elephants that they have every incentive to preserve animals that were once merely competitors with their cattle.

Suppose a rich Texan wants to spend three weeks in Tanzania next year hunting a lion, a leopard, an elephant and a variety of antelopes: an eland, an impala, a waterbuck and a kudu. The package will cost him around $40,000 without air fares, about half of which will stay in Tanzania and much of it locally. That dwarfs the value to Tanzanians of a minibus full of tourists taking photographs of tame lions in the Serengeti. Kenya, which banned hunting for sport in the 1970s, has just changed its mind under the influence of such figures, and the western wildlife charities are not objecting. They have welcomed the new "sustainable-use" policy of the Kenya Wildlife Service.

The Russians are also taking notice. Bears in Kamchatka, salmon near Murmansk, snow sheep in Siberia, moose in Khabarovsk—all are for sale to westerners at prices to gladden the hearts of their human neighbours. Managed properly, they are a renewable resource.

Yet, despite this, blood sports are becoming steadily more politically incorrect in the West, especially among urban people. In California there are now insufficient people prepared to hunt deer. Deer numbers are increasing unchecked. In many parts of suburban America, they have become a menace. In Britain anybody who hunts foxes must be prepared to be regularly abused and occasionally attacked by protesters. Even fishermen have recently had their lines cut by campaigning frogmen.

The main complaint people have against blood sports is the infliction of cruelty. This argument is frankly unanswerable, not least because the critics of blood sports are often more concerned with the cruelty of the human than the suffering of the animal. The two are quite different. Killing an animal may be cruel, though the animal may suffer more if its population is not culled or it is allowed to die a natural, and probably less sudden, death. But neither argument seems to be winning the day. For every son of a hunter who would rather ski, there is a son of a factory worker who would like to spend his new-made fortune satisfying a primeval urge to hunt.

Both sides in this bitter debate claim to have the animals' interests at heart. But whereas the conservationists and animal lovers value the animals, they do not want to pay the price. Hunters, by contrast, are prepared to put that price on the animals' heads. If asked by an African or Russian native, "How much will you pay me to keep wildlife in this area?", the hunter usually has the more lucrative answer than the animal lover. Until economic incentives are abolished or values change, therefore, blood sports will thrive.

Matt Ridley: former science editor and American editor of *The Economist*; columnist for the *Sunday Telegraph*; author of "The Red Queen: sex and the evolution of human nature" (Viking Penguin).

THE BEST WAY TO UNDERSTAND YOUR CUSTOMERS IS TO BE one OF ours.

GET move USE IT™

The better you can manage your customer information, the better you can understand your customers. The more you know about us, the more you'll realise we're the best way for you to achieve this aim.

AT&T Global Information Solutions is the only company to properly combine computing and communications. It's a combination achieved by combining two companies.

AT&T is the world leader in communications and networking. It processes over 140 million voice, data, video and fax messages every day.

NCR has vast and relevant experience which can affect every aspect of your business. From obtaining information at the point of customer contact, to the design and manufacture of automated teller machines for banks, for which they have 68% of the UK market. And as a major player in the field of massively parallel processing, no-one else comes close in helping you turn customer information into action.

So what does this combination mean to you?

It means you have the ability to obtain vast amounts of customer information, move it to whoever you want, wherever you want.

This data can then be turned into usable information in any form you need.

It means you have a better understanding of what your customer wants. And the more you understand your customer, the more successful you'll be.

This success can only come with our help. So call the Information Centre on 071 725 8989.

Now that NCR and AT&T are one, computing and communications have come together to help you get, move and use information.

AT&T
Global Information
Solutions

Office quality print wherever you read this magazine.*

*Whenever you have your new HP DeskJet 320 with you.

Crisp, clear 600 x 300 dpi. You can switch to colour printing in seconds. All from a printer that weighs the same as two bags of sugar. So take the new HP DeskJet 320 wherever your business takes you. For more information, telephone HP on 0344 369222.

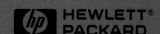 HEWLETT® PACKARD

DIARY FOR 1995

JANUARY

The World Trade Organisation takes over from GATT as the governing body of world trade.

Austria and the Nordic countries join the European Union (EU). France takes over its presidency. Jacques Santer becomes president of the European Commission.

A trade agreement signed by Colombia, Venezuela and Mexico starts to create a common market of 140m.

The annual World Economic Forum, Davos, Switzerland.

Brazil's new president, Fernando Henrique Cardoso, is inaugurated.

Bill Clinton's "state of the union" address.

Ban on political activities in Nigeria is lifted.

The German state-owned telecommunications and postal company is split into three joint stock companies.

Centenary of the National Trust, Britain's biggest charity and guardian of its heritage.

In Sweden same-sex marriages become legal.

Betting shops in Britain open on Sundays.

The London School of Economics celebrates its 100th anniversary.

FEBRUARY

Presidential election in Portugal.

Parliamentary election in Sri Lanka.

Chinese year of the pig begins.

MARCH

General elections in Finland, the Sudan, Estonia and Chad.

First conference on climate control in Berlin. The 150 signatories at Rio will attend.

World summit in Denmark on social development. Heads of governments discuss job creation, poverty and social instability.

Arab League council of foreign ministers meeting in Cairo.

Grammy awards in New York and Academy awards in Los Angeles.

March 21st is the first day of the Muslim year 1374.

APRIL

The first round of the French presidential election.

Presidential and legislative elections in Peru. President Alberto Fujimori could face a challenge from his wife.

The American artist Christo wraps up the German Bundesrat building in 100,000 square metres of heavy silver-grey fabric.

Nuclear non-proliferation conference in New York.

The IMF/World Bank spring meeting in Washington, DC.

40th Eurovision song contest in Ireland.

MAY

The second round of the French presidential election.

Presidential election in Argentina could rock the incumbent, Carlos Menem.

Greece gets a new president as Constantine Karamanlis steps down; prime minister Andreas Papandreou is the favourite.

Polls in Iraqi Kurdistan and Armenia.

Election for the Philippine senate.

50th anniversary of the end of the second world war in Europe.

The 1995 rugby world cup in South Africa.

Mike Tyson released from prison.

JUNE

EU heads of government summit in France, Spain takes over its presidency.

Foreign ministers of the NATO countries meet in the Netherlands.

OECD finance ministers in Paris.

Taiwan to abolish its tobacco and wine monopoly system.

The host city for the 2002 winter Olympics will be decided.

The Le Mans 24-hour race.

JULY

The Uruguay round of tariff reductions comes into effect.

G7 summit in Halifax, Nova Scotia. Economic issues to be debated by the seven but when political affairs are discussed Russia's presence makes it eight.

ASEAN annual meeting in Brunei.

Tour de France.

AUGUST

50th anniversary of the end of the second world war in Asia.

World championship athletics, Gothenburg, Sweden.

Edinburgh International Festival.

The traditional Palio horse race in Siena, Italy.

SEPTEMBER

Annual meeting of trade representatives from Canada, the EU, Japan and America.

The IMF annual meeting in Washington.

Legislative Council elections in Hong Kong. China says it will wipe out the results when the colony returns to Chinese rule in 1997.

German budget presented to the Bundestag.

American moratorium on nuclear weapons testing expires.

Fourth UN conference on women, in Beijing.

Jewish New Year 5756.

OCTOBER

Parliamentary elections in Portugal, Latvia and the Côte d'Ivoire..

General election in Switzerland.

Socialist international summit; who's left? Well, Tony Blair, leader of the British Labour Party, will be there.

Nobel prizes announced.

A new European law means that most goods sold in Britain will have to be in metric quantities. Notable exceptions will be beer, cider and road signs.

Inaugural Afro-Asian games, New Delhi. The games have been postponed three times.

Fifth anniversary of the unification of Germany.

The United Nations is 50 years old.

NOVEMBER

Presidential elections in Poland, Lech Walesa's swansong?

State elections in America.

General election in Belgium. A victory for Jean-Luc Dehaene will help him get over his failure to become European Commission president.

Egypt's 258-member consultative body, the Shura, is elected.

Presidential elections in Sierra Leone and Guatemala.

EU-American summit.

UNESCO annual meeting.

The 13th Commonwealth conference in Auckland.

British budget.

The cricket world cup in India, Pakistan and Sri Lanka.

DECEMBER

NATO summit.

OECD to release its economic outlook.

Japanese budget.

Deadline for a NAFTA agreement on anti-dumping and subsidy code.

Final date for withdrawal of Russian troops from Georgia.

EU heads of government summit in Madrid, Italy takes over its presidency tomorrow...

Source: Future Events News Service. To find out how to receive regular updates contact FENS: +44 81 672 3191

HOW WALES PROVIDES THE INNER STRENGTH FOR FORD.

For the technologically advanced Mondeo, Ford chose its Bridgend plant in Wales to produce the new 1.6 and 1.8 engines.

Why did Ford decide on Wales to provide the "inner strength" to power Ford's new global car?

Because Wales has an excellent quality workforce with the precise skills and track record to tackle such a prestigious and exacting task.

Wales' other big advantage is, of course, the support and invaluable assistance of the team at the Welsh Development Agency, whom Ford have

known for some years to have a "beauty with inner strength" all of its own.

To get your project motoring in Wales put the Welsh advantage to your advantage.

Write or post your business card to The International Division, Welsh Development Agency, Pearl House, Greyfriars Road, Cardiff, CF1 3XX.

Or telephone 0222 222666 or fax 0222 668279.

THE WELSH ADVANTAGE.

Should we celebrate peace or victory? Next year we will try to do both. The May Day bank holiday will be on May 8th, rather than the 1st, coinciding with the 50th anniversary of VE day. The focus will be on peace. Heads of states of all the nations involved in the war will march through the streets of London. They will be joined by a youth parade and a concert in Hyde Park. However, in August, another day has been set aside for VJ day celebrations. This time victory will be celebrated. The old boys will be on show again, reeling with nostalgia and justifiable pride.

A grumpy country

Anthony King

The British economy will grow, albeit sluggishly, in 1995, unemployment will fall, inflation will remain low, but by and large the British people will still be discontented with the present and apprehensive about the future. The celebrations to mark the 50th anniversary of the Allies' victory in the second world war will serve only to remind Britons of how far the nation's fortunes have declined.

The paradox is obvious. The British people are far better off than they were in 1945—better housed, better educated, more widely travelled. They centrally heat their homes, buy new cars and take holidays in Florida. Yet only a minority think things are going well at home.

Part of the problem is the neighbours. The British are happy to belong to the European Union, but they resent

Anthony King: professor of government at Essex University, election commentator for the BBC and regular contributor to the *Daily Telegraph*.

Brussels officials telling them which potatoes to grow or how many hours they can work. The continental Europeans, like the Japanese, are orderly; the British, for all their willingness to stand in line, are by nature anarchic.

Britons also suffer, though not all are aware of the fact, from the half-century-long decline in their country's standing abroad. To be British is no longer anything special. Britain's blue passports have turned Euro-red. Britain's highly capable foreign secretary, Douglas Hurd, will spend most of 1995 trying to make Britain's now-diminished voice heard above the international hubbub in Brussels, Moscow, Washington and New York. Britain's ever-diminishing status—in 1995 its population will drop below 1% of the world's total—is unsettling.

In some ways even more unsettling is what many Britons perceive to be the country's loss of social cohesion. The war and the welfare state combined to create

"one nation". Full employment helped too. The British looked down their noses at the Americans for their racial conflicts and violent crime. Now Britain, too, has inner-city deprivation, rising crime rates, a burgeoning drugs culture and a visible underclass. In post-war Britain there were toffs and manual workers but no real outsiders. Now 10% of the population lives on income support.

The middle classes feel the effects. They fit security alarms to their houses and lock their cars. They tell the opinion polls (sometimes truthfully) that they would pay higher taxes to relieve poverty. More immediately, many of them fear loss of their own income and status. Middle-class unemployment rises as firms "down-size" and strip out layers of middle management. Jobs for life have become jobs for now. Middle-class university graduates think themselves lucky to gain old-fashioned middle-class employment. In 1995, the housing market will remain sluggish and there will be little or no rise in middle-class equity. The middle classes remember the Thatcher boom of the 1980s. They now reckon they were conned.

Anxieties about the future will similarly prevent growing material well-being, where it exists, from translating itself into spiritual well-being. The "feel-good factor" will continue to improve as the country puts the recession further and further behind it, but doubts about security of employment, the country's moral health and the welfare state's long-term viability will remain. After the Thatcher bust, the mood is one of "Never glad, confident morning again."

Who is to blame for all this disquiet? Other nations at other times would have blamed foreigners. The British, more amiably, blame the government. The Conservative administration, in its 16th year, will continue in 1995 to be held in almost universal derision and contempt. The proportion of voters approving of the government's record is unlikely to struggle above 20%. The proportion satisfied with the prime minister's personal performance will be higher, but not much. The Tories will again lose seats in the May local elections.

Blaming the government is too easy. Ministers can hardly be held responsible for worldwide economic developments affecting all of Europe. But ministers in the present government, fractious as well as stale, seem determined to make matters worse. In 1995, they will continue to fight over the Thatcherite inheritance—whether to consolidate the gains she made or press ahead with what Mr Hurd, in one of his rare forays into domestic politics, called a Tory version of Mao's "permanent revolution".

Fortunately for the Tories, no national election is due in 1995; they do not have to face the electorate again until 1997. They are especially fortunate because the Labour Party under Tony Blair is now a serious opposition party for the first time for a generation. Labour under Michael Foot and Neil Kinnock never looked like winning. Labour under Mr Blair does, at least for now. In 1995 Labour will appear moderate while the Tories often appear extreme.

The Conservatives will be apprehensive about one feature of Mr Blair's popular appeal. A believing Christian as well as a socialist, Mr Blair is a convinced communitarian. He believes individuals are (or should be) formed by communities and that without a strong sense of community individuals seldom thrive. In a country increasingly out of sorts with itself, Mr Blair's calls for a renewal of national solidarity are bound to resonate. As luck would have it, calls for national solidarity used to be a central theme of Tory propaganda. The Tories in 1995 will find the Tory-sounding Mr Blair an unusually tricky opponent to handle.

A lost last chance

Anatole Kaletsky

Believe it or not, the best is over for Britain. The economy will decelerate in 1995, living standards will slip and 1994's sharp falls in unemployment will slow to a crawl. There will be no return to recession nor will there be any kind of inflationary explosion. But humiliatingly for John Major, who has become accustomed to bragging about Britain's place at the head of the European league of economic performance, the country will slide back to its traditional place near the bottom of the international pile.

Already Britain's interest rates are higher than in any of the core countries of the European Union. The growth rate in 1995 still looks like being the highest among the big four European economies, but is well behind that of Norway and Ireland. Germany and Italy are catching up, and even France, the perpetual laggard in Europe since the mid-1980s, will be making ground.

Among the G7 countries, Britain's position will look even less impressive. Interest rates are the second highest, after Italy, and growth will by 1996 be the second lowest after France. Only in terms of inflation will Britain continue to be among the best international performers, illustrating yet again that small differences in inflation have little effect on the ultimate objectives of economic policy such as employment, productivity and growth.

This kind of depressing news may be hard to believe as 1994 draws to a generally comfortable close, with Britain's growth rate comfortably exceeding economists' 3%-plus forecasts, and with the markets, egged on by the Bank of England, fretting about inflationary overheating. But then, two years ago, readers of *The World in 1993* may have found it hard to believe that Britain was about to become the strongest economy in Europe—not when the government was behaving as if the world had come to an end, when industrialists were preparing for another round of swingeing job cuts and financial analysts were predicting

Anatole Kaletsky: economics editor of *The Times*.

The jobs jigsaw
Britain's workers
25,225,000

Female employees
10,600,000*

Male employees
10,799,000*

Services
15,305,000**

Production
4,534,000**

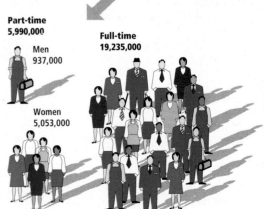

Part-time
5,990,000

Men
937,000

Women
5,053,000

Full-time
19,235,000

* Excluding the self-employed ** Excluding the self-employed; HM Forces; Government training programmes
Source: Department of Employment

that the devalued pound would produce no new exports, but only inflation.

What has gone wrong since those happy days? The answer is simple—government policy. Kenneth Clarke, the chancellor of the exchequer, quite rightly undertook a drastic tightening of fiscal policy, announcing the biggest round of tax increases in post-war history for 1994 and 1995. But he failed to counterbalance this with a corresponding monetary relaxation. The result was bound to be a slowdown in the economic recovery. This was just becoming apparent in the late summer with the weakening of consumer spending, car sales and housing, when the Bank of England bizarrely piled on the monetary pressure with a half-point increase in rates.

This masochistic mix of monetary and fiscal tightening, combined with the sharp increase in long-term interest rates caused by the worldwide collapse of bond markets and the Bank of England's misguided warnings about inflation, is sufficient to explain Britain's deteriorating prospects. With macroeconomic incompetence like this, there will be no need to look for sob stories in the alleged deficiencies of the economy's supply-side—deficiencies like low skills, inadequate training or unwillingness by industrialists to invest for the long term.

In fact, the flexibility of Britain's supply-side will continue to shine out in comparison with the rest of Europe. That is why Britain will go on attracting the lion's share of overseas investment directed at the EU market. In the long term, the Thatcherite strategy of turning Britain into an aircraft-carrier for the Japanese and American industrial assault on Europe will reap rewards. But that is a game that will take the rest of the decade to play out. In the meantime, Britain's halting efforts to catch up with the living standards and productivity levels in the rest of Europe and the G7 will suffer a painful setback.

With Germany and Italy again overtaking Britain in terms of GDP growth, Britain will slip even more decisively into seventh place among the G7 countries in terms of productivity and GDP per head. In Europe, it will drift further into the limbo area between the backward peripheral countries of the Mediterranean and the prosperous nations of the future "core" EU—northern Europe plus Italy.

The weakest components of GDP will, of course, be housing and consumer spending, as the simultaneous tightening of fiscal and monetary policy begins to bite, just as the pent-up demand left over from the recession for houses, cars and other consumer durables runs out. But

Major's economy won't take off

investment, too, will probably prove disappointing, despite the bullish projections from surveys of business opinion in 1994. Businessmen are rarely good judges of economic prospects. The fact that they were so confident in the late summer, predicting that tax increases would have no impact on demand, suggests their bullish investment plans are riding for a fall. For any competent economist could have told them that a tax increase implemented in April would not begin to become apparent in weak demand figures for at least four to six months—which is exactly what began to happen from September onwards.

Exports galore

Nevertheless, with corporate profits high, wages subdued and company balance sheets strong, there should be enough additional demand flowing in from export markets to keep large parts of Britain's manufacturing sector busy and to prevent the inevitable downgrading of investment plans turning into a slump. To that extent, the Treasury and Bank of England will prove right in their judgment that Britain can now rely on the recovery in Europe and Japan.

Exporters will find further support because the pound is more likely to fall than to rise in response to the government's new lurch towards deflation. But British-owned manufacturers will do less well than largely export-oriented foreign firms such as Honda, Toyota and IBM. Indigenous manufacturers, generally far more dependent on the domestic market, will be reluctant to increase investment in the face of subdued demand, with the

prospect of more tax increases and still-higher interest rates ahead.

One of the advantages of the aircraft-carrier export strategy was to insulate a large part of Britain's manufacturing sector from the Treasury's mismanagement of domestic demand, though not the exchange rate. But the other side of this coin is that the relative prosperity of large foreign-dominated exporters can give false signals about the prospects for the manufacturing sector as a whole.

Thus, while Britain's big exporters may continue to hit new records, domestically oriented manufacturers will struggle and the country's industrial base as a whole is more likely to shrink than expand. The service sector, too, will find the next year hard going and is unlikely to invest in new capacity as long as consumer demand remains weak and still further monetary tightening is threatened. At the same time, the stagnation of domestic demand will further increase the natural rate of unemployment, as more workers give up looking for jobs and consign themselves to the scrapheap.

As a result, Britain will become more prone to inflation in the long run. This malady will again be more threatening from 1996 onwards, when the government suddenly takes its foot off the monetary brakes and steps on the fiscal accelerator ahead of the general election. That would have been the right time for the authorities to put on the brakes against a traditional boom-bust cycle. But when did the Bank of England or the Treasury ever do the right thing at the right time?

Scotland's secret prosperity

Magnus Linklater

Scotland has every reason to celebrate 1995. Its economy will grow faster than in the previous two years, its unemployment will fall and its exports accelerate. It will outperform the rest of the United Kingdom. All the forecasts say that this pace will continue into 1996. Business confidence has crept back. Yet none of this has produced a greater fondness either for the union with England or for the Conservative government to which some of the credit, at least, is due.

The state of the governing party in this, its northern territory, has slumped to a level unprecedented since the war. Support for the Tories is down to a disastrous 12%, less than half the level the party achieved in the 1992 election. By contrast, Labour has moved up to 51%, with the Scottish Nationalist Party (SNP) reasserting its case for independence on 27%.

The search for reasons as to why things are so bad for the Conservatives goes some way to explaining the state of Scotland today, and to predicting its future course.

First, these are still dogdays on the political scene—the trough between elections when parties begin looking forward rather than back. The SNP's support in both local and European elections, in which they achieved a remarkable 30%, is seen as more of a protest vote than a genuine surge in favour of independence. Having said that, the party is building steady grass-roots support, particularly in the north-east, and has avoided the mistake of claiming too much too soon.

The Labour Party in Scotland is equally intent on consolidating its position. It has its eyes firmly on victory at the next election, which means that old splits between left and right have been cemented over, at least for the time being. Labour MPs, like their colleagues south of the border, are firmly behind the man they regard as a prime minister-in-waiting—Tony Blair. Winning the general election has become more important than making a strong Scottish statement.

That does not mean that the case for

Magnus Linklater: former editor of the *Scotsman*.

devolution—the establishment of a parliament in Edinburgh, which remains the most distinctive aspect of the party's Scottish policy—has melted away. Mr Blair has committed himself to carrying forward John Smith's plans for devolution and constitutional reform, and has made several speeches in support of them.

But the Labour Party recognises that devolution is not currently a burning issue with the electorate, and that if they

Un-Tory tribal rites

are to rekindle enthusiasm they have to sell the idea rather than take it for granted.

They may have an uphill task. Other issues are considered far more important at present. There is continuing anger, shared by many Tories, about the imposition of value-added tax on fuel. The franchising plans for Scottish water (full privatisation has been abandoned by the Scottish secretary because of the strength of public opinion) continues to arouse hostile opinion, with a recent poll in Strathclyde revealing a massive 90% majority in favour of keeping it in public ownership.

But the major argument next year will be over the reform of local government in Scotland. The government is committed to wholesale changes in the administration of Scottish affairs, including breaking up the large regional councils which have wielded such influ-

ence over the past 20 years. This will see the end of monoliths like Labour-dominated Strathclyde, representing half Scotland's population, and Lothian, which covers the capital. They have in a sense represented the opposition in Scotland for as long as a Tory government has been in power in Westminster, and their dissolution will change the political face of the country. It remains to be seen, however, whether the changes bring actual improvements in local government or simply a large and very expensive shake-up.

Scotland has had its share of industrial setbacks, which will have implications far into the future. Cutbacks in the defence industry, including the announced closure of the naval dockyards at Rosyth, have not only led to thousands of job losses but threaten the future of a whole infrastructure, particularly in Fife, which depended upon it. The building and construction sector has been through a difficult year, with little sign of light on the horizon. Metals, chemicals, man-made fibres, and textiles, once such a vital part of Scotland's industrial profile, have barely marked time.

It remains the case, however, that business confidence has returned to an astonishing extent. Order books have picked up, the electronics sector continues to perform well, and the oil industry is back on course, with a forthcoming auction of several new blocks west of the Shetlands.

It may be somewhat misleading to judge Scotland's relative prosperity from the vantage point of the new Festival Theatre, Edinburgh's long-delayed opera house, which finally opened in 1994 to great plaudits from the critics; or from the ultra-modern conference centre in the same city which opens in 1995.

It may be tempting fate to stand in Aberdeen's Union Street and conclude that Europe's oil capital is back in business; or listen to Glasgow's ebullient leader, Pat Lally, as he promises yet another resurrection for the "dear green place"; or hail a further $1 billion investment by NEC in a new microchip plant.

Given all these achievements, however, it is hard to resist the conclusion that Scotland, for all its problems, is well-placed for 1995. The sound you may hear, however, is the grinding of Tory teeth.

To the moon and back, four times a day.

The United Airlines fleet covers 2 million miles, carrying 190,000 passengers, every day of the week.

That helps to make us one of the world's biggest airlines.

But it's the fact that we go to the ends of the earth to please you that makes us the best.

Come fly the airline that's uniting the world. Come fly the friendly skies.

For reservations, see your travel agent or call United on 081 990 9900 (0800 888 555 outside London).

UNITED AIRLINES

WHEN YOU'RE TAKING RISKS YOU DON'T WANT TO TAKE CHANCES

In the midst of fierce competition when the pace quickens and the game gets tough, you need to be well equipped and fully protected.

It's the same when you're managing assets or liabilities – you're looking to minimise risk and maximise performance. That's where Credit Suisse Financial Products can help.

As an authorised bank in the UK, we specialise in developing tailor-made derivative packages for clients all over the world. We work closely together to make sure that our strategies are well adapted and well understood. And because it's all we do, we do it better.

Rated AAA by S&P, we can help you manage your financial affairs even more successfully, by devising creative but responsible ways of reducing risk or exploiting opportunities.

So, if you want to be secure and well protected, with the support of a world-class team, call us on any of the numbers below.

CREDIT SUISSE
FINANCIAL PRODUCTS
USE YOUR IMAGINATION. PROFIT FROM OURS.

Money makes the arts go round

Martin Vander Weyer

There will be festivals of Verdi at Covent Garden, of de Kooning at the Tate and of literature in Swansea, but the biggest theme in British arts in 1995, right across the country, will be a festival of raging argument about money.

That may not sound like anything

Martin Vander Weyer: associate editor, the *Spectator*.

new. But a poignant combination of circumstances—largesse from the proceeds of the new National Lottery on the one hand; on the other, extreme frugality in arts-funding on the part of a government desperate to find relatively painless ways to restrain public expenditure—will force Britain's arts administrators to focus more closely than ever on their finances.

Britain is the last country in Europe to launch a lottery—even the Albanians got there first—but the new national pastime, managed by the Camelot consortium, will immediately become one of the biggest gaming ventures in the world. According to a former heritage minister, Peter Brooke, it will be a "bonanza for good causes". Camelot has predicted that the arts, heritage and the conveniently vague Millennium Fund (three of the five categories to benefit, the others being sport and charities) will each receive £150m ($233m) in the first full year of operation.

These figures dwarf the sums currently available for spending on arts pro-

Photos of a fading friendship

Anthony King

The British used to make much of their "special relationship" with the United States. Americans were always more sceptical. In 1995, the special relationship will go the way of the dodo. America, ever more Asian, Hispanic or black, is ever less

Anglo in its history or trade.

And the relationship *was* special. Britain and America not only had a common enemy. They spoke the same language. They shared a common political philosophy. Both were committed to free trade. Mutual trust made possible the nuclear sharing that took place after 1958. To this day Britain uniquely buys nuclear-weapons technology from America. America uniquely sells such technology to Britain.

But the extraordinary post-war intimacy—punctuated only

by the allies' temporary falling-out over Suez—was not fated to last. Britain's relative economic decline led to political and military decline. The post-war "Atlantic generation" died off. To the extent that it survived, the special relationship became personal. Churchill had flattered Roosevelt. John F. Kennedy had a fellow-professional's respect for Harold Macmillan's wiles. Jimmy Carter leaned heavily on the older and more experienced James Callaghan. Margaret Thatcher clucked over Ronald Reagan—"Poor dear," she said in an unguarded moment, "there's nothing between his ears"—but she did like him. Reagan's America assisted Britain during the Falklands conflict. Thatcher's Britain, grateful, allowed Reagan's America to use British bases to launch air strikes against Libya.

In 1995, the Clinton administration will not have much use for Britain. Now that the GATT/WTO negotiations are complete, Britain's commitment to free trade is no longer as crucial as it was. Britain's limited utility to America still lies mainly in its unusual willingness—a legacy of Empire—to commit troops overseas.

For their part, the British are desperately keen for the United States to remain engaged in Europe. They fear being left alone with a resurgent Germany and a turbulent Russia. They also have a post-Imperial need to feel wanted. Once the world's captain and then America's first lieutenant, the British recoil at the thought of being reduced to the ranks.

Even the personal dimension of the relationship seems unlikely to be re-established. Bill Clinton and John Major are scarcely buddies, and the Clinton camp still resents the help that the British Conservatives rendered George

Bush's election campaign two years ago. The two men's political philosophies differ, and they are too close in age for Mr Major to attempt to play the role of solicitous uncle in the style of Macmillan or Callaghan.

Anxious to please Washington, Mr Major will nevertheless be more preoccupied in 1995 with the newly re-elected German chancellor and the soon-to-be-elected French president.

In the 1950s Harold Macmillan used to muse that Britain might in future play Athens to America's Rome. America had the power, but Britain in the end was a far more civilised country and had vastly greater experience of the wider world. In 1995 that vision is no longer tenable. America has less power than it did. Britain no longer resembles ancient Athens.

The castle will be 600 years old, the National Trust 100

jects, whether from public sources or from private bodies like the football pools-funded Foundation for Sport & the Arts. The National Heritage Memorial Fund, the state agency which will distribute the lottery's "heritage" pot, had only £8.6m to play with in 1994.

The Arts Council expects 30,000 applications for lottery money. Potential applicants are already well prepared to start carping at the bureaucratic delays involved, at the council's own operating costs (more than double those of a well-run charity, as a percentage of expenditure) and at the inevitable perceptions of bias, whether towards London rather than the provinces or towards political correctness rather than excellence.

Most importantly, commentators will be watching for substitution of lottery cash for funding which would otherwise have been provided by the Department of National Heritage. Stephen Dorrell, the arts minister, has warned that his office (once referred to as the "Ministry of Fun") is no longer "a money fountain": it is prepared to act as a catalyst, but not to be a guarantor of arts projects which would otherwise fail for lack of popular support or corporate sponsorship.

The Arts Council suffered a £3.2m budget cut (from £190m) in 1994, and seems unlikely to do better in 1995—making life extremely difficult for many grant-dependent arts bodies. Among these are English National Opera, English National Ballet, Opera North and

several of the most prominent provincial orchestras and theatres. The Royal Opera House, anxious to proceed with its redevelopment plans and perpetually trapped by the need to maintain world-class standards in competition with hugely subsidised European houses, remains first in the subsidy queue.

As they struggle for short-term survival, many of these companies and buildings will at the same time be promoting long-term plans for the Millennium, an opportunity for celebration and architectural display which the lottery will fund to the tune of some £1.6 billion. Ideas for the capital, which will be vigorously debated in 1995, include Richard Rogers's scheme to encase the South Bank arts complex in glass (possibly with a giant Ferris wheel alongside), the Tate Gallery's "Bankside" annexe, and the "Albertopolis" redevelopment of South Kensington's museum district. Outside London, the Cardiff Opera House project is a leading contender. With so much to spend, so many projects jockeying for position and the clock ticking towards 2000, there will be increasing pressure on the ten-man Millennium Commission to define its objectives and demonstrate a sense of direction, notably lacking in its deliberations so far.

In the private sector, arts promoters who over-estimated the economic recovery in 1994 will be proceeding with caution. Ticket sales remain unpredictable, and there are unlikely to be repeats of

expensive stately-home fiascos like the Bolshoi Ballet's cancelled tour to Leeds Castle and Castle Howard. But we will see more of the ubiquitous "popular classics", modestly priced concerts invariably accompanied by fireworks, for which there is now a proven mass audience. West End theatre producers will continue to play safe, with productions like "Oliver!" at the Palladium guaranteed to sell to the tourists. And there will still be plenty of other highlights for the public to choose from. The Royal Academy offers major shows of Nicolas Poussin and African art; we wait to see whether the Summer Exhibition can recover its lost verve. The Tate in February will bring 76 works of Willem de Kooning across the Atlantic.

Birthday parties

The Royal Opera House launches a six-year programme commemorating Verdi's centenary, with Domingo and Carreras in "Stiffelio". The ENO (struggling to shake off accusations of waywardness) celebrates Sir Michael Tippett's 90th birthday with "King Priam"; the London Symphony Orchestra joins in with Tippett concerts at the Barbican. The Royal National Theatre (also under the critical spotlight) mixes *avant garde* work from the Théâtre de Complicité with a more traditional diet of Pinter, Orton and Terry Hands's production of "The Merry Wives of Windsor".

Under the Arts Council's "Arts 2000" initiative, 1995 is the Year of Literature, and Swansea in South Wales is the host city for a populist festival of world literature "on every street", everything from South African novelists to sports-writing and comic-strips.

Populism and accessibility are the constant mantra of initiatives in every arts discipline, whether that means building a better visitor centre at Stonehenge, or Opera North's proposal to create mass-participation community opera on the North York Moors. The theme recurs in what may well be the happiest arts event of 1995: the centenary of the National Trust, custodian of over 200 historic houses, 8,000 paintings and 160 beautiful gardens. Events range from the reopening of Uppark, a Sussex mansion struck by fire in 1989, to a lecture by Lucinda Lambton on the history of the lavatory.

In a year characterised by endless wranglings over cash, however, perhaps the most important attribute of the National Trust to be celebrated, and imitated, is its self-reliance: 2m members, 10m annual visitors, and never a penny of government money.

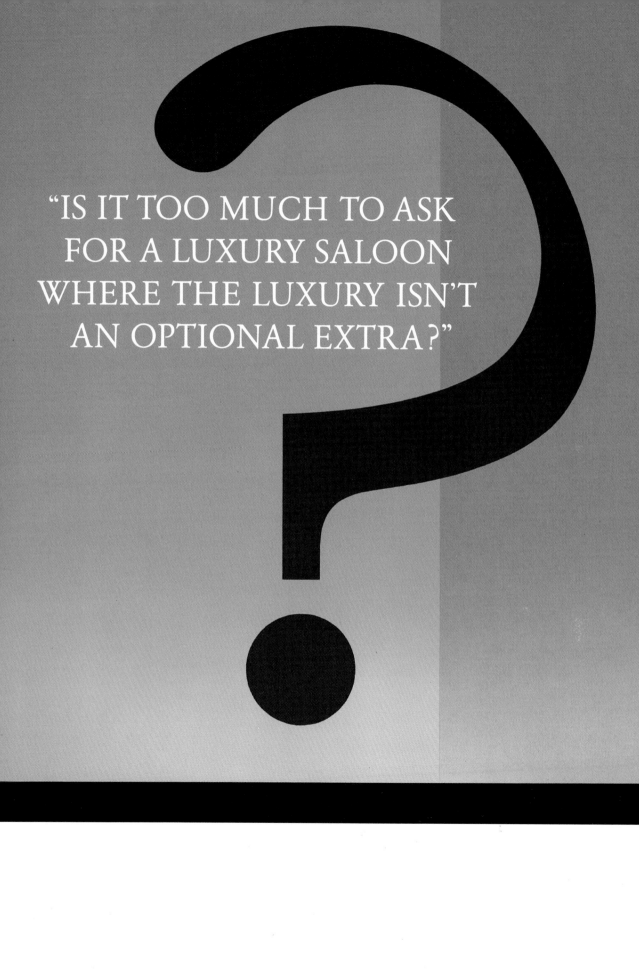

THE OMEGA ELITE FROM VAUXHALL HAS EVERYTHING, EVEN AN ELECTRIC REAR SUNSCREEN

The new Omega Elite from Vauxhall. £27,515.

Price includes low energy air conditioning system, leather seats, 6 disc auto-change CD/radio/cassette with 8 speakers and speed-sensitive volume, electrically controlled front seats with a three position memory that adjusts the rear view and door mirrors as well, an electric sunroof with nine preset positions, full size driver and passenger airbags, traction control that stops the car slipping when you accelerate, ABS that stops it slipping when you brake, twelve on-board computers, multi-function display unit (including radio station display, outside temperature, fuel consumption, average speed,

range, and stopwatch), cruise control, 3.0 litre V6 24 valve engine, 4 speed automatic gearbox, infra-red remote controlled three-way immobiliser and alarm with 69 billion possible combinations, speed sensitive power steering, 12 month road tax, delivery, number plates and electric rear sunscreen as standard.

If you can think of any extras, they're extra.

For more information on the Omega Elite, talk to your local Vauxhall dealer or telephone the Omega Information Service on 0800 040 041.

THE OMEGA FROM VAUXHALL

The engines are quietly humming at 37,000 ft. above the Indian Ocean. And you wish you could sleep. Then you remember who you are flying with.

 **Lufthansa**

Zzzzzz.

A love affair with monopoly

The World in 1995 asked **Richard Branson**, chairman of Virgin Group, to put the case for a more competitive Britain

Both government and business in Britain have a love affair with monopolies and regulation. The great privatisations of the 1980s are now behind us. In only 14 years entire sections of British industry have moved from being state-controlled monopolies to being public limited companies.

The problem is that little has been done to increase the competitiveness of British industry. More efficient these privatised companies may be; more competitive they are not. Most Britons now believe that the privatisation programme was not about competition at all, but had more to do with reducing the burden of taxation, the public-sector borrowing requirement and the state's involvement in industry.

After privatisation the thorny problem of managing these capitalist monopolies rested firmly with a new group of regulators: Ofgas, Oftel, Ofwat. (Sadly, from Virgin's point of view, no Ofair.) These regulators were not given clear guidelines. Were they supposed to act in the interest of the consumer, and to call the shots on pricing? Or were they supposed to introduce competition into these industries with the same long-term effect as price controls would have in the short term?

The fact is that nobody knew the best way forward. The uncompetitive morass in which the regulators found themselves, in their respective industries, dragged them into conflict with both industry and the consumer.

Almost all of them have fallen for the temptation of setting complex pricing formulae to assuage the consumer. Very few of these pricing mechanisms have been effective. None of them encourages competition, which is the best way of keeping prices down.

Telecommunications has been the exception. During the 1980s there were two major privatisations, British Telecom (BT) and Cable & Wireless. Here was an industry that was not simply a monopoly moving from the public to the private sector. Two newly quoted telecommunications companies were going to battle it out for the hearts, pockets and ears of the nation. So the regulator was able to establish some competitive benchmarks.

Oftel has not fallen into the trap of providing any form of protectionism for Mercury or BT, though there have been considerable arguments about Oftel's role in managing access to the bottle-neck points in BT's communications network to other players. So Mercury and BT have started to compete aggressively with each other over price, as they see Hutchison, AT&T, MCI and others moving over the horizon towards them.

The benefits have been felt immediately. Not so in other industries. In 1987 BA was hailed as one of the

"Britain needs a decent set of antitrust laws modelled on those in America."

most successful of all the Thatcher privatisations. In theory there was no need for the government to set up a structure to regulate this privatised state monopoly because they already had a pro-competitive aviation policy, the CAA and the Department of Transport. What is more, BA said that it faced "vicious competition" all over the world from carriers much larger than itself.

From fortress Heathrow, it would stand and proudly defend Britain's airline interests, fighting on the beaches, the hills and in the corridors of Whitehall. That was the myth; but it failed to mention the power that BA had at Heathrow—the world's busiest international airport at which iniquitous grandfather rights secured BA almost 40% of all landing slots in perpetuity.

With the enormous strength that this provided BA, it went on the acquisition trail, first acquiring British Caledonian in 1988, then stakes in a variety of airlines including Brymon Airways, GB Air, TAT, Dan Air and most recently USAir and Qantas. The stated aim in privatising BA was to increase competition in the airline industry. In

the years since 1986, BA's dominance of British aviation has increased; it now controls over 90% of Britain's scheduled airline industry.

In these circumstances regulators are caught between the devil and the deep blue sea. On the one hand they can set prices in the consumer's interests and control the monopolists, on the other hand they can unfetter the monopoly and allow it to destroy vibrant and healthy independent businesses.

The solution is for regulation to always be pro-competition. The regulator should operate on the premise that eventually it wants to put itself out of business—having no real place in the market. It would be there only to achieve circumstances from which it can gracefully withdraw. In the case of the airline industry, our pro-competitive Ofair would, if it existed, break up all the barriers to competition that still remain in the airline industry. Target number one must be the rules governing slot allocation at Heathrow, which are designed to preserve old-established oligopolies and shut out troublesome new entrants that would satisfy passengers the best. Safety issues would be left to the CAA.

The whole management attitude to competition needs to change in Britain, if we are truly to regain our competitive edge over the rest of the world. The British consumer is at the mercy of a very small number of providers each with high market shares in their particular sectors. The laziness of these oligopolists—each charging their brand tax to the consumer—has contributed considerably to the relatively high cost of living in this country since the 1970s.

Equally it is certain that continued exposure to competition and challenge sharpens management's ability to satisfy customers and run efficient enterprises, as well as adding to the interest and satisfaction of the task.

There can be no doubt left about the immense advantages of the market economy. The leaders of all three British political parties now support it. Now is the time to update the British system to get rid of monopolies and oligopolies and make the market really work. Britain needs a decent set of enforceable antitrust laws modelled on those in America. With luck, politicians will start to debate how we are to meet this need in 1995.

WALLONIA, EUROPE'S MEETING POINT.

Where the roads from Brussels (38 miles), Berlin (375 miles), Paris (190 miles) and London (250 miles) meet, qualification and productivity have also joined forces (according to the U.S. Labor Force Report) to attract the world's largest companies. The technology is there. We are ready to meet your industrial challenges.

PROBABLY THE EASIEST WAY TO INVEST IN EUROPE: WALLONIA, BELGIUM'S FRENCH-SPEAKING REGION

Robert COLLIGNON.
President of The Walloon Government.

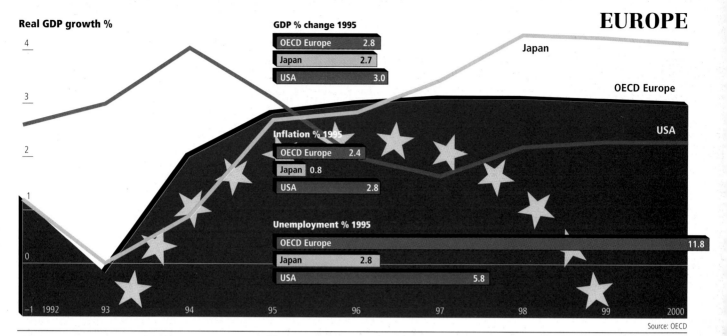

Real GDP growth %

GDP % change 1995
OECD Europe 2.8
Japan 2.7
USA 3.0

Inflation % 1995
OECD Europe 2.4
Japan 0.8
USA 2.8

Unemployment % 1995
OECD Europe 11.8
Japan 2.8
USA 5.8

Japan
OECD Europe
USA

Source: OECD

Europe rests between courses

Bob Taylor

1995 will be the year that the European Union takes a much needed look at itself. Expect no grand gestures. EU newcomers will be feeling their way as full members. The commission will be looking ahead to the next wave of entrants from Eastern Europe. Member states will be putting round the first drafts of what the Union might look like after 1996. Those ambitious for grander stuff will first have to wait to see how the Franco-German axis shakes down after the French election. The new European Commission will also be settling down under the unconvincing presidency of Jacques Santer.

France, which holds the six-month rotating presidency of the EU from January until June, will keep anything vaguely ambitious or in the slightest controversial off the Union agenda until its presidential election is safely over in May. One exception will be the EU's future relations with its East European neighbours.

Although the two countries do not entirely see eye-to-eye on this issue, the French joined the outgoing German presidency to ask the commission to prepare proposals for the spring of 1995 on how the EU can bring the most advanced East European countries into the Union as quickly as possible. Economically, the first newcomers—Poland, Hungary, the Czech Republic and Slovakia— will be unlikely to qualify to join until after 2000.

Bob Taylor: writes for *The Economist* from Brussels.

The search is on for some new status, short of full membership, that will satisfy impatient East Europeans while reassuring cautious EU countries. Spain, which is in the president's chair for the second half of the year, is among the least keen on further enlargement. It will no doubt try to prevent the EU from moving too fast.

The other big debate of 1995 will be on the future shape of the existing European Union. This has to be decided before any more new countries can be admitted. This debate, the subject of the coming 1996 intergovernmental conference to review and update the Maastricht treaty on European Union, was well and truly launched last autumn. It will preoccupy Europe's chancelleries throughout the coming year and will manage to fill many column-metres in the European press.

The skirmishes taking place in 1995 will foreshadow the bruising constitutional battle to follow. All governments agree the rules need changing; a Union heading for 20 members cannot be run by consensus politics. The British and Danish opt-outs over monetary union and (in Britain's case) over social policy in the Maastricht treaty already reveal the limits of this process. But there is no agreement on the way forward.

As the debate progresses through 1995, the divide will deepen between those keen to push further ahead with integration—the majority—and a small

minority led by Britain who are happy with the Union's free market achievements but unwilling to pool monetary or political sovereignty. During the year, rows will break out within the majority camp. Not all are pleased at suggestions from France and Germany for a core group of countries to move ahead by themselves, leaving the others to catch up later if they can—or if they wish. Events will also show that besides agreement on monetary union as a priority goal, Germany and France have not yet agreed on the rest of the post-Maastricht agenda.

In contrast to the Franco-German alternative of a multi-speed Europe, Britain would prefer a Europe *à la carte* where each country would be free to pick and choose the areas of European policy in which it wants to participate, providing it signed up to the principles of the single market.

On one big issue for the 1996 conference, the Germans, French and British are on the same side. This is that the power of the European Commission should be reduced and that of individual governments increased. Although such a development is opposed by smaller members who see the commission as a bulwark against big-country hegemony, it is to some degree already happening. As it steps down at the end of 1994, the Delors commission has long since shed the last remnant of its pre-Maastricht boldness. Jacques Delors's final strategic initiative, a white paper on growth, competitiveness and employment, will get a formal burial in 1995. The coming months will show that the cyclical economic recovery now gathering pace will do more to help jobless Europeans back to work and to improve the competitive position of European firms than any number of white papers ever could.

With luck, a few sections of the white paper may survive 1995. These will concern a series of projects to give Europe an integrated transport and communications infrastructure through the creation of trans-European networks. But infrastructure deregulation, particularly in the telecoms sector, is advancing rapidly in most countries. Without early action, the EU may end up doing little more than rubber-stamping what has already been done.

Brussels grandees

Do not look to Mr Delors's successor, the affable but timorous Mr Santer, to reverse the commission's fortunes. He has neither the vision nor the energy for such a task. He will be hard put just to assert his leadership over his colleagues on the commission. Mr Santer has inherited several prominent members of the Delors team who have signed up for another five years. They include Leon Brittan, Martin Bangemann of Germany and Karel Van Miert of Belgium, a trio of Brussels grandees with their own views and their own agendas who owe him no personal loyalty. Add to them strongminded newcomers like ex-French prime minister Edith Cresson (who once dismissed all Japanese as workaholics and all Englishmen as homosexuals) and former British Labour leader Neil Kinnock, and his task looks daunting.

One early test of the calibre of the new commission will be its actions (if any) to stop governments backsliding on their commitments under the European single market. Unchecked, the flouting of already-adopted frontier-flattening legislation risks undoing the Union's most significant achievement to date. Business leaders complain to the commission virtually every day about how governments twist the rules to block the free flow of goods and services across EU frontiers. It is to the discredit of Mr Delors and his colleagues that they did not act decisively to stamp out such law-breaking at an earlier stage.

If he has the stomach for it, this is a fight Mr Santer could actually win. He can certainly count on support from the European Parliament, which will be keen to find causes to uphold with the new powers it acquired under Maastricht.

Two men in search of one job

France votes, little changes

Jean-Marie Colombani

Three men will throw their hats in the ring to be France's new president in 1995. They are Edouard Balladur, Jacques Chirac and Jacques Delors: the current prime minister, the former prime minister and the former president of the European Commission. One will take over from the longest-serving ruler in modern French history since Napoleon III. For the French, 1995 will indeed be the year of succession to François Mitterrand, the year that closes, with this "socialist" president, the post-war era.

Socialist label, capitalist practice: conservative label, social welfare. Henceforth, left and right in France will not be distinguished by their economic policies. In future, both will follow common rules. And this is not the least of President Mitterrand's legacy. Europe's strong ambitions and France's strong currency can be added to it. Europe was the "grand plan" of two seven-year terms of office, achieved by this larger-than-life character, a man who by turns exasperated and charmed, and, ultimately, fascinated his countrymen.

With such an outlook, Mr Mitterrand became part of a French continuum bent on creating a European identity around a hard Franco-German core, one that has found its ultimate success in the Maastricht treaty and the promise of a monetary union. As for the currency, that is to say the "franc fort" policy, that is another example of the coherent, rigorous and unyielding attitude that has allowed France to turn her back on her traditional method of economic management, namely inflation.

If he looks back, Mr Mitterrand can enjoy the satisfaction of knowing that, regardless of which governments succeed him, France will continue to move forward along the path he—and his predecessor Valéry Giscard d'Éstaing—have trod. France is better equipped today in terms of foreign competition. The country has preserved and developed its national industries and has encouraged intra-European co-operation wherever possible.

This, however, is not all there is to it. It would be astonishing if a man accustomed to nothing but compliments delved more deeply into the balance sheet. At the very most he will concede that he was not able to reduce inequality as much as he would have liked. This is not the least of the paradoxes: this socialist president oversaw a neo-liberal administration of the economy. This translated into a record level of unemployment (12.5% of the working population) which shook the whole of society.

Pockets of deprivation have grown at

Jean-Marie Colombani: editor of *Le Monde*.

the same time and poverty, hitherto controlled by a system of social welfare that was the most "protective" in Europe, has increased in scope. Above all, a rift has deepened between the ruling classes and the country as a whole. This found its clearest expression in a revolt of the magistrates who attempted to set up a "clean hands" operation, Italian style. It is also the case that the very foundation of the republic—an educational system that has functioned like a great up-escalator for society, guaranteeing a perpetual hope for the future—has found itself under attack. The process itself has seized up.

As Mr Mitterrand ponders on the economic failures of his presidency, Mr Balladur can feel quietly pleased with the recent upturn—for which he will take the credit. The economy is growing by over 3% a year in real terms and the Balladur administration is also increasing government expenditure, concentrating on housing and incentives for car purchasers. A further cheer comes from the low level of inflation—despite spectacular growth in consumer demand—which will remain well below 2% next year.

Mr Balladur also has in his favour the fact that he is not a man who has made promises and thus has none he is obliged to keep. Another major boost to Mr Balladur's electoral hopes is the prospect of a real decline in unemployment, now a credible prospect. The prime minister is engaged in reducing unemployment by a million people at a rate of 150,000 a year, so this policy will take (wait for it) seven years.

All these factors will undermine Mr Chirac's campaign, armed only with a partisan legitimacy, that of his own party, the RPR. The other component of the majority, the liberals of the UDF, have already rallied behind Mr Balladur.

Mr Balladur's main difficulty will be the wrath of an electorate fed up with the bitter wranglings of recent political rivalries. The French right, as always, divides between support for the prime minister and Mr Chirac. Even within the present cabinet discussions are heated. Alain Juppé, the foreign minister who supports Mr Chirac, has made public insults against his cabinet colleague, Charles Pasqua, the interior minister.

Mr Balladur will also face the charge next year that his administration is sleazy and corrupt. Prominent resignations—Alain Arignon, the communications minister, and Gérard Longuet, the industry minister—have given credence to this accusation.

The only card that the left holds is Mr Delors, returning from Brussels. But Mr Delors will need to rely heavily on the right tearing itself apart. So long as the rivalry between the right's contenders quietens, 1995 will be the first time in 21 years that the presidency is within their grasp.

Kohl's ambitions

Jonathan Carr

Helmut Kohl enters 1995 with high ambitions for his fourth and final term as German chancellor. Whether he can realise them despite his crumbling domestic power base is quite another matter.

Three main developments have reduced Mr Kohl's political clout. First, his centre-right coalition only just scraped back to power in the October federal election, its Bundestag (lower house) majority cut from 134 seats to ten. Mr Kohl's Christian Democratic Union and its Bavarian ally, the Christian Social Union, mustered only 41.5% of the vote between them, their worst result since 1949.

But it is the dismal state of the Liberal Free Democrats, junior partner in the alliance, which gives Mr Kohl his biggest headache. With colourless leaders and fuzzy policies, the Liberals have been

Jonathan Carr: author and freelance journalist living in Germany.

booted out of one regional parliament after another. They have seen their share of the national vote slump from 11% to 6.9%. They know they now have to give themselves a much sharper profile vis à vis the Union parties or face obliteration at the next election. That presages a lot more friction in the coalition and a constant threat to its slim majority.

Second, thanks to a string of regional election wins the Social Democrats who are in opposition in the Bundestag now dominate the Bundesrat, the upper house where the *Länder* (federal states) are represented. The Bundesrat has the power to veto legislation, including tax, directly affecting *Länder* interests and can delay much else.

Hence the Social Democrats have a powerful, direct influence on law-making which forces Mr Kohl to work with them, like it or not. This informal "grand coalition" could be the forerunner to a formal

Belgium 1995

Jean-Luc Dehaene, despite being vetoed as the next president of the European Commission, will still enjoy high office in Brussels, staying on as prime minister after elections in November 1995. Despite a plethora of political difficulties, including a series of financial scandals, the current coalition is expected to form the next government.

This is hardly a daring political projection because there is no real alternative. Belgium is a tapestry of linguistic and political divides, and the federal government will be a combination of the francophone and Flemish centrist parties—the Christian Democrats and the Socialists.

After the general election, legislation providing for a truly federal state will be implemented. The federal parliament, at the centre, will be a modified version of the present national parliament. The Chamber of Representatives, the main law-making body, will be slimmed down from 212 to 150 members, while the veto powers of the Senate will be removed.

The powers of the federal parliament and federal government will cover foreign affairs, defence, justice, finance, the budget and social security. All other powers will be devolved to the regions and communities.

The huge public debt, projected to be equivalent to 145% of GDP in 1995, remains the biggest economic headache. Debt-interest payments are commanding an increasing share of budget expenditures (about 16%). The new federal constitution, which limits the control of the federal government over the fiscal powers of the country's communities and regions, will make spending more difficult to control.

Real GDP will benefit from stronger investment growth in 1995. A two-year real-wage freeze will commence in 1995, which will have a depressing impact on private consumption. Exports will be the fastest-growing segment of the economy, although import growth will also be buoyant.

KEY INDICATORS

	1993	1994	1995
GDP growth (%)	-1.3	1.5	2.1
Inflation (%)	2.7	2.8	2.8
3-month money market rate (%)	8.2	5.7	5.2
Exchange rate			
BFr per DM	21.0	21.0	21.0
BFr per $	34.7	34.9	35.1
Current account ($bn)	10.0	10.3	10.0
EIU COUNTRY ANALYSIS AND FORECASTING			

Europe's survivor

one in the Bundestag even before the next election if, as many believe, the centre-right alliance fails to hold for the full four-year term.

Standing down

Third, Mr Kohl has surprisingly weakened his own position (and his party's) by announcing he will not stand again in 1998. The hunt is already on behind the scenes for a successor. At the latest, by mid-term Mr Kohl will be a lame duck chancellor—meaning he has a maximum of two years in a tougher political environment to realise his remaining ambitions. What are they?

Easily topping his foreign-policy agenda is the need to give another decisive push to European integration. Mr Kohl is already sure of a place in the history books for leading the Germans to unity in 1990. He also wants to be remembered as the man who tied his country irrevocably into a united Europe.

Mr Kohl will plan a campaign in tandem with France to try to ensure closer integration between those countries able and willing to go ahead. This will be despite further extension of the European Union (EU) to the east, which Mr Kohl also backs. That implies a multi-speed Europe with a "core group" of states in the fast track.

The integration drive is due to start in earnest after the French presidential election in May. Mr Kohl hopes that France will elect Jacques Delors, departing president of the EU, into the Elysée. The two have long been chums, especially since 1989 when Mr Delors was quicker than most European leaders to endorse Mr Kohl's dash for German unity.

Mr Kohl believes that pressure from Germany and a Delors-led France would influence the other EU countries at the Maastricht follow-up conference in 1996. He has plans for that conference to endorse economic and monetary union, including a single currency. He also wants an agreement to strengthen Europe's institutions, not least the Strasbourg parliament. Mr Kohl will press for greater European co-operation in foreign and security policy, arguing that Germany is now ready, after four convulsive years of unity, to play a weightier role in both.

None of this will be easy for Mr Kohl to push through at home. Although all main parties support a united Europe in principle, most Germans hate the idea of losing the D-mark. The *Länder* (not least Mr Kohl's Bavarian allies) will fight to avoid a further drift of power to Brussels. Nor, despite the rhetoric, is there much enthusiasm in Germany to take on bigger tasks abroad.

In principle a constitutional court decision in 1994 opened the door to far greater use of German forces abroad, not just for UN peacekeeping. In practice, such use will be subject to approval in each case by parliament—and in the current parliament the strengthened left wing plus the jittery Free Democrats will act as a brake.

Is Germany now better able to use its financial muscle to solve international problems—for instance in Eastern Europe, Russia and the Ukraine, which are so vital to its security? It may seem to be, thanks to its improving economy. Germany is heading for another year of more than 2% real GNP growth in 1995, inflation will drop again and the current deficit is on its way down. Parts of eastern Germany are in the midst of a boom greater than anywhere else in Europe, thanks not least to around DM500 billion ($330 billion) worth of investment pumped in since unity.

The bad news is that unemployment remains high at close to 4m and new public-sector debt still looks set to total over 6% of GNP in 1995. Mr Kohl knows that the current economic upswing alone will not solve either problem.

Germany needs another hefty dose of deregulation and privatisation to stay competitive. It also has to slash subsidies and do more to slim its still bloated social-security system to cut its debt. A tall order for a chancellor short on time and with Social Democrats breathing down his neck.

Climbing Italy's learning curve

Beppe Severgnini

1995, for Italy, is the last boat. If the country misses it, no political upheaval or major economic slump will follow, no social unrest, no withdrawal from the European Union. Italy will merely coast unspectacularly towards the end of the century.

It will be a difficult year for the country. More so than 1994. Then, the size and number of the scandals uncovered by the *Mani Pulite* (Clean Hands) investigation—more than 7,000 people were charged, including 438 members of parliament—convinced Italians that a break with the past was necessary. A sense of urgency, and the feeling that the country had to prove something—to itself and to the world—inspired the nation and created hope.

Pulling down the old system, though, has proved to be easier than building a new one. In 1995, Silvio Berlusconi, the prime minister, will need to stop being a charismatic figure and start being a competent politician. The pressure to do so will come from his own allies (the populist Northern League and the right-wing National Alliance), who won't want to waste an historic opportunity: post-war Italy, unlike the United States, France or Britain, never had a conservative government.

The coalition, in other words, is likely to stay together. Gianfranco Fini, leader of National Alliance, is aware that without Mr Berlusconi's appeal (and television stations), his party would still be floating in a post-fascist limbo. Umberto Bossi has spent 1994 playing the part of the opposition from inside the government. However, he knows that in a general election his Northern League would be routed, as lower-middle-class voters in the north switched their allegiance to Mr Berlusconi's *Forza Italia*. Expect Mr Bossi to thump his chest from time to time, and nag Mr Berlusconi with pro-

Beppe Severgnini: American editor and columnist for *la Voce*, an Italian daily newspaper; author of "Inglesi" (Rizzoli; Hodder & Stoughton).

First flight of the day-U.A.

The first to JFK, every day, from London Heathrow.

Come fly the airline that's uniting the world. Come fly the friendly skies.

For reservations, see your travel agent or call United on 081 990 9900 (0800 888 555 outside London).

 **UNITED AIRLINES**

DUBAI DUTY FREE'S
finest surprise

BMW 850 Ci Arktis Grey And Porsche 911 Carrera Cabriolet Green Metallic

YOUR OPPORTUNITY TO WIN LUXURY CARS AT THE WORLD'S FINEST DUTY FREE

Dubai Duty Free, pioneers of the luxury car promotion, now in its fifth year, offer you a choice. Tickets may be purchased for one or both cars.

For each car, tickets are priced at Dhs 500/ US 139 and limited to 1000 bonafide travellers either departing or transiting through Dubai International Airport.

The draw date and winning numbers will be published, and each participant will be advised.

The cars will be shipped to the winners' address free of charge.

The finest collection at the world's most elegant duty free.

For The World's Finest. — **Fly-Buy-Dubai** — السوق الحرة دبي DUBAI DUTY FREE

For further information please call Dubai (9714) 206-2433 or Fax (9714) 244 455

CONGRATULATIONS!
DUBAI DUTY FREE'S FINEST SURPRISE WINNERS

<u>342nd Winner</u>
TERESA ANNE PAGE
(Series # 342 - Ticket # 0292)
British, from Al Ain, UAE, winner of
a white Mercedes Benz S 500L

<u>343rd Winner</u>
GANSHYAM DEVIRAM CHHATRY
(Series # 343 - Ticket # 0873)
Indian, from Sharjah, UAE, winner of
a red BMW 850 Ci

<u>344th Winner</u>
JORG HEYER
(Series # 344 - Ticket # 0132)
German, from Dubai, UAE, winner of
a red Porsche 911 Carrera

<u>345th Winner</u>
GHOLAM HOSSEIN M.H. JAVAHERI
(Series # 345- Ticket # 0258)
Iranian, from Dubai, UAE, winner of
a calypso red BMW 850 Ci

Berlusconi has some thinking to do

posals of antitrust legislation. But that will be it.

1995 will be a year of learning for Italy. The government parties will gradually improve their performance, and will tame some of the arrogance shown in 1994. Mr Berlusconi himself will learn to accept media criticism (some, at least), and will be forced to distance himself from his own enormous business empire (expect some Byzantine, amazingly complicated Italian version of a "blind trust"). Northern Italy—home of Mr Bossi's League and of the original *Mani Pulite* investigation—will also be learning. Since the new political leadership is seen as a "Northern one" (a total of 18 ministers and under-secretaries are from Lombardy, including the prime minister), expect caution, more sober behaviour, and no more talk of secession.

The opposition will also be learning. After an unexpected (and therefore shocking) electoral defeat in 1994, it will regroup into two loose formations. A mellowed Democratic Party of the Left will consider dropping "Left" from its name, trying to capitalise on the aura of the Democratic Party in America. Purged by scandal and chastened by the first taste of opposition, a new centre movement will revolve around three men: Romano Prodi, a professor of economics, former chairman of the IRI conglomerate (the huge Istituto per la Ricostruzione Industriale), Catholic philosopher Rocco Buttiglione, the new leader of the Popular Party; and Mario Segni, the man who launched the "Italian revolution", but then proved indecisive and fared poorly at the polls in 1994.

The government will show remarkable activism next year. There will be moves to help small businesses (the bulk of Mr Berlusconi's support), and to reduce the national debt. Law and order will be a priority, and there are successes to be scored in this field.

Unfortunately, the frictions and the misunderstandings between the government and the magistrates will continue. The bone of contention, as in 1994, will be Mr Berlusconi's past, and his vast business empire.

Three things the government will not do: it will not change the electoral rules (despite pressure to do so); it will not speed up privatisation of the bloated state sector of the economy, as the present pace is all that it can handle; it will not do away with ubiquitous "political appointments"—Italy's crude version of the American "spoils system".

Foreign policy will be lively. Farnesina, the Foreign Ministry, will enjoy a measure of independence. Having complained for years that Rome was too careful, Italy's friends will realise that the new conservative government wants to make up for those lost years. Some of its actions will be cheered; the British government, for example, will find in Antonio Martino, the foreign minister, an ally with the same "minimalist" view of Europe. Other initiatives are going to leave some people uneasy. Rome will not allow itself to be shoved aside when it comes to major international appointments, and it will mount a vigil in order to prevent Japan and Germany from becoming permanent members of an enlarged UN Security Council.

The Netherlands *1995*

With a new government in August 1994, after more than three months of coalition negotiations, observers will be watching for any sign of weakness in 1995. After 80 years as the linchpin of the Dutch tradition of consensus politics, the centre-right Christian Democrats were kicked out of power, losing 20 seats in parliament.

Their erstwhile colleagues in the Labour Party have joined a coalition with avowedly right-wing Liberals, with the Labour Party leader, Wim Kok as prime minister. Despite Mr Kok's pragmatism, the stability of the new coalition cannot be taken for granted.

The main stumbling block will, as always, be the budget. The prime minister cannot afford to alienate his party's left wing by giving in to Liberal pressure for across-the-board cuts in the generous Dutch social-security benefits. Liberal supporters, already sceptical about the coalition with Labour, will be insisting that the prime minister does.

Despite the political upheavals, prospects for the economy in 1995 are better than for several years. More favourable conditions in the Netherlands' main European trading partners will stimulate export growth, which, in turn, should help business and consumer confidence.

However, this will be partly offset by high unemployment and expected cuts in public subsidies and welfare payments. The government will struggle to reduce the budget deficit and to reverse the upward trend in public debt in line with the requirements of the Maastricht treaty.

Inflation will be fairly stable in 1995. One factor will be low wage growth as a result of high unemployment.

Monetary policy is conducted by the independent central bank which will suppress inflation by aligning the guilder closely with the D-mark. Against the dollar there will be very little movement, helping to stabilise the import prices of both commodities and manufactured goods.

KEY INDICATORS			
	1993	1994	1995
GDP growth (%)	0.2	1.8	2.3
Inflation (%)	2.6	2.9	3.0
Bond yield (%)	6.5	6.8	6.8
Exchange rate			
G per DM	1.12	1.13	1.13
G per $	1.86	1.88	1.89
Current account ($bn)	9.0	9.1	9.4
EIU COUNTRY ANALYSIS AND FORECASTING			

Long before the world woke up to the potential of optical fibre, BICC saw the light.

We were investing in the technology and building up our manufacturing facilities as long ago as 1972. With the result that BICC, in partnership with Corning, is now the largest producer of optical fibre outside the USA.

It's a far-sighted strategy, in optical cable as well as fibre, that is now reaping rewards for our business.

WE'RE SATISFYING THE WORLD'S APPETITE FOR FIBRE.

With the telecoms market alone set to double within a decade, the BICC Group is in excellent shape to capitalise on the global communications revolution.

Which should prove beyond all doubt something we recognised sooner than most.

Fibre is good for your business.

BICC Group

BICC Cables

ENGINEERING TOMORROW'S WORLD

Balfour Beatty

Skint Scandinavia

Christopher Brown-Humes

The Nordic countries will spend 1995 adjusting to their new relationship with the European Union. It will not be easy. The Finnish referendum in October 1994 decisively endorsed EU membership, a vote that will take this strategically important part of the world further down the road from neutrality towards the common defence of the Western European Union. This is a move that would have had the old Russia fuming; as it was, it passed almost without notice.

The Nordics will be net contributors to the EU budget. This means that they will want influence in return, and influence "above their weight". Don't be surprised to see them make an early mark in Brussels, particularly in areas like welfare policy, unemployment and the environment. And watch the way cultural affinities with other North European countries quickly tilt the EU axis northwards. The Nordics will also be hoping that EU membership provides a domestic pay-off, particularly in terms of much-needed investment.

On the political front, the shade of colour across the entire region will be decidedly pink in 1995. The chances are that there will be Social Democratic dominated governments in all four Nordic countries by March—a swing to the left which is against the trend in the main European economies. In 1994, the Swedes ousted a right-centre coalition in favour of a Social Democratic government and the Danes voted back a left-dominated administration. In March 1995, there is every chance that the Finns will get rid of the centre-right coalition which has presided over the country's deepest recession for 60 years.

This trend reflects disillusion with the market liberalism of the past few years, a nostalgic longing for the way things were, and a reaction against some of the deeply unpopular, but necessary, policies pursued by right-leaning governments to counter economic difficulty. It confirms the view that the Nordic governments which try to rein in bloated welfare budgets are likely to end up paying a heavy price on election day.

There is an air of unreality about this. Both Sweden and Finland have huge budget deficits and in 1994 the financial markets spent much of the year punishing them for not doing more to

Christopher E. Brown-Humes: Stockholm correspondent for the *Financial Times*.

curb a steady growth in state debt. The natural thing for them to do would be push through bigger savings programmes.

The extent to which fiscal constraint forces a further dismantling of the lavish benefits systems will be a process to watch out for in 1995. Denmark, with a budget deficit of 5% of gross domestic product, may just be able to entertain thoughts of welfare expansion, even though state spending already accounts for 60% of GDP. Sweden, with a budget deficit of 11% of GDP and state spending

Santa heads for Europe

amounting to 70% of GDP, emphatically cannot. Indeed, the Social Democrats will almost certainly get their first real taste of the paradox of politics. It will fall to them to chip away at the Swedish model which they built.

There is another big question for the Nordics in 1995. Can ambitions to promote private-sector job growth be accomplished, given generous unemployment benefits, cultural resistance to the creation of a low-wage service sector and some of the highest tax levels in the world? In the past 40 years virtually all net job creation in the Nordic area has come from the public sector. There have been all too few incentives to encourage new private-sector business.

If this does not change, the Nordic region will have to get used to permanent-

ly high unemployment rates, however unpalatable for governments which have prided themselves on a virtual absence of joblessness in the past. In 1995 Finland will have an unemployment rate of at least 16%, while Sweden and Denmark will both struggle to get their jobless totals below 12%.

The good news is that the Nordics will not be without ammunition in their struggle. The region will experience a second successive year of economic growth, supported by a gathering economic recovery in Europe.

The Danish and Norwegian economies, which in 1994 enjoyed some of Europe's best growth rates, will have another good year, with economic growth of around 3%. Both countries have seen a strong rise in consumer spending following fiscal expansion.

In Sweden and Finland, the recovery which has been export-led since the sharp depreciation in their currencies in 1992 should also reflect increased consumer confidence in 1995. The Finnish economy will grow by as much as 4% in a strong rebound from the deep recession of 1991-93, when GDP sank by 13%. Sweden will be the laggard, and economic growth may be as little as 3%.

There is every indication that short-term interest rates will have to move up again to choke off an early surge in inflation. The Nordics have reason to be sensitive on this point: they have a generally poor record on inflation and they know the markets will punish them severely in 1995 if they show any sign of returning to their bad old ways.

From the Urals to the Atlantic

The World in 1995 asked **Leon Brittan**, a longstanding European Commissioner, to predict what will occupy and worry the European Union in the coming year

1995 will prove to be the year when Europe finally stops vacillating over whether to reunite the two halves of the continent, and focuses instead on how to achieve it. The rhetoric for and against European reunification will gradually give way to a hard-nosed, fractious but ultimately fruitful debate on the internal changes needed to bring Europe fully together after 45 years of official separation.

Three developments will dominate this process. The first is the progress that the countries of Central and Eastern Europe are themselves making. They are all throwing off the last vestiges of their communist past and evolving into mature democracies, bolstered by competitive market economies. That market reform is taking hold throughout the region is not in doubt. The speed of this process varies considerably from country to country.

Some East European governments may slacken the pace of their reform; none of them will abandon the course altogether. The determination of the Poles, Hungarians, Czechs and others to become equal players in one European market is often overlooked in Western Europe.

The European Union's plans to accelerate this process of reform will take tangible shape in 1995. Through the "pre-accession" strategy, devised by the European Commission and likely to be endorsed by the EU's members in December 1994, we will remove the few remaining barriers to trade with Eastern Europe. The commission will produce, by June 1995, a white paper to show our Eastern partners what laws and practices we think they will have to adjust in their economies before participating fully in the single European market.

The second development is change within the EU itself. Ever since communism collapsed, the notion that Western Europe could integrate further without changing the way in which it takes collective decisions has been collapsing with it. Two years ago, the EU's governments put off the evil day when these reforms would have to be tackled: the trauma of the Maastricht treaty saw to that. But change in the

way the EU works will now be the dominant theme of the intergovernmental conference in 1996.

The effect can already be felt. Throughout 1995 governments will test each other with talk of a "hard-core", "multi-speed" or "à la carte" Europe. This is likely to be the most divisive debate Europe has known since the war. Several governments are already setting the scene for the next wave of reform after the 1996 conference. Whether

"Change in the way the EU works will be the dominant theme."

reform of the farming, budget and regional policies will require an intergovernmental conference beyond 1996 is not immediately obvious. Many are already booking the best seats for that show well in advance, rightly predicting that European reunification will make Europe's costliest policies costlier still.

The third development—in foreign and defence policy—is the hardest to predict. It involves forces beyond Europe's borders and beyond its control. Europe's ability to become an autonomous defence entity will depend to quite a degree on the superpowers that dominated the balance of power in Europe throughout the cold war. America has made its choice. The protector of war-torn Europe against communism, America has repeatedly served notice that Europe should share more of the burden of its own defence. The United States carried this message one crucial step further in January 1994 when President Bill Clinton formally encouraged Europeans to develop defence capacities and priorities

separate from those of their main NATO partner. For their part, the Europeans pre-empted this parental nudge to the edge of the nest by agreeing in the Maastricht treaty to develop their own foreign and security policies, albeit in step with America.

Russia, however, has yet to decide its position on the evolution of Europe's defence. Anxious to reform its economy along market lines without losing the political and military clout it wielded in the old Soviet Union, Moscow has been taking a higher profile of late, notably towards its "near-abroad" in the Baltics and Caucasian republics.

The effect has been to intensify the debate in Europe—east and west—over how defence should be handled as the continent reunites, without alienating America or, more immediately, Russia.

The Yugoslav conflict came too early to test Europe's fledgling defence policy. The ink was hardly dry on the Maastricht treaty before civil war broke out over Serbia and Croatia. This war will continue to overshadow Europe's attempts to create a common foreign and security policy. It will convince some people that Europe urgently needs such a policy; others that it cannot have one. The groundwork for a separate identity in foreign and military policy has yet to be laid. Work has started and will accelerate in 1995. Watch out for the first joint foreign-policy initiatives, such as common European positions in the United Nations and joint military exercises through the multi-national Eurocorps brigade.

The Single European Act responded to Europe's need to create economies of scale in order to restore Europe's competitive position in world markets. The Maastricht treaty sought to answer calls for deeper economic and political integration to face the unpredictability of the post-cold war era. The act came when economic times were good; Maastricht was conceived when they were turning sour.

The next episode of European integration is clear: to enhance Europe's ability to take decisions in preparation for the biggest decision for a long time, namely the reintegration of Europe as one continent, not two. Sceptical politicians and frosty electorates will need much convincing. Thank goodness the economic climate is improving.

Tim Wright, Managing Director. "Power Macintosh™ is the best value in personal computing today. They're extremely fast, so our people get more done in less time. They're easier to use than PCs, which saves us a bundle in training and support costs. They give us the option to run MS-DOS, Windows and Macintosh™ software on the same desk. And the price was less than comparably equipped PCs. We've installed Power Macs in our London office and will probably have them in Paris by year-end." **Power Macintosh. It's a better future than you expected.**

Why is it that so many large corporations are investing in Power Macintosh?

What is it about this radically advanced new personal computer that appeals to business managers?

The power to stand out.

For one thing, its advanced RISC architecture enables a Power Macintosh to outperform even the fastest PCs.[†] In fact, the Power Macintosh 8100 is the most powerful mainstream personal computer *ever* built – giving your people the ability to get significantly more done, in significantly less time.

For another thing, a Power Macintosh is still a Macintosh. They're easier to set up, learn and use than an ordinary PC, which can result in substantial savings in training and support. In fact, studies have consistently shown that Macintosh users are more productive than people who use PCs equipped with Windows.[††]

And finally, Power Macintosh is extraordinary value. Not only are the prices surprisingly low, they also include things that most ordinary PCs don't: built-in networking, file-sharing, Ethernet, plug-and-play expansion capabilities and much more. So you can buy Macintosh computers now, without having to worry about buying lots of expensive additional pieces later on.

The power to fit in.

Power Macintosh computers work with the networks, servers and PCs you already have.

Ethernet and AppleTalk™ networking are standard. And Power Macintosh supports everything from Novell netware and TCP/IP to Token Ring.

Every Power Macintosh has a built-in SuperDrive disk drive that enables users to exchange files between a PC and a Power Mac on a standard 3½″ floppy disk.

And, with the addition of optional SoftWindows software from Insignia Solutions, a Power Macintosh can actually run thousands of MS-DOS and Windows applications (as well as thousands of Macintosh applications).

So when you buy Power Macintosh computers for your department, you can run your new accelerated Macintosh programs, without abandoning any of your current software. No other computer offers this kind of flexibility.

The power of Apple, IBM and Motorola.

At the heart of Power Macintosh is the PowerPC microprocessor. The first of a family of RISC chips developed in an unprecedented three-year collaboration between Apple, IBM and Motorola.

So when you invest in Power Macintosh, you can invest with confidence. This helps explain how Apple has become the world's largest manufacturer of desktop RISC-based computer systems in less than just ten months.

The power of RISC for as little as £1299* (excluding VAT).

Many experts have written that RISC technology is the future of personal computing. RISC chips are smaller, faster and require less energy than the conventional CISC chips found in other PCs.

They're also less expensive to manufacture. Thus, we can offer Power Macintosh systems for as low as £1299 – complete with a 160Mb hard drive, 8Mb of RAM, 16-bit video support for up to a 17″ monitor, sound, built-in Ethernet networking and built-in file sharing.

You can then add SoftWindows** (to run MS-DOS and Windows software), Apple A/V technologies to record and play digital video, up to 1Gb hard drive and up to 264Mbs of RAM. There's plenty of room to grow.

There is nothing more convincing than a demonstration. For the name of an Apple Authorised Reseller near you, call free on 0800 127753 today.

You'll find that Power Macintosh is here. And the future is better than you expected.

A selection of software available for Power Macintosh.

ClarisDraw
CLARIS CORPORATION

ClarisImpact
CLARIS CORPORATION

ClarisWorks
CLARIS CORPORATION

Dimensions
ADOBE SYSTEMS

Excel MICROSOFT

Freehand ALDUS

Illustrator
ADOBE SYSTEMS

MacWrite Pro
CLARIS CORPORATION

Mathematica
WOLFRAM RESEARCH

Office MICROSOFT

PageMaker
ADOBE SYSTEMS

Photoshop
ADOBE SYSTEMS

PowerPoint
MICROSOFT

Premiere
ADOBE SYSTEMS

QuarkXPress QUARK

SoftWindows
INSIGNIA

Word MICROSOFT

WordPerfect
WORDPERFECT

Works MICROSOFT

Apple
Power Macintosh

For further information about the Power Macintosh range call the Apple Information Centre free on 0800 127753.

Ireland   1995

Ireland will soon fulfil most of the criteria for currency union in Europe as set out in the Maastricht treaty. In 1994 it had a general budget deficit of less than 3% of GDP, very low inflation and converging long-term interest rates. Only on public debt, which was over 90% of GDP, did Ireland exceed the stipulated maximum. However, that debt has been falling for some time and may be considered as under control.

In terms of growth, Ireland is probably Europe's most dynamic economy. In 1990-94 real GDP grew by over 5% a year, compared with an average of only 1.2% for the EU as a whole. The outlook is favourable, with real GDP forecast to expand by 4% in 1995 and inflation not to exceed 3%. Private consumption and exports will continue to drive the economy, while the current-account surplus will be sustained, thanks largely to generous transfers from the EU.

Despite this strong outlook, three problems will persist. One is fixed investment, which has shown only volatile growth since 1990. The second is unemployment which, at around 15%, will remain among the highest in the EU. The third is its trade dependence on Britain, which will absorb 30% of Ireland's exports in 1995. This means that the punt might not be able to participate in European currency union if Britain's policy is to keep sterling out.

The peace process in the British province of Northern Ireland should inspire confidence in the Republic's economy and help it to attract extra foreign investment.

The IRA ceasefire of August 1994 was a triumph for modern Ireland. A referendum (probably in July 1995) on divorce law will be the next test of its cohesiveness. It will also provide the electorate with a chance to show northern protestants that the Republic is not an outpost of the Vatican, but a progressive and thriving nation within Europe.

KEY INDICATORS

	1993	1994	1995
GDP growth (% pa)	4.0	4.8	4.0
Inflation (%)	1.4	2.5	3.0
Bond yield (year end %)	7.7	7.3	7.3
Exchange rate			
IR£ per DM	2.43	2.42	2.43
IR£ per $	1.47	1.46	1.46
Current account ($bn)	3.8	3.0	3.2

EIU COUNTRY ANALYSIS AND FORECASTING

Will they wave back?

Felipe Gonzalez's honour

Juan Luis Cebrián

"I am going to get through the end of my term with honour. I will not bow my head." This statement, dramatically announced before the Spanish parliament by the socialist prime minister, captures the roughness and uncertainty of current Spanish politics. Throughout 1994 Felipe Gonzalez has been a cornered boxer, flailing without much effect at an emboldened opposition that is trying to remove him at any price.

The situation could not be worse for Mr Gonzalez. The former governor of the Bank of Spain, whom he himself had defended from press accusations, has been in jail accused of corruption. The Spanish Workers' Socialist Party stands accused of illegal financial practices. Many thought that the government would not last through the summer. A kind of collective embarrassment and shame has pervaded the socialists, who have called for "a dignified retirement", an orderly transfer of power to the opposition.

The right-wing is certainly in the ascendancy. It secured great gains in the European elections and now has its eye on the municipal and provincial elections which will take place in the spring of 1995. These, it believes, will show that the socialists are finished. An opposition triumph may force the retirement of Mr Gonzalez; it would be unlikely to lead to a general election, as this need not take place before 1997.

Few believe that the government has the strength to finish a full term, but Mr Gonzalez seems to be obsessed with making it until 1996, which would enable him to hold, from June 1995, the presidency of the European Union.

With time, he will also benefit from Spain's coming economic recovery. In the coming year growth is forecast at 2.5%. Unemployment will continue to fall, though remaining Europe's highest at over 20%. New labour legislation—more flexible and less protectionist—and a recovery in tourism following the devaluation of the peseta will help further. Interest rates, in the short term, may continue their moderate downward trend. Long-term rates, however, will continue to rise, due to inflation, which may reach 4.5% in 1994, although the government had predicted it would be only 3.5%.

The local elections in May 1995 promise a defeat for the government and, although different, some may try to

Juan Luis Cebrián: chief executive officer of PRISA and publisher of *El Pais*.

compare them to the municipal elections of 1931. On that occasion, the defeat of the pro-monarchy parties forced the king to abandon Spain and gave rise to the republic. The right, which has made intellectual efforts to take over some liberal-republican values, likes to quote this example to show what could happen. As they see it, an overwhelming victory—which is what they expect—by the Popular Party in local governments will force Mr Gonzalez to resign and dissolve parliament.

Much depends on Mr Gonzalez's interpretation of his own honour, which he so theatrically invoked. It is not known whether he will run in the next general election or if he is willing to remain as head of the party in opposition, in the event of a socialist defeat.

The leaders of the Popular Party say that the prime minister "has nothing to fear" but then they maliciously compare him to Bettino Craxi in Italy or Carlos Andreas Perez in Venezuela. However, there is not any indication that Mr Gonzalez has been involved in influence-peddling practices.

Mr Gonzalez has repeatedly said that his honour will not be stained by any further revelations. Despite the turbulent end that the socialist era may experience, his record of public service is remarkable.

The refusal by the opposition and the press to give credit to him for making the new Spain may be one reason he dwells so much on something so typically Spanish as honour. If Jose Maria Aznar, the right's leader, managed to discover what honour actually means for Mr Gonzalez, he would gladly give it all to him in exchange for the other thing that motivates any politician: power.

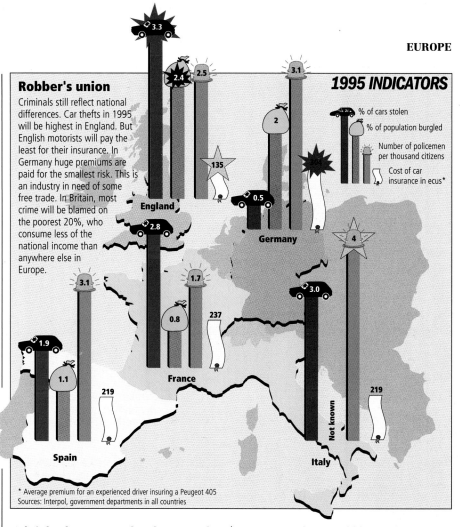

Robber's union

Criminals still reflect national differences. Car thefts in 1995 will be highest in England. But English motorists will pay the least for their insurance. In Germany huge premiums are paid for the smallest risk. This is an industry in need of some free trade. In Britain, most crime will be blamed on the poorest 20%, who consume less of the national income than anywhere else in Europe.

1995 INDICATORS

% of cars stolen
% of population burgled
Number of policemen per thousand citizens
Cost of car insurance in ecus*

England
Germany
France
Spain
Italy
Not known

* Average premium for an experienced driver insuring a Peugeot 405
Sources: Interpol, government departments in all countries

Turkey's unhappy turnaround

Tim Hindle

What a difference a year can make to a nation's fortunes. Turkey entered 1994 full of economic promise and youthful political zest—GDP growth in 1993 was a dizzy 7.3%, and the leaders of three major parties were newcomers under 50 years of age. But Turkey enters 1995 with a shrinking economy, and with its political leaders once again bogged down in the country's old political mire.

In a few respects the scene bears a chilling resemblance to the Turkey of the late 1970s. Then, as now, the economy was dependent on the outcome of recurrent discussions with the IMF, and the country was an international pariah

Tim Hindle: editor of *EuroBusiness*; formerly on *The Economist*.

where civil liberties were abused in an over-reaction to gruesome acts of terrorism. This sense of déja vu is reinforced by the remarkable resilience of many of the nation's political leaders. Of the three most prominent figures of that time—Suleyman Demirel, Bulent Ecevit and Necmettin Erbakan—Mr Demirel is now president and the other two are still at the head of significant political parties.

This changelessness is a weakness in Turkish politics. The nearly simultaneous arrival of three new party leaders is exceptional; in Turkey it is extremely difficult to remove the head of any political party who does not want to go. Regular military coups turn politicians into heroes when, in the natural course of civil-

ian events, they would be made answerable for their political mistakes.

For that reason alone it is a fair bet that the glamorous economist, Tansu Ciller, will survive as prime minister at least until the next general election due in 1996. And that despite an extraordinary demand last summer for a parliamentary inquiry into the apparent imbalance between her considerable wealth and her tax payments. Turks are now waiting for some sign that Ms Ciller can apply her wealth-creating abilities as effectively to her country as to herself.

In April 1994, as the overheated economy came close to melt-down, she introduced a series of strict economic measures. When they began to bite, things like the trade deficit and triple-digit inflation improved dramatically. Almost the only thing not to improve was economic growth itself.

In order to keep the economy growing at all in the pre-election year of 1995, Ms Ciller will be under pressure to compromise her short-lived victory against inflation. This should increase her determination to push ahead with a programme of privatisation, so far the source of much talk and little action. The revenue from the sales of state enterprises would greatly help her budgetary

Greece 1995

The Greek parliament will need to elect a new president in May, when Constantine Karamanlis steps down. The prime minister, Andreas Papandreou, has indicated a willingness to stand, his increasing frailty making him more suitable for the non-executive position of head of state. This could lead to an early general election if he does not receive enough support from parliament. The main parties will seek to avoid this if possible.

The struggle to succeed Mr Papandreou is on. The front-runner is Akis Tsohatzopoulos, a former interior minister. Another strong contender is Theodoros Pangalos, who effectively ran the Greek presidency of the European Union (EU) in 1994. His forceful personality and populist brand of socialism may yet get him Mr Papandreou's personal backing.

The Greek economy will see only slightly stronger growth in 1995. Policies aimed at reducing the burgeoning public-sector debt will keep the lid on demand. Both monetary and fiscal policy will be tight.

The five-year convergence plan agreed with the EU in 1994 will determine economic policy. This aims to reduce inflation and the budget deficit. Central to the plan is the freeing-up of government revenue to repay the country's debt. The reward for this thrift is 16.8 billion ecus ($20.75 billion) of EU structural funds allocated up until 1998.

An onslaught against tax evasion will yield significant results, and the partial privatisation of the state telecom (OTE), utility (DEH) and oil (DEP) companies will boost government revenue. A budget deficit of 11% of GDP is likely, and public-sector debt will remain stubbornly high.

The current-account deficit will remain below 2% of GDP, bolstered by good tourism receipts and the flows of EU funds. However, the strong drachma has damaged the performance of exports and is unsustainable in the long term.

KEY INDICATORS

	1993	1994	1995
GDP growth (% pa)	0.0	0.7	1.3
Inflation (%)	14.3	11.0	10.0
Bond yield (year end %)	18.3	21.0	16.0
Exchange rate			
Dr per DM	139	150	180
Dr per $	229	245	300
Current account ($bn)	-0.7	-0.6	-0.3

EIU COUNTRY ANALYSIS AND FORECASTING

arithmetic (though official projections of raising over $20 billion by the end of 1995 are exaggerated).

Ambitious politicians in Turkey have to wait for dead men's shoes, or go off and start new parties—a route followed recently and prominently by Cem (pronounced "gem") Boyner, a handsome young Istanbul businessman and former chairman of Tusiad, the industrialists' association. Yusuf Ozal, younger brother of Turgut Ozal, the former president and political colossus of the past decade, has done the same.

Although Turgut Ozal died in April 1993, the Ozal name is still more of a liability than an asset, largely on account of the flamboyant spending patterns of the late president's immediate family. But it is sure to be venerated soon as Turgut's achievements are increasingly compared with those of the political pygmies who have followed him. When that time comes, the moderate and gifted Yusuf will benefit.

Meanwhile the sparkling Cem steals the headlines as he charms unlikely parts of the electorate with his New Democracy movement. Yesterday's buzzword in Ankara was "pluralism", an aspiration for cultural diversity that died a sorry death in the spring anti-terrorist offensive against the Kurds in the southeast. The new political buzzword is "synthesis", the synthesis of Islam with the nation's republican heritage.

Pluralism and synthesis are ways of talking about the two main conflicts in Turkish society: between Kurds and Turks, on the one hand; and between Islam and the secular tradition of Ataturk on the other.

The recent manifestations of religion that frighten western-minded Turks (such as the increased decibels of the pre-recorded calls to prayer from the minarets) are unlikely to assume anything like Iranian proportions among a people so rapidly going through the process of "middle-classification". The continuing spread of Turkey's middle class, and its preoccupation with consumer durables and the payment of standing orders, is the surest guarantee against Islamic excess.

Islamic manifestations are not always what they seem. The main religious party, the Welfare Party, had such a resounding success in the municipal elections in 1994 that it now supplies the mayors of both Istanbul and Ankara. But it attracted votes from the disillusioned

Ciller will last, the smile won't

as well as from the faithful. Its success owed much to the failure of the socialist parties to provide any left-of-centre alternative.

The proliferation of the veil is also multi-faceted. An influential sociologist, Nilufer Gole, points out that it is not the veil of female modesty; it is more like a Muslim manifestation of the worldwide feminist movement. Today's veil-wearers seem to say, "Look at me; I'm an individual, not just the attachment of a man." Why else are they more visible on university campuses than in farms and villages?

The main threat to Turkish prosperity next year lies with the Kurds. As a consequence of the country's continuing failure to undermine foreign-influenced Kurdish terrorism by meeting its own Kurdish citizens' reasonable demands, Turkey is the world's fourth biggest importer of arms; it has a military budget that breeds triple-digit inflation; its tourist industry fails to reap several billion dollars a year; and it strains almost to breaking point the forbearance of its international friends.

Ms Ciller has thrown her headscarf in with the military and, capricious though she is, nothing is likely to change that before the elections. Turkey's young electorate can be sure there will then be plenty of candidates to choose from. They will be lucky if one of them is a leader.

Eastern Europe's western problems

Delia Meth-Cohn

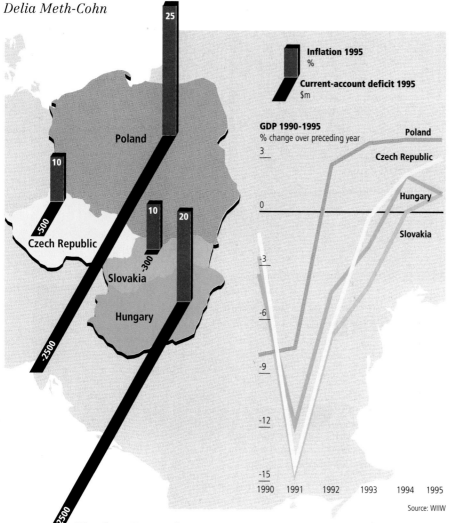

Inflation 1995
%

Current-account deficit 1995
$m

GDP 1990-1995
% change over preceding year

Poland

Czech Republic

Hungary

Slovakia

Source: WIIW

The four Visegrad countries—the Czech Republic, Hungary, Poland and Slovakia—will have good economic growth and political stability in 1995. There will be problems aplenty but they will be the problems of increasing prosperity: problems similar to those that will be found in any West European country. There are miles to go before these East European countries can boast of a life as rich as that of their neighbours, but 1995 will show how much terrain has been covered in the past few remarkable years since the death of communism.

The Czech Republic will still be cited as the model reformer. The major problem for Vaclav Klaus's government is the slow industrial turnaround. Elsewhere in

Delia Meth-Cohn: economics and politics editor of *Business Central Europe.*

Eastern Europe the manufacturing sector is driving growth, but in the Czech Republic industrial output has only just bottomed out. The economy is unapologetically service-driven.

As long as the country's exports remain competitive (an undervalued currency and wage controls help on that score), many will wax lyrical about the Czech miracle.

But 1995 will see pressure on the trade account. Much more industrial reform is needed. That means bankruptcies, higher unemployment and a budget deficit, which will not look too good for Mr Klaus with an election coming up in 1996. But the pick-up in Germany will give export demand an extra boost and could have German companies shifting factories across the border at a much faster rate.

In Hungary, nobody is looking at the future quite so blithely. With elections in the distance and a huge majority in parliament, the finance minister Laszlo Bekesi will be taking some hard and unpopular decisions. There will be no easy dash for short-term growth. Instead, expect the government to spend the year sorting out a current-account deficit that equals 10% of GDP, a budget deficit screaming out for cuts in social spending and a growing foreign-debt problem.

Poland's 1995 will, on the surface, be dominated by October's presidential election. Lech Walesa will in all probability lose. His best work has long since been finished. The likely winner will be Aleksander Kwasniewski, whose pragmatic socialist party dominates the governing coalition.

But chaotic politics will have little impact on Poland's economic course. The private sector's vibrant growth, now in its fourth year, has been joined by a recovery in manufacturing, fuelled by exports and strong domestic investment. The challenge in 1995 will be to transform these heated spurts into measured, sustainable growth. That means keeping real-interest rates at a level that will boost savings rather than imports.

That is a problem Slovakia will have to deal with too, along with budget and trade deficits. The mix is not quite as explosive as in Hungary, but Slovakia still has to tackle the whole issue of industrial restructuring. It inherited the Czechs' go-slow approach without the fundamentals—low inflation and low unemployment—to make such a policy viable. But it is no longer going down the route of irresponsible politics and no-hope economics that threatened to cut it off from the rest of Europe. The governing coalition, led by Vladimir Merciar, has a chance in 1995 to produce real growth.

Although the problems of each country differ, there is one concern that they will all share—how to keep exports growing. The traditional answer was to re-orient trade westwards. But the West's protectionist backlash to the early success of that policy has made intra-regional trade look more attractive.

Under the Visegrad free-trade agreement, tariffs on most products will be gone by 1998. Although the Czech Republic still tends to regard regional initiatives as an impediment to joining the European Union (EU), the other three are beginning to see that membership is out of the question without joint integration first. The EU begins discussions on Eastern Europe's membership next year, so the importance of standing together will become much clearer.

People's capitalism catches on

Russia's coming boom

Andrew Cowley

By next year, Russia will have lost almost all interest in politics. It is now hard to imagine anyone bothering to shell the parliament or take to the streets. Opinion polls show that under 5% of Russians take an active interest in politics. What Russians are interested in is money. The raw capitalism which has captured Russia's imagination will turn around the economy in 1995.

On the surface, the idea of an economic boom in Russia seems ludicrous. The country is now in its fourth consecutive year of a recession, which has seen industrial output decline by more than half. America's industrial output, for comparison, fell by less than one-third during the Great Depression. Inflation is still uncomfortably high and 20m Russians (from a population of 148m) live miserably below the official poverty line. Critics of the government charge that its much-touted privatisation programme has involved a lot of shuffling of paper but has not raised any new capital for industry.

Large as all of these problems loom, they should not be allowed to obscure the real achievements of Russia's eco-

Andrew Cowley: Moscow correspondent for *The Economist*.

nomic reforms. It could have moved forward more quickly and coherently but, since the liberalisation of most prices in January 1992, Russia's government has stuck to the three main pillars of reform: further liberalisation of prices and trade; efforts (sometimes fumbling) to achieve macroeconomic stability; and privatisation. In the process the government has laid the foundations of a market economy to take off in 1995.

Look beyond the casinos—Moscow alone has over 60 of them—and the institutions of a market economy have appeared. Russia has more than 3,000 commercial banks, 800 insurance companies, 600 mutual funds and 200 commodity and stock exchanges. That not all of these fledgling institutions are scrupulously honest should come as no surprise. That they exist at all in a society where most forms of private economic activity were a crime four years ago is remarkable.

The process of building a market has changed the structure of Russia's economy. Grigory Yavlinsky, an economist who now leads a reformist party, jokes that the problem with the Soviet economy was not that it was under-developed, but that it was mis-developed. His point is a

serious one. The economy which Russia inherited was over-industrialised. The decline in industrial output has reduced industry's share of GDP from over 50% in 1991 to around 30% in 1994. Services, noticeable in the Soviet economy only by their absence, now account for an estimated 50% of Russia's GDP. This means that the structure of Russian output is now comparable to that of a normal middle-income country. As important is who the producers are. By 1995, the private sector will produce about 60% of total output. Over 1m Russians own small businesses such as shops and cafés. 17,000 medium-sized and large enterprises have been privatised and 40m Russians own shares in them.

The more thoughtful opponents of Boris Yeltsin's government admit that reform has led to some positive changes, but claim that the price has been too high. It is hard to get an accurate picture from official statistics of how living standards have changed, because most of them record only what is happening in the dying state-owned economy and capture little of what is happening in the emerging private economy. However, there are haphazard clues to suggest that Russians are living better than they used to. Regular surveys of what households buy and eat will show rising consumption during 1995. Car ownership in Moscow has increased by 40% over the past two years. One in three families in Siberia has started building a new house. The average monthly wage has risen from $8 in January 1992 to $113 in August 1994. (Measuring the average wage in dollars is a useful measure of the standard of living, as Russia does not produce much that consumers want, forcing them to buy imported goods.)

For Russia to develop a more efficient market, which delivers the goods to most of the people most of the time, its government needs to do two things in 1995. First, it has to continue to squeeze inflation: a target of 1-2% a month by late 1995 would be quite realistic. Second, it has to show the will to bankrupt the ex-Soviet industrial behemoths which have no chance of surviving in a market economy without massive subsidies.

If the government were to do these things, then the Russian firms and individuals which have salted away $20 billion in capital flight would start to bring their money home next year. That is a huge prize. Add in foreign investors, keen to get into the world's largest emerging market at the bottom, and a possible rise in the oil price and the foundations would be in place for a boom.

Slavs over all

Andrew Cowley

"Jesus Christ was not a Jew, as Zionist propaganda wants him to be. He was a pure-blooded Slav from Novgorod, who went to Palestine to stop Jewish expansion into the Roman empire. That was why he was executed." This is part of what new recruits to Russian National Unity are taught. It is just one of over 80 groups of extremists lurking in Russia's political undergrowth. Some of these groups make the Liberal Democrats, led by Vladimir Zhirinovsky, look like lambs. Russia has textbook conditions for the rise of extremism in 1995. Many of its people still feel a profound sense of humiliation at their country's loss of superpower status. This feeling is particularly strong in the armed forces. The roots of democracy have yet to penetrate beyond the top-soil of Russian society.

The spawning ground for Russian extremism is Pamyat ("memory" in Russian), an organisation set up as a historical society by Sergei Vasiliev in 1986. Pamyat today calls for a restoration of the monarchy and a mystical version of Russian orthodoxy. Its political offspring are less ethereal.

Take, for example, Alexander Barkashov. He left school to train as an electrician. He served briefly in the army, where he rose to the dizzy rank of lance-corporal and became a brown-belt at karate. Mr Barkashov was an active member of Pamyat from 1987 to 1990, when he left the group to found Russian National Unity.

The new party is organised along classic fascist lines. New members join first as "sympathisers", of whom Mr Barkashov claims to have tens of thousands. Some are then promoted to "associates". Of these, around 600 have become the shock troops of the party, known as "companions". To become a companion, a member has to be pure-blooded Slav and to serve a year's probation. All companions swear an oath of loyalty to their leader (Mr Barkashov) and promise "to be ruthless to the external and internal enemies of Russia." Several of them died defending the old parliament against forces loyal to Boris Yeltsin in October 1993. In the mythology of Russian National Unity, they were martyred by "snipers from NATO's 6th brigade" sent to Moscow to prop up the western puppet, Boris Yeltsin.

Russian National Unity and its largest rival, the National Republican Party of Russia, espouse similar ideologies. If they came to power, they would rebuild the Russian empire, remilitarise Russia's economy and undertake substantial ethnic cleansing: "Jews and gypsies will be eradicated as soon as possible."

Silencing the lamb

Both parties also display profound contempt for Mr Zhirinovsky, who achieved notoriety by winning 24% of the votes cast in parliamentary elections last year. Seen through the ultra-extremists' eyes, Mr Zhirinovsky is more of a help to Mr Yeltsin than a danger: Mr Zhirinovsky has helped to split the mainstream opposition to the president; without his assistance the new constitution adopted in December 1993, which gave Mr Yeltsin greater powers, would not have been passed; and, most usefully to those in power, Mr Zhirinovsky is disposable—his Jewish father and weak grip on sanity see to that.

Too young to die

Andrew Cowley

The average Russian is lucky if he lives long enough to receive a pension—by 1995 life expectancy for Russian men will have fallen below 59, putting Russia on a par with India. 360,000 more Russians died in 1993 than in 1992—that's more extra deaths than total American losses during the second world war—while the annual number of births has almost halved since 1987. "It is hard to find a historical precedent for such a severe mortality crisis, outside war or famine," says Judith Shapiro, an economist at London University.

The cause of the problem, which will get worse before it gets better, is not the number of births. Although it has been falling since the second world war and collapsed after the advent of *perestroika*, the decline in the birth-rate is now levelling off. The death-rate, however, is still rising—10% more people died in the first half of 1994 than they did in the same period of 1993.

Conventional wisdom says that the main causes of premature death are violence, disease and industrial accidents. All of these have risen sharply, but they are still dwarfed by the number of Russians who die as a result of cardiovascular disease. Russian men aged between 45 and 50 drink too

Russians meet their maker early

much, smoke, eat fatty food and do little exercise. With the health system in collapse, many people die unaided after a relatively mild heart attack.

An improvement in health care might save a few lives, but it would not address the root cause of Russia's problem with heart disease, which is stress. Those with the weakest hearts often feel too old to adapt to the new Russia, but are too young to retire. The biggest cause of stress is not poverty but a sense of not being in control, which leaves people with nothing to do but to sit, worry and drink vodka.

Even if the death-rate were to improve at the same rate it did in other countries that have seen a sharp improvement in life expectancy (such as China), it would take Russia a quarter of a century to reach Western Europe's current level of life expectancy. In the meantime, the Russian attitude to death is likely to remain as fatalistic as it was 150 years ago, when Nikolai Gogol wrote, "If a man has died, then he's dead."

Connecting Moscow to the world.

Your business in Russia is international. You need fast and reliable international voice, fax and data communications. Welcome to Combellga.

A UNIQUE SERVICE

Combellga offers you a rapid and dependable telecommunications service to and from Moscow via its own private satellite network. Our international telephone code 7-502 connects you immediately to any country in the world.

FULL RELIABILITY

The Combellga network is based on a combination of Alcatel Bell's state-of-the-art technology,

Belgacom's (Belgian RTT) international network and the local expertise of Comincom and MGTS. Every part of the Combellga network is backed up to guarantee you absolute reliability for your business calls.

COMPETITIVE PRICES

Combellga charges your calls on a 12 second basis thus guaranteeing you the lowest overall prices on the market.

Combellga subscribers in Moscow receive:

(Clear, immediate telephone communications

(Data transmission via modems with a speed up to 9.6 Kbit/sec

(Fax transmission with a speed up to 9.6 Kbit/sec

(Leased/dedicated lines for extension to Moscow of existing virtual private networks

(X25 electronic mail

(VSAT services

(Many additional services

For more information call or visit our sales office at

Ulitsa Mitnaya 3, Entrance 2, 14th floor

117049 Moscow, Russia

Via Moscow telephone: (7 095) 239-1149, 239-1259, fax 239-1474

COMBELLGA Via Combellga: (7 502) 222-1432, fax 222-1435

The president and supporter

Clinton's vital year

Stacy Mason

1995 will be the defining year of Bill Clinton's presidency. It will determine whether Mr Clinton is a one-term or a two-term president. And his fate, in turn, will ultimately shape America for the rest of the decade and fashion the condition of the only remaining superpower as the world enters the 21st century. Whatever Mr Clinton accomplishes or fails to accomplish in 1995 will decide his strength in November 1996. Anything after 1995 is too late.

The third year of a first-term presidency historically has been crucial. In 1991, George Bush was still reeling from his fateful decision to raise taxes and renege on his famous pledge: "Read my lips. No new taxes." In doing so, he became a one-term president. Throughout 1983, Ronald Reagan enjoyed America's spectacular recovery from economic hard times and coasted to re-election in 1984. In 1979, Jimmy Carter was suffering the consequences of sky-rocketing oil prices and the kidnapping of American hostages in Iran. He, of course, was defeated in 1980.

For Mr Clinton, the major initiatives of the first half of his administration will start to show their colours in 1995. And it is on this scorecard that pundits and voters will rate the president in 1996. In

Stacy Mason: editor of *Roll Call*, the twice-weekly newspaper of Capitol Hill.

1995, it will become clearer whether his controversial budget (approved by a one-vote margin) has succeeded in maintaining growth. More than a year after the passage of the North American Free Trade Agreement (NAFTA), it will no longer be guesswork whether the United States is losing jobs to Mexico at the breathless pace critics predicted, or whether Mexico is snapping up American goods with the appetite supporters promised. And it will be known whether the crime bill's call for, among other things, more police on the streets is actually making the streets safer (or at least feel safer).

Early indications are that Mr Clinton may reach his goal of creating 8m new jobs during his first term. In fact, he is more than half way there: between January 1993 and August 1994 about 4.3m workers were added to payrolls at private businesses and government agencies, according to the Bureau of Labor Statistics. Such tangible success will be key to his popularity next year.

The second half of Mr Clinton's administration will be played out in a radically different political climate. The reason? Congress. The Republicans will control both the House and the Senate throughout the next two years. This guarantees more gridlock and partisanship than ever before. And while the

ranks of Republicans in Congress have become more conservative, the ranks of Democrats are becoming more splintered. Moderate Democrats feel abandoned by their liberal leaders in Congress. They will threaten to side with the Republicans on key votes. Conservative-minded politicians will, therefore, have the upper hand on the controversial issue of welfare reform. Liberal Democrats want to spend generously on new welfare programmes. Virtually all Republicans and most moderate Democrats want a stricter, less costly, version of reform.

There are other factors contributing to the disjointed Congress. By 1995, more than half of all members of Congress will have been elected since 1990, signalling a major shift in the institution. This is certain to dilute the power and influence of the old guard. Long-time committee chairmen are fighting mightily to resist the reformist tendencies of younger members. These, for example, want to limit the number of years of service of a committee chairman and abolish voting by proxy in committee, a powerful tool for chairmen.

There will also be some significant changes in congressional leaders. A new Senate Democratic leader will replace George Mitchell of Maine. Newt Gingrich will be anointed as the House Republican

Gingrich comes on strong

leader. The Gingrich era will be lively. Mr Gingrich is a highly partisan intellectual who has experienced a coming-of-age in recent years. He first gained fame as a bomb-throwing ideologue but has toned down his rhetoric lately and worked tirelessly to bring Republicans of all stripes into his fold. In doing so, he has won the respect of his colleagues; he was virtually unchallenged for his new leadership post. For this reason, Mr Gingrich is likely to eclipse the Senate Republican leader, Bob Dole, as Mr Clinton's primary Republican foe in Congress.

Someone to blame

The fortified Republican ranks in Congress could spell big trouble in this critical year of Mr Clinton's presidency. Or, in an ironic twist, it could help him. In contrast to the first years of his administration, Mr Clinton will be able honestly to blame Congress for his failures. And his successes may be of the more moderate variety, which is after all in line with the mood of the country at large.

But perhaps most significantly a controlling Republican class in Congress will provide Mr Clinton with an escape hatch on the issue that was once the centrepiece of his agenda: health-care reform. Heralded as the single most important piece of legislation the nation's officeholders would tackle—so critical that the president named his wife to lead the effort—health-care reform has come off the rails. Now the question is whether it will be revived in 1995. The likely answer: probably not. With the Republican majority in Congress there is little chance of sweeping reform. Congress may enact such popular health-care initiatives as malpractice reform, coverage for children, coverage for pre-existing conditions, and portable health insurance. Anything more is unlikely.

In another irony of this presidency, the failure of comprehensive health-care reform is likely to have little effect on Mr Clinton's re-election outlook. In fact, according to polls, voters place the economy and crime far higher on their lists of

priorities than health care. However, if Mr Clinton is re-elected in 1996, expect the issue to return once again to the front-burner—and once again to come under the stewardship of Hillary Rodham Clinton.

With health care off the agenda, look for Vice-President Al Gore to play an increasing role in this administration. His "reinventing government" initiative—an effort to curb government bureaucracy and introduce more technology into the system—will be likely to get a push from

the president. Mr Gore's ideas are generally well-received by Republicans and the public, so this initiative could see rare bipartisanship and co-operation.

Other items on the agenda include re-authorisations of the Clean Water Act, Farm Bill and the Endangered Species Act. Also, expect a raging fight over whether telephone companies can sell information services.

But in the end Mr Clinton, like every president that has come before him, will be judged by the state of the economy.

The cycle starts to turn

David Hale

The United States economy in 1995 will be in the fifth year of a business expansion which began during the spring of 1991. In the modern era, three expansions have extended through a fourth year, while only two have survived to enjoy a fifth: the Reagan expansion of the 1980s and the Vietnam war expansion of the 1960s. In both cases, these long expansions experienced mid-cycle pauses either because of monetary tightening (1966) or because of disinflation shocks resulting from falling oil prices and a strong dollar (the mid-1980s).

Most American economists believe that the current expansion will slow to a

Exchange rate

65.6
65.9
65.7

93
94
95

IMF index, 1985=100

nancial chaos caused by huge losses in the banking system. This severely curtailed the ability of small and medium-sized companies to obtain capital. As a result, their hiring slowed dramatically, whereas during the 1980s they had created more than 20m new jobs. Meanwhile, the *Fortune* 500 companies continued the lay-offs which have reduced their total employment by one-third since the 1980s.

The American economy enjoyed a more pronounced cyclical recovery during 1993 because the financial system got steadily stronger. There was a record boom in small-company financing on Wall Street. Nearly 600 non-financial initial public offerings raised $25 billion of new equity capital. A rebound in the high-yield bond market (junk-bond market) produced another $60 billion of new funding. The banking

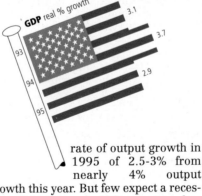

GDP real % growth

3.1
3.7
2.9

93
94
95

rate of output growth in 1995 of 2.5-3% from nearly 4% output growth this year. But few expect a recession. This time round, the economy has not generated any of the cyclical imbalances or financial excesses which often culminate in a slump. On the contrary, the United States economy was so subdued during the first two years of the expansion that many households and businesses did not notice it until 1993. Inflation, at only 2.6% in 1994, will still not rise above 3.5% next year.

The United States economy grew at a subdued pace during those first two years of the recovery because of the fi-

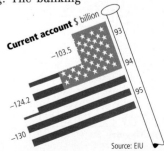

Current account $ billion

–103.5
–124.2
–130

93
94
95

Source: EIU

David Hale: chief economist, Kemper Financial Services, Chicago.

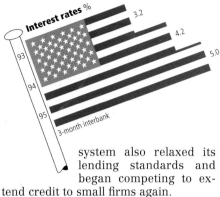

Interest rates %

3.2
4.2
5.0
3-month interbank

system also relaxed its lending standards and began competing to extend credit to small firms again.

As a result of the rebound in both demand and output since the autumn of 1993, the Federal Reserve is now concerned about supply-side constraints in the economy reviving inflation. The unemployment rate has fallen below 6% in the nation and is well below 5% in a group of states accounting for one-third of the labour force. The capacity utilisation rate of manufacturing has risen to the 83-84% range compared with 85% at the peak of past business cycles.

Many small businesses are now starting to report a scarcity of skilled workers and even entry-level applicants. Industrial commodity prices have increased by more than 20% since last year. In addition to supply constraints in the industrial sector, the housing market could soon fuel inflation. Falling vacancy rates for apartments and homes in several western states have begun pushing rents up by more than 5%. As rents account for 27% of the inflation index, further declines in vacancy rates could add half a point to the inflation rate next year even if the economy slows.

In order to head off a resurgence of inflation, the Federal Reserve began raising interest rates in early 1994 for the first time in five years. In past monetary-policy cycles, excluding the oil-price shocks of the 1970s, the Fed typically hiked interest rates by as much as 400 basis points. American money-market yields are now under 5% and will probably be hiked by at least another 75

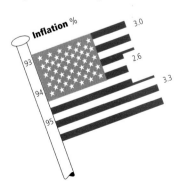

Inflation %

3.0
2.6
3.3

basis points before mid-1995. Most Fed officials do not believe that monetary policy will be truly restrictive until real short-term interest rates significantly exceed 2%.

The financial markets expect that money-market yields will rise to at least 6% by 1996 but whether they peak at that level or higher will also depend upon the strength of the coming world recovery. There is a risk that strong world growth could continue to drive commodity prices higher during 1995.

There is also a political wild card in prospect. So far, Bill Clinton has been presiding over a voteless recovery. Hence the Clinton administration may decide that it will have to change its fiscal policy in order to regain popular support. Instead of emphasising deficit reduction and carefully targeted spending programmes (such as retraining workers), the administration might engage in a political bidding war with the Republican congressional leadership to offer a 1996 middle-class tax cut.

How about a foreign policy?

Daniel Franklin

Bill Clinton has the opportunity to make 1995 the year of the Great Revision of his presidency: the year that the focus shifted from domestic to foreign policy. He came to the White House with ambitious plans to set America to rights at home. Foreign affairs have often seemed an unwelcome distraction, not given consistent thought or attention by the president. Aides even had trouble getting him to set aside regular time for meetings with his top foreign-policy advisers. The result, almost inevitably, has been a series of embarrassing flip-flops—over Somalia, China and Bosnia, to name but three examples—which have unsettled America's European allies and given the Clinton administration a reputation for foreign-policy incompetence.

A reputation for incompetence, once established, is not easy to reverse. But imagine how it could happen. The operation in Haiti turns out to be a success, contrary to the near-unanimous predictions of doom by foreign-policy experts in Washington. America avoids the dangers of "mission creep" and extricates most of its forces from Haiti as planned. Haiti, of course, still has huge problems to sort out, but the exercise of American power there comes to be seen as benign and virtually bloodless.

Success in Haiti and the president's rapid deployment of American strength aimed at Iraq when Saddam Hussein began military manoeuvres along Kuwait's border in October leads to a general reassessment of Mr Clinton's foreign-policy record. The reassessors discover that it is not nearly as bad as they had thought. On some of the big issues, such as the handling of Russia and the promotion of peace in the Middle East, the Clinton administration has been con-

Daniel Franklin: Washington bureau chief for *The Economist.*

sistent and on the whole sound. It has stumbled into a sensible policy towards China. On the margins, it has helped nudge the peace process forward in Ireland. As for trade liberalisation, Mr Clinton has had to battle with his own instincts as well as with the protectionists in his own party, but in the end he has managed to deliver both the North American Free Trade Agreement (after the most courageous political fight of his presidency) and the GATT agreement.

On most of these issues, the policy process has been anything but smooth (look at the troubles in passing the GATT enabling legislation, for example, or the climbdown on human rights in China, or the furore over the decision to let Sinn Fein's Gerry Adams into America). But, in the end, the results have not been bad. And if Mr Clinton wants to become newly engaged in foreign policy in 1995, he will have no shortage of options.

On trade, there is the challenge of extending NAFTA-like liberalisation to the rest of the hemisphere. Over the next couple of years, how America handles questions of nuclear non-proliferation, from the Korean peninsula to the Indian subcontinent, will affect everyone's security. Then there are the random foreign-policy crises—in Cuba, perhaps, or maybe the Gulf—that are bound to arise and demand a response.

The most predictable test of Mr Clinton's ambitions is likely to come in Bosnia. This has been a source of repeated friction between America and its NATO allies, as well as a potential cause of a bust-up with Russia. Unless Bosnia's Serbs have an unlikely change of heart and accept the peace deal on offer, the question of lifting the arms embargo for Bosnia's Muslims will again threaten to divide America, its allies and Russia. In his first two years, Mr Clinton has bowed

Fashion forever new

Andrew Sullivan

American culture delights in change. To help you in 1995, here are some predictions of the new trends coming soon to a neighbourhood near you.

The absence of feminism

Finally, all the participants in the feminist/anti-feminist debate will expire from sheer boredom. Camille Paglia will become a question for Trivial Pursuit; and Julie Burchill will stick to novel-writing. Gloria Steinem will decide to write about smoking.

Catholic chic

The drift of the Church of Rome ever further to the right will unleash a new fashionability for American Catholicism. Suddenly, it catches two trends at once: doctrinal conservatism and ethic trendiness.

Bagel bonanza

Already growing, the bagel craze will finally sweep mainstream America. From being largely inedible, extremely dense dough-rings, bagels will become the new muffin, only this time fat-free! Every kind of fruit is mixed in; eventually cappuccino bagels will sweep the market. The key sign of the mainstreaming of what was once a Jewish oddity: they show up in Cleveland shopping malls.

The new seriousness

As all forms of media start falling into the O.J. Simpson cesspool, a backlash will gather force. Extremely long, boring articles on very worthy topics will appear in what used to be popular magazines. Norman Pearlstine, at Time-

Warner, will transform *Time* back into a staid journal of record. The *New York Times* will scale back its livelier writers in favour of stolid reporting prose. Cable channels will vie with one another to be more upmarket. c-span will be seen as the model of the new media. Rupert Murdoch will follow suit.

Airport heaven

Suddenly, the hip new place to hang out won't be the local mall, but the local airport. Denver's extraordinary new aeroplane complex will rival Mall of America in its array of specialist shopping. Chicago O'Hare's architectural splendour will attract intellectuals keen to appreciate the transience of post-modern life; bistros will pop up where once there were only hot-dog stands and over-priced coffee. Douglas Coupland's next novel is set in a baggage-claim area. There will be spin-offs on MTV.

Republicans all

As Republicans control or dominate both houses of Congress, political scientists will realise that the Republican comeback in presidential elections in the past 30 years is not restricted to that particular branch of government. Suddenly, real bipartisanship will be a necessity; and Bill Clinton will become a Republican ally on a whole range of issues. But this temporary truce will unravel as the 1996 presidential election draws near.

The kiddie backlash

As baby-boomers finally tire of their squealing kids, the boom in products geared to young parents will subside. Suddenly, bachelorhood will be chic

again; single, childless women will be portrayed as role models; and movies that portray children as sinister menaces will crop up.

Hairs apparent

In advertising and modelling, the hirsute will return as a male sex symbol. Calvin Klein ads place underpants next to mountains of dark stomach hair. Jews and Italians will score big; Aryans, in another blow to WASP hegemony, will retreat. Alec Baldwin will become an even bigger star at the box office. Companies will manufacture hair-growing products for chests. Articles will appear about the new misogyny.

Andrew Sullivan: editor of the *New Republic*, Washington, DC.

to French, British and Russian concerns and backed away from the idea of lifting the arms embargo and launching air strikes against the Serbs. The new Clinton might be less timid about exercising American leadership.

The revitalisation of American foreign policy would not come about in a systematic, orderly way. That is not Mr Clinton's style. Nor is he likely to satisfy critics who demand a clear, convincing definition of American interests abroad in the post-cold-war era (while failing to suggest one themselves). Progress will have to come through more stumbles and zig-zags, and despite some difficult obstacles.

One is Congress. Law-makers were

angry about Mr Clinton's failure to let them vote in advance on the planned invasion of Haiti. Through their control of the purse strings, they may seek to constrain the president if he develops ambitions for further foreign ventures. Another constraint is the inward-looking mood of the American people. It seems to have become axiomatic that almost no military engagement nowadays is worth the loss of American lives. That imposes awkward inhibitions on the actions of a supposed superpower.

To revamp his foreign-policy reputation, many argue, Mr Clinton has to get himself a more sparkling foreign-policy team. He has already replaced his defence secretary. A favourite Washington

sport is to speculate over the future of his nice but uninspiring secretary of state, Warren Christopher, and his national security adviser, Anthony Lake, who is so inconspicuous that a caption to a picture in the *New York Times* identified him as an "unidentified man". One version of the merry-go-round would have Mr Lake replaced by Strobe Talbott, the deputy secretary of state and a friend of Mr Clinton's from Rhodes-scholarship days at Oxford, while ex-Vice-President Walter Mondale is recalled from the embassy in Tokyo to be secretary of state. But Mr Clinton hates shuffling his friends out of jobs, and the real problem with the foreign-policy team has anyway been the captain, the president himself.

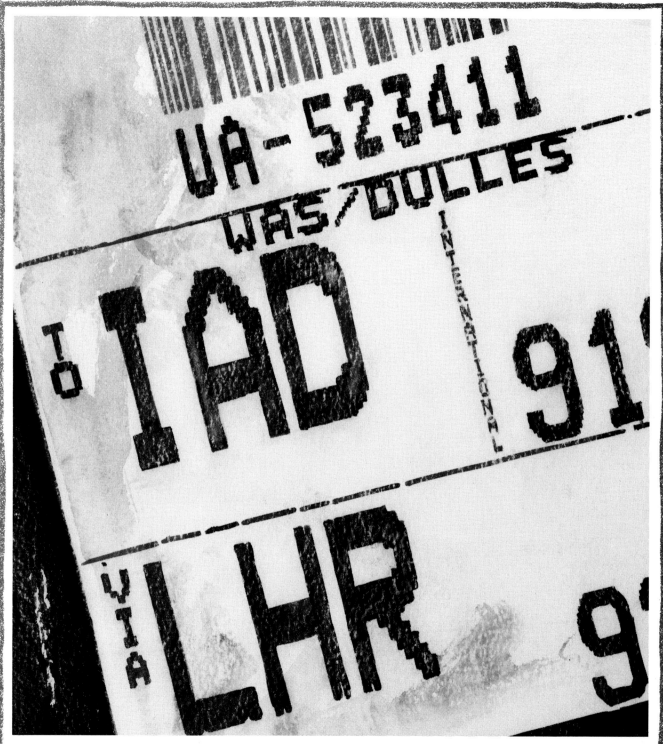

Non-stop every day-U.A.

Uniting London and Washington D.C. non-stop every day from Heathrow.
Come fly the airline that's uniting the world. Come fly the friendly skies.
For reservations, see your travel agent or call United on 081 990 9900 (0800 888 555 outside London).

 **UNITED AIRLINES**

Some People had a Lifetime to make Things perfect.

Fortunately, now you have your Epson Stylus™ Color.

Isn't printing all about reproducing one's intellectual output, sharing it with others?

A painstaking task in the past - always done with loving care. To share precious knowledge.

We at EPSON believe that perfect print quality is not the ultimate goal. It is a means of recording perfected thoughts.

EPSON printers represent a new generation of printers - precision instruments that give you a much better presentation performance.

Take the EPSON Stylus Color for example. It's an ink jet color printer with close to photographic print quality (to 720 x 720 dpi). With a palette of more than 16 million colors and 256 grey scales that are easy to manipulate with software specially designed for EPSON.

What's more, the EPSON Stylus Color prints amazingly fast. Special transparencies and papers are available for producing superlative color presentations.

And if ever the ink runs out, you only need to replace the cartridge - not the entire print head.

You also get our world famous service and support. Because we're EPSON. It's our guarantee to you of each and every one of our products.

The evolution of the ink jet printer has taken a giant step with the EPSON Stylus Color. It's all because of our passion and dedication. Intertwined with expertise and experience.

Or as we say: practice made perfect. For more information, call your local EPSON dealer.

WARRANTY 3 YEARS EPSON STYLUS

EPSON *Stylus* COLOR
INK JET PRINTER

EPSON®

EPSON EUROPE B.V. PROF. J.H. BAVINCKLAAN 5, 1183 AT AMSTELVEEN, HOLLAND / SEIKO EPSON CORPORATION, 3-5, OWA 3-CHOME SUWA-SHI, NAGANO-KEN JAPAN.
EPSON IS A REGISTERED TRADEMARK AND EPSON STYLUS IS A TRADEMARK OF SEIKO EPSON CORPORATION.

The Republican agenda

The World in 1995 asked **William Weld**, the governor of Massachusetts, to spell out the ideas that the Republican Party needs to follow if it is to win the White House in 1996

The federal government in Washington is grey and tired. National politics has become something even less than "the art of the possible"—with Washington reduced to practising little more than the statecraft of artifice.

Unbalanced budgets are accepted as inevitable; meagre reductions in projected spending increases are brandished as cuts. Those who would raise taxes are preposterously lauded for their "courage". Those who cut waste are assailed for lacking compassion. The average American family will, in 1995, pay nearly a quarter of its income in federal taxes, compared with just 2% in 1950.

Despite this growth in the tax take, most Americans believe that their schools are deteriorating, their cities are dangerous, and government has become intrusive and inefficient. Republicans believe they are right.

Republicans are not only more closely aligned with the prevailing inclinations of the electorate; the party can also return to Washington blessed with an exile's availing ignorance. Republicans can restore themselves to executive power with an optimism that refuses to accept debt-heavy budgets and their corollary impulse: the lazy reflex that compels tax increases rather than tight management and real spending reductions.

As a foundation, we need a balanced budget amendment. In addition, a line-item veto for the president would be a natural complement. The governors of 43 states have the power to strike the wasteful, the redundant, and the ludicrous from their budgets. The president in the White House, absurdly, has no such weapon. He needs to be similarly empowered if we are to control spending and taxes in the future.

The next president ought to commit himself, on the record, to submitting only a balanced budget, even in the absence of an amendment that requires it, and vetoing each year any unbalanced budget passed by the Congress. Deficits are not inevitable. In 1993, the House nearly passed the $100-billion Penny-Kasich spending-cut plan. Despite the defeat of Penny-Kasich, it held a hopeful clue to the future. A majority of newer

congressmen supported it.

Certain agencies announce themselves loudly as candidates for termination: the Bureau of Reclamation's water projects and the Rural Electrification Administration, for example (mission accomplished, both). And just what goes on at the Departments of Energy and Education? If the question cannot be adequately answered, those agencies ought to be abolished, as well. If the objection is,

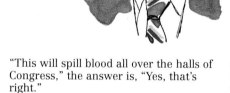

"Government ought to stay out of your wallet and out of your bedroom."

"This will spill blood all over the halls of Congress," the answer is, "Yes, that's right."

Just as obsolete agencies tend to exist in perpetuity, American politics has become, in too many instances, an endless run for re-election. Congress has re-election rates that make Britain's House of Lords look dynamic by comparison, with flagrant venality, extreme incompetence, or death being the typical causes of an incumbent's demise. We need to limit congressional terms, and consider a single, six-year term for the president. Meanwhile, the Republican nominee in 1996 should publicly vow to serve only a single term. Nothing so focuses the mind of an incumbent on the common good as not facing an election.

As Republicans, we do have a special burden to demonstrate that our aversion to costly bureaucratic programmes and high taxes is not in fact a lack of commitment to social justice and compassion. Republicans are well-versed in the virtues of the free market, but in order to be fully credible, we also have to be alert to those areas

where the free market falls short.

In "The Tragedy of American Compassion", Marvin Olasky argues that private charitable organisations in America's earlier days were able to make greater demands on individual behaviour because those organisations stood closer to the misfortune they were trying to redress. Mr Olasky's thesis is that we have inverted compassion. "Entitlements" are now administered from afar and without discrimination between the deserving and the undeserving poor—that is, those who are willing to work and those who are unwilling. The task for Republicans is to show that an anti-statist approach, particularly with regard to welfare, is more consistent with true compassion than the left's concession to defeat. Government should help those who want to work or are unable to work. The obligation to those who refuse to work is, frankly, non-existent.

The Republican Party has been properly critical of the Democrats when they seek to extend the long arm of the government where it does not belong. We should be true to that conviction on all issues. If we do not trust the government even to tie its own shoes, why should we trust government to divine solutions to a matter so ethically, theologically and scientifically complex as abortion? Government ought to stay out of your wallet and out of your bedroom.

As for foreign relations, Republicans must recognise that expanding global free trade has supplanted the defeat of imperial communism as the chief aim of United States foreign policy. Republicans must be in the vanguard of building upon NAFTA and extending the reach of the World Trade Organisation in future rounds.

Rather than being a negative vision, the minimalist Republican view of government represents a new idealism—grounded by a proven faith in liberty. In fact, it is the left's view of government that is meagre and unambitious, content to tolerate poverty, give reparations through entitlements, and preside over a society of victims.

Friedrich Hayek distilled all of this into a "fundamental principle that in the ordering of our affairs we should make as much use as possible of the spontaneous forces of society, and resort as little as possible to coercion." Republicans would do well—will do well—to abide by Hayek's creed.

TOMO

"We are positioned for sustainable, significant increases in both sales and earnings"

*Joseph T. Gorman,
Chairman and Chief Executive Officer*

RR**O**W IS HERE

We used to say "Tomorrow is Taking Shape at a Company Called TRW." While TRW has been helping to shape our world, we have also been working hard to streamline and strengthen our company.

We have set a course that aims to delight our three key constituent groups – customers, shareholders, and employees – by providing each with superior performance. The facts demonstrate we are doing just that.

Several years ago, we set for ourselves some tough objectives. We are meeting those objectives. Today, we are number one in our key markets. We are the world leader in occupant restraints, in steering systems, in certain automotive electronics markets, in advanced spacecraft technology, in defense communications, and in consumer credit information, among others. We are also the world leader in complex systems integration.

Our businesses are in segments of industries that are outgrowing the markets themselves, and we are managing that growth for profit. Cost structures have been improved dramatically, and we are beginning to experience the benefits of our strategic investments over the past five years.

Further, technology leadership, always a core TRW strength, is now helping to make us more competitive in all of our businesses.

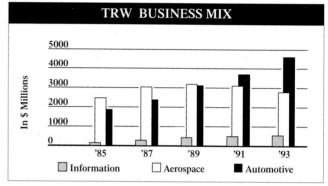

TRW BUSINESS MIX

In $ Millions — 0, 1000, 2000, 3000, 4000, 5000

'85 '87 '89 '91 '93

☐ Information   ☐ Aerospace   ■ Automotive

TRW aerospace technology is contributing to the rapid growth of TRW's automotive business.

Management is also stronger. Supporting a seasoned group of top managers, we have a highly qualified, energetic, and experienced team around the globe.

What are our priorities? Delivering on our commitments to customers, shareholders, and employees. We are positioned for sustainable, significant increases in both sales and earnings.

We are doing what we say we will do, and we will continue to deliver on our promises.

Automotive. Aerospace. Information. Innovation.

Unconfident Canada

William Thorsell

In 1994, the United Nations ranked the quality of life in Canada as the highest in the world. Why, then, in 1995, will Canada be convulsed by self-doubt?

Its doubt grows out of its virtue: it is an exceedingly successful country that doubts whether it is, or should be, a country at all. There is so much diversity that it is not surprising that there should be quite a lot of paradox too. The opposition in Canada's Parliament now comprises the separatist Bloc Québécois, a party devoted to Québec's independence. And the newly elected government of the province of Québec itself is the separatist Parti Québécois (PQ), which promises a referendum on independence before 1995 is out.

The Canadian federation is already among the most decentralised in the world, with much of the legal jurisdiction, such as education, health, social welfare, urban affairs, civil law and commerce vested in the provinces. There isn't much dirigisme by the national government over the regions. With an annual deficit still exceeding 3% of GDP, the central government has neither the money, the cause, nor the will seriously to challenge the constitutionally powerful provinces.

Québec is already largely free to adopt its own economic policies. In fact its slow growth rate stems from the mess it has made in running its own affairs. Chastened, it has been turning to free trade and deregulation to escape the torpor of "Québec Inc".

Like Canada itself, the current momentum behind Québec's independence is largely an accident of political history. In Ottawa, the Bloc Québécois is a protest against the bruising failure of several other provinces to ratify constitutional amendments of symbolic importance to Québec in 1990. The new PQ government in Québec City reflects the desire of Québéckers for a change in provincial leadership, rather than independence, after nine years of Liberal Party rule.

Canada is not so much a country as it is a series of pragmatic arrangements. Strong nation-states may sneer, but in

William Thorsell: editor-in-chief of Toronto's *Globe and Mail*.

the years running up to the turn of the century this may prove the best way of running a country. In a world of increasingly strong international government, who needs a bossy national parliament? Canada is wise to ask such a question and is further along than most countries in answering it.

Canada's doubt about its nationhood is, in part, assuaged by the consensus, even among Québec separatists, that many of Canada's current arrangements would have to be recreated should Québec become independent. Separatists

Too heavy by half

say that Québéckers would continue to use the Canadian currency and carry Canadian passports, that Québec would continue to share a common market (or at least free trade) with Canada, and that Québec would continue to pay its "fair share" of interest and principal on Canada's national debt. Some joint administrative mechanisms would be necessary, perhaps along the lines of the European Union. Québec would become independent only immediately to reassociate.

The Canadian economy will recover nicely in 1995, fuelled by higher productivity, free trade with the United States, rising commodity prices and the 73-cent Canadian dollar (down from 89 US cents four years ago). Inflation remains very low. With the notable exception of high government deficits that generate high taxes and high real interest rates, Cana-

da has been able to deliver on most of the things that matter to its citizens.

The unemployment rate, still near 10%, reflects generous unemployment insurance and regional development subsidies as much as it does real mismatches in the labour market. Canada's generous social safety net will be increasingly under review next year, both because of its cost and its perverse effects on work.

Jean Chretien, the Liberal prime minister, makes the low-key argument that Canada is a solution that has become much too skilled at inventing problems for itself. In fact, the population is turning away from constitutional politics, despite the high profile now enjoyed by Québec separatists in national and provincial parliaments. The intellectual arena is filled with debate about multiculturalism and immigration, the state of the family, education, culture, new technology and quality of life in Canadian cities.

With a population of only 29m, Canada adds a million immigrants and refugees to its population every four years, most of them from Asia, Africa and Latin America. Toronto is now among the most multiracial cities in the world, followed by Vancouver and Montreal. This is a logical extension of Canada's past, which was never lacking in a hyphen, even when the people of New France took up with the aboriginals to form the Métis. There is some risk that the hyphen will break along the borders of Québec in 1995, but the productive inertia of a 203-year-old relationship suggests otherwise.

Li Peng, Qiao Shi, Zhu Rongji and Jiang Zemin form an elderly, orderly queue

China's post-Deng turmoil

Dominic Ziegler

Deng Xiaoping's imminent death will start a full-blooded fight for the leadership of China next year. The Chinese Communist Party is too venal, and the future of economic reform too uncertain, for the coming power-grab to be as decorous as the body of international opinion wishfully predicts. Political instability at home will be matched by a militant Chinese chauvinism abroad. That could mean military skirmishes with Vietnam in the disputed South China Sea; strident hostility towards Taiwan's growing international acceptance; loud threats directed at seditious Hong Kong; and a new hostility in its relations with America, particularly if China's dream of joining the World Trade Organisation at the start of 1995 is dashed.

In some ways, the Communist authorities behave as if Mr Deng were already dead. Certainly, the man's presence is no longer as important as his "Thought", which by the end of 1994 was being honoured alongside Mao's. Deng Thought—slogans concerning "socialism with Chinese characteristics"—is largely vacuous stuff meant rhetorically to disguise the country's abandonment of Maoism. But in 1995 expect the first questions to be asked privately by political heavyweights about Mr Deng's economic legacy. Leadership bids will be staked on the claim that the legacy was, after all, not all good for China.

Ever since late 1978, when Mr Deng threw the country into economic reform, such a contention has appeared not only

Dominic Ziegler: China correspondent for *The Economist*.

blasphemous, but also irrelevant. China's opening brought more millions out of penury more quickly than any episode in economic history, for annual growth in China over the past 15 years has averaged 9%. Just what are the limits of such growth? With 1994 came the possibility that the limits might already have been reached. Following a year of gung-ho, Deng-exhorted boom, the country has been saddled with growth that is barely slowing but with inflation that is climbing towards 30%.

Not all of China's leaders will draw the obvious conclusion that, far from having gone too far, the Deng reforms have so far failed their biggest challenge: getting rid of the state-owned industrial sector. The sector runs, for a big part, on machinery commissioned before the Great Leap Forward. It is an all but insupportable drain upon the national finances. By engendering inflation, and by hogging national investment, it is

Jagged economy

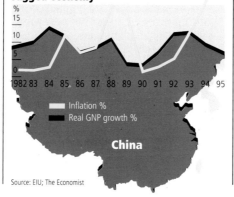

%
15
10
5
0
1982 83 84 85 86 87 88 89 90 91 92 93 94 95

Inflation %
Real GNP growth %

China

Source: EIU; The Economist

now a predatory threat to the private sector that is Mr Deng's greatest legacy.

This is not a conclusion that any of China's leaders are willing to voice. The state sector has been the bedrock of the Communist Party's authority since its power waned in the countryside with Mr Deng's rural liberalisations. So even those in the Politburo most closely identified with the Deng reforms—for instance, Jiang Zemin, the country's president and Mr Deng's anointed heir, and Zhu Rongji, known in the West as the economics tsar—will now not hear a harsh word spoken against the state-owned giants. Previously they payed lip-service at least to state-sector reform.

All of which has implications for the leadership fight. The assumption of most westerners is that Mr Deng's mantle will pass to the collective leadership that now supposedly embodies "Dengism": Mr Jiang, Mr Zhu and Li Peng, China's premier. And so it might pass, briefly. Yet these three are no towering force within the hierarchy; moreover, their alliance is not strong enough to survive the conclusion of any one of them that rivalry might best further his interest.

Mr Jiang's wealth of titles—state president, party secretary-general and head of the Central Military Commission—belies his rather shaky authority, in both party and army. Mr Zhu's authority, always exaggerated by the western press, hangs upon the outcome of his anti-inflation drive. Mr Li, an as-good-as adopted son of Zhou Enlai's, has supporters among the party's conservative gerontocrats; but he is charmless, bu-

Red stars and the deep blue sea

Dominic Ziegler

In the coming year western governments will be forced to admit what China's Asian neighbours have long been warning. The rise of China's navy has altered the balance of power in the region.

It is not the current state of the navy that appears alarming, but the speed at which it is modernising. In technology, it is still far behind America's navy, and Russia's. Nonetheless defence spending is on the increase, growing by a third in 1994 alone. The official defence budget of $6 billion excludes all sorts of other military spending, for instance, on research and development. So the final figure is up to six times that, and much is being lavished upon the navy.

Over the past decade missile-equipped destroyers and conventional submarines have been built at a rate of one a year, and missile-armed destroyers at three a year. China is developing submarine-launched ballistic missiles with a 5,000-mile range, and has started building nuclear-driven submarines to launch them. It is in the market for at least one aircraft carrier. This is in addition to two dozen Su-27 fighter-bombers it has bought from Russia, and 100 S-300 surface-to-air missiles. China is now building a handful of deep-water ports to house the new goodies, notably at Dalian on the Yellow Sea and Zhanjiang in southern Guangdong. The goal that bullish admirals occasionally let drop is, sometime between 2000 and 2050, to have a rapid-deployment force based upon aircraft-carriers. If China keeps up its enthusiastic buying of Russian weaponry, says Shigeo Hiramatsu of Kyorin University, the job will be finished well ahead of time.

What does China want with all this hardware? In 1988 China seized half-a-dozen atolls in the Spratly Islands. With its investment in military installations since then on both the Spratlys and the Paracels (370 miles from the Chinese mainland), China is almost in a position not just to stake territorial and mineral claims in the South China Sea, but also to enforce them. It already has more than enough power to wreak havoc with shipping lanes.

America, Russia and even Japan have chosen to let all this pass. China looks set to strut in the East China Sea as it has already further south. It has drilled enthusiastically for oil in its half of the sea's continental shelf. In 1992 it claimed Japan's Senkaku Islands for its own, a subject that the Japanese, for the sake of a quiet life, would rather not have to think about. Soon China will try to enforce jurisdiction over the whole of the East China Sea's continental shelf, pitting it not only against Japan, but also against the Koreas and Taiwan. Next, it will announce grand plans with Myanmar's military thugs to build a route down from China and out into an Indian Ocean port. By then China will have covered all the region's deep-water pockets.

China's imperial pull

reaucratic and probably inept.

Just as Mr Zhou's death in 1976, and Hu Yaobang's in 1989, provided the spark for spontaneous popular protests in Tiananmen Square against the regime, so Mr Deng's death could do the same. Such an occasion would inevitably lead to a reappraisal of the violence used against civilians during the 1989 crackdown. Several politicians could serve their own purposes by repudiating government violence. Hu Jintao, who as a whipper-snapper of a little over half-a-century is the standing committee's youngest member, was not present at the Politburo's crucial 1989 vote on the matter. Qiao Shi, another member, abstained. Mr Qiao's authority comes from his security background and his control of the party's personnel files; he is now trying, as parliamentary chairman, to turn the National People's Congress from a rubber-stamp parliament into a working power base.

Finally, there is Zhao Ziyang, the second of Mr Deng's three chosen heirs (the first was Hu Yaobang), who was ousted as secretary-general just before the 1989 killings. That year Mr Zhao opposed the hard-line approach that his colleagues were adopting; now that he has emerged from internal exile, it is clear that he is unrepentant. He represents the best leadership hopes of those that might call themselves reformists.

In the meantime the stronger hand is more likely to be played by a wing of the Communist Party that may soon be happy to have itself openly dubbed "neo-Maoist". This wing bemoans inflation and is the loudest promoter of command-economy controls to rein it back. It objects to the wide discrepancies in wealth—among individuals and between regions—that have sprung up during the Deng era; and to the rise of lawlessness across the country. It is appalled at the lack of party discipline and at the way many provinces, such as Guangdong, next to Hong Kong, have largely been able to forge their own paths.

It is this wing, in the pell-mell of a fight over the party's soul, that is most likely to raise the flag of national chauvinism, though plenty of other causes could rally around it. Hong Kong will be the first to feel the new mood. In 1995 Hong Kong's vigorous press and public opinion will be branded as exporters of sedition to the mainland. The colony will by the end of the year be left in no doubt about the future of free expression once Hong Kong reverts to China in 1997.

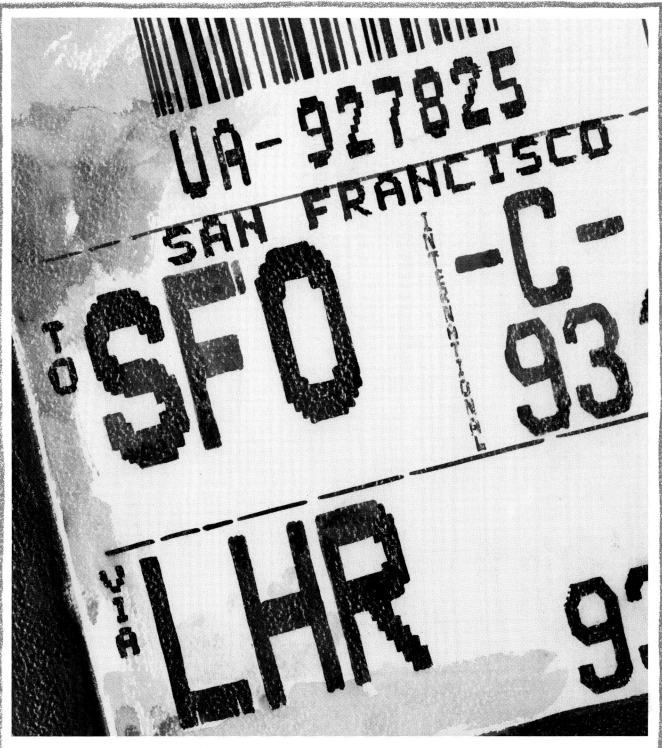

Non-stop every day-U.A.

Uniting London and San Francisco non-stop every day from Heathrow.
Come fly the airline that's uniting the world. Come fly the friendly skies.
For reservations, see your travel agent or call United on 081 990 9900 (0800 888 555 outside London).

 **UNITED AIRLINES**

BORDERLESS

When the leaders of nations and celebrities traveled to the East, NYK provided the services to help make history. Today, too, on a worldwide scale but in the same tradition, NYK is making extraordinary advances in shipping history with a fleet of some 400 ships including containerships,conventional vessels, tankers and specialized bulk carriers. Now more than ever before, NYK services have expanded to meet the challenge of global economic interdependence.

Borders between nations, between carriers, borders between products and between people and ideas are being dissolved. NYK's integration of global logistics and megacarrier capabilities opens fresh vistas on the borderless society.

NYK LINE
NIPPON YUSEN KAISHA

Head Office: 3-2, Marunouchi 2-chome, Chiyoda-ku, Tokyo 100, Japan   Tel. (03) 3284-5151

Japan's new politics

Sebastian Mallaby

The urban masses have their say

1995 will test the depth of Japan's political renewal. There will be local elections in the spring; a national election for parliament's upper house in the summer; and, quite possibly, a third election for the more powerful lower house in the autumn. These contests should ensure that Japan's politics do not merely drift. Indeed, the process of creating a new parliamentary order will probably be hastened.

The old system fell apart in 1993, when the corrupt Liberal Democratic Party (LDP) lost its grip on power after 38 continuous years in government. Most Japanese were thrilled: the coalition that took over scored approval ratings three times higher than its LDP predecessor. Commentators declared that a political system widely held in contempt would at last cede to something worthy of Japan's miracle economy.

In 1994, however, these hopes were rudely deflated. The reformist coalition collapsed, regrouped, then fell apart again, opening the way for the LDP's return to government. Admittedly, this was a chastened LDP: defections have deprived the party of the clout to rule on its own, so it shares power with two left-leaning parties. The question for the coming year, therefore, is whether the

Sebastian Mallaby: bureau chief for *The Economist* in Tokyo.

hopes of 1993 or the doubts of 1994 are to be vindicated.

The elections are likely to show that on the issue of bribery, at least, optimism is largely justified. Japan's big companies used to shower the LDP with cash because the alternative was so awful: the biggest opposition group was the Social Democratic Party, which clung to hard-line, left-wing policies. But the political turmoil of 1993-94 has reduced the SDP to a smallish force, and the party has anyway ditched its extremism. The new alternative to the LDP is a coalition of reformist groups, led by LDP defectors. As a result, businessmen no longer mind which party is in government.

The decline of bribery will be quickened by the political reforms of 1994. These include curbs on raising campaign funds. They also change the electoral rules. The vast multi-member constituencies that were previously used to choose candidates for parliament's lower house have been replaced with a mixture of British-style single-member districts and German-style proportional representation.

This removes one cause of money politics. Under the old system, two or three LDP men were elected from each constituency. Being from the same party, they could not differentiate themselves by policy; they therefore resorted to buy-

ing votes with cash sealed in neat white envelopes. The cash came from local businessmen, who thus secured the parliamentarians' support in lobbying for government licences and contracts.

The new electoral system attacks this set-up in three ways. The constituency boundaries have been moved, so undermining the candidates' well-oiled ties with local businesses. The new single-member districts will end the contests between members of the same party, so enabling candidates to compete on policy. Lastly, 200 out of 500 members of the lower house will be elected by proportional representation: bribing voters across these huge electoral districts will be beyond the power of even the best-organised candidates.

Electoral reform may also promote the second change that optimists foretold: that politicians will no longer put the interests of producers before consumers. Fewer business bribes will make politicians less beholden to producers; at the same time, direct appeal to voters, based on policy, is likely to result in pro-consumer promises. The farm lobby will be weakened by another part of the electoral reform, which reduces the over-weighting of rural constituencies. At last, urban consumers will have the clout to push for lower farm subsidies.

Let's debate ideas

That leaves the third hope aroused in 1993: that policy may come to be more vigorously debated. Again, the decline of money politics will create room for the politics of ideas. The Social Democrats' decline will help too: in the past the party's extremist views (hostility to America, sympathy for Stalinist North Korea) rendered moderate debate futile. Now that politics is dominated by two moderate groups, reasonable argument at last seems possible.

On all three counts, therefore, politics seems set to change: there will be fewer bribes, less producer influence, and more discussion of policy. Yet the final prediction for 1995 gives this optimism a cruel twist: the parties that worked to bring about the change will not benefit from it. One of the most remarkable features of politics in 1994 has been the extreme unpopularity, both in parliament and among ordinary Japanese, of Ichiro Ozawa, the man most associated with the drive for policy-based politics. Next year's elections will give the Japanese a chance to choose between the LDP and Mr Ozawa's reformist block. Even though they will have Mr Ozawa to thank for that choice, the Japanese may vote against him.

Will memories stir?

Sebastian Mallaby

The 50th anniversary of Japan's defeat in the second world war—August 15th 1945—will shatter a taboo that is already looking fragile. For years the Japanese remembered only their own sufferings in the war, glossing over those they inflicted on their neighbours. But in August 1993 the prime minister called Japan's invasion of Asia a "war of aggression", and the recognition of Japan's responsibility for starting the conflict began spreading. The stage is set for a cathartic half-centenary.

Since the prime minister's admission, war veterans have unbuttoned their memories in public. The emperor's uncle has spoken out against the war. A new museum has opened in Hiroshima, which was flattened by an atom bomb in August 1945 and so symbolises Japan's

suffering; this explains that Japan was an aggressor in the war, not merely a victim. Next year's commemorations will no doubt bring more of this. To be complete, however, they need just one thing more: a popular film that undams private guilt and pain, washing the collective conscience.

In Germany the film was "Holocaust", a Hollywood tear-jerker that ran on television in 1979. Fully 20m watched "Holocaust", half the adult population of western Germany.

Nothing will quite match this in Japan. For one thing, the Japanese are less weighed down with angst, so the exorcism, when it comes, will be less thorough and traumatic. For another, Japan's crimes were less awful than Hitler's were: prisoners of war were abused, civilians were murdered, but

there was no genocide. All the same, the Japanese case does resemble Germany's in one big way. Soul-searching has started with earnest museums and political pronouncements. It will flower with something more popular.

There is a decent chance that Japan will have its equivalent of "Holocaust" in 1995, probably in August, when the anniversaries of the atom bomb and of Japan's surrender are commemorated. Starting early in the year, Japan's newspapers will run features about the war; the *Asahi*, a left-leaning daily, plans to stress Japan's mistreatment of Koreans and Chinese during the years of occupation. Television documentaries and books will jostle each other for the public's attention. Just possibly, one will match the cathartic power of Hollywood's magicians.

Rising sun, falling prices

Sebastian Mallaby

Economic recovery has been long predicted in Japan. In 1995 it is genuinely going to happen. After zero growth in 1993 and not much in 1994, next year should see real growth hit 1.7%. There is nothing very remarkable in this; after three years of restraint and saving hard, Japan's consumers want to live a bit. But recovery will have its surprising side. Many firms will be grumbling.

This is because inflation, a familiar guest at recovery feasts, will be disconcertingly absent. Indeed, prices will

probably fall, although official statistics (which overlook discount stores) may fail to record this. Because of falling prices, Japan's nominal GDP will remain roughly flat even while the real economy is growing.

Discounting

The main force driving down prices will be Japan's discount revolution. The Japanese used to frequent only two kinds of shop: the cosy mom-and-pop stores, supplied by armies of delivery vans bringing goods in tiny quantities, and the vast department stores, filled with bowing sales girls, where even the most modest purchase is wrapped like a jewel. Both sorts of shop are wildly expensive. Both will increasingly lose out to the nonsense neon of the discounters.

The discounters are cheap not merely because they avoid cornerstore tininess and big-store extravagance. They also take advantage of the strong yen by buying supplies from foreigners. In 1993-94, by-passing Japanese suppliers (and so putting locals out of jobs) was something only a few rebels would stomach. Next year even staid supermarkets will be at it.

The recovery will therefore be fun for consumers (at least those who keep their jobs), but grim for producers that are forced to slash their prices. Lumbered

with the tradition of lifetime employment, big firms will be slow to cut labour costs in line with falling revenues. As a result, they will lose out to smaller, newer firms that are not burdened by hordes of long-serving employees.

Meanwhile firms of all sizes will face a nasty financial problem. Their debts are fixed in nominal terms; in real terms, therefore, they will be growing. The burden of debt service (part of which is also fixed in nominal terms) will weigh heavily on revenues that decline along with prices. To avoid taking on more burdensome debt, some firms will delay investments. This, in turn, will prevent economic recovery from gathering steam: which is why growth in nominal GDP will be so slow.

Deflationary recovery will confuse debate on Japan's notorious trade sur-

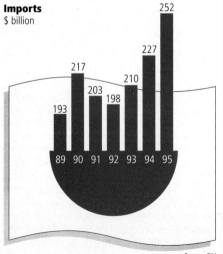

Imports
$ billion

193 · 89
217 · 90
203 · 91
198 · 92
210 · 93
227 · 94
252 · 95

Source: EIU

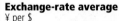
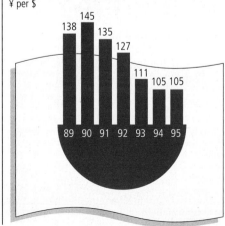

Exchange-rate average
¥ per $

138 · 89
145 · 90
135 · 91
127 · 92
111 · 93
105 · 94
105 · 95

Inflation
%

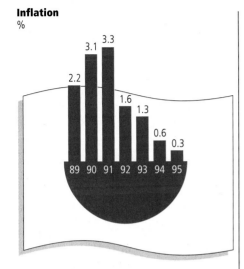

2.2 3.1 3.3 1.6 1.3 0.6 0.3
89 90 91 92 93 94 95

plus. Falling prices will encourage a strong yen, since investors will be delighted to hold a currency whose real value is rising. This, in turn, will goad retailers to fill their shelves with cheap imported goods, so shrinking Japan's trade surplus.

Japan will export less, as its companies are undercut by cheaper foreigners (often these "foreigners" will be the overseas subsidiaries of Japanese companies). But the strong yen will mean that, in dollar terms, the value of Japan's exports will stay high. Trade tension will therefore stay high also.

The flood of imports will submerge Japan's famous singularity. For years Japan banned imports of foreign rice, declaring that it would never suit Japanese palates. Next year Californian rice (which is indistinguishable from the Japanese sort and costs much less) will be lustily shovelled from bowl to mouth by a million Japanese chopsticks. The

Japanese will drive foreign cars and take even more foreign holidays than they do already.

The strong yen will also dent Japan's singular employment system. The tradition of lifetime employment at Japan's big firms was sustained only because of high growth; and high growth depended until recently on steadily expanding exports. Now that the strong yen is choking export volumes, Japan's prestigious manufacturers have no use for their white-collar armies. Service firms are under pressure too: for example, cheap foreign airlines will lure so many Japanese customers away that Japan's carriers will have to fire workers.

So far most big firms have resisted drastic action, preferring to freeze the appointment of new graduates rather than sack middle-aged workers. This has created a jobs crisis among young Japanese, who are taking part-time jobs and travelling abroad while they wait for real work to become available. This may have profound social effects. A period of disenchanted heel-kicking may make young Japanese more cynical than their workaholic parents.

The jobs crisis among the young will be much discussed throughout 1995, and the discussion will eventually shift policy. At present Japan's government subsidises the lifetime-employment system. Firms that hit hard times receive hand-outs in return for not laying people off; and employees that stay in one firm for their entire career retire with a generous bonus on which they pay no taxes. The government will eventually remove these incentives to keeping employees on. This will trigger the firing of mid-career workers, and the end of lifetime employment.

Baby dragons look to mummy

John Burton

1995 will find the four dragon economies adjusting to the growing regional dominance of the Middle Kingdom.

Hong Kong will revert to Chinese sovereignty in mid-1997. Sino-British confrontation over democratic political reforms in the territory is not likely to abate. China will offer minimum co-operation to the British colonial administration. The British will be increasingly isolated. Influential segments of business

John Burton: Seoul correspondent for the *Financial Times*.

and the civil service will slip over to the Beijing camp as 1997 draws near.

The continued political confrontation and China's threat to dismantle the recently introduced electoral system will provoke further polarisation in Hong Kong society. The much-heralded elections to the municipal and legislative councils will take place in 1995. Expect lots of damaging (but democratic) rhetoric during the campaign. The longer-term effect will be that Hong Kong's talented officials will flee the

Australia — 1995

The sun will shine on Australia's economy in 1995. Economic growth will exceed 3% for the third year running. Unemployment will fall and inflation will remain acceptably low. Australia's mining companies will benefit from higher world prices. Its manufacturers will make further inroads into booming South-East Asian markets. One sector that is likely to perform poorly is agriculture. Drought in 1994 will dent output in 1995.

Strong economic growth will be accompanied by a worsening of the current-account deficit. Import growth will outstrip export growth. More confident consumers will want to indulge in foreign goodies. More confident industrialists will need imports to upgrade their factories.

Expect trouble. The financial markets already do. The current-account deficit will exceed 4% of GDP in 1994. The Australian dollar looks susceptible to a shock.

This would come at a bad time for the prime minister, Paul Keating. He will be suffering from internal rows in the ruling Labor Party. Left-leaning elements in Labor will remain unhappy with the government's privatisation policy. Mr Keating may also have to contend with a new deputy prime minister, possibly Carmen Lawrence, who will covet his job. Most difficult of all, the opposition Liberal/National alliance may at last have pulled itself together under its new leader, Alexander Downer.

Mr Keating does not have to call a general election before May 1996. But, on the expectation that the economic situation will deteriorate, he may go to the country in late 1995. Expect a good contest: the experienced, street-wise Mr Keating versus the gaffe-prone but able Mr Downer.

Both may be spouting surprisingly similar policies. The opposition has already ditched the radical reform agenda that lost it the 1993 contest. Both men are good talkers. But, after 12 years of Labor Party rule, the advantage will be with the challenger, not the incumbent.

KEY INDICATORS

	1993	1994	1995
GDP growth (% pa)	3.2	3.7	3.3
Inflation (%)	1.8	2.3	3.0
Prime lending rate (year end %)	9.0	10.0	11.5
Exchange rate			
A$ per $	1.43	1.39	1.42
Current account ($bn)	-10.8	-12.5	-13.7

EIU COUNTRY ANALYSIS AND FORECASTING

WORLDWIDE

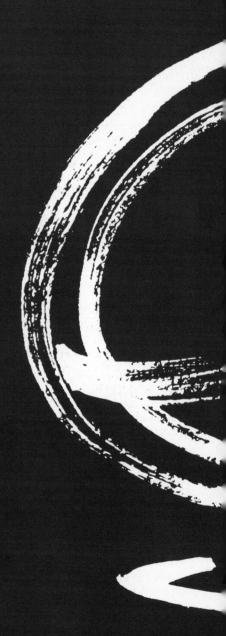

From the heart of Asia we fly to 42 cities arou

CATHAY PACIFIC

...he world. Cathay Pacific. The Heart of Asia.

colony. The quality of public administration will nosedive. This is happening already. In 1995 the divided loyalties in the colony, between present and future masters, will become ever-more apparent.

The political dispute, however, should not greatly affect the Hong Kong economy, which is stable, but lacklustre by regional standards, with a GDP growth rate of 3.6% in 1995. Hong Kong's integration with China in trade and investment is forcing Beijing to take a pragmatic approach on these matters. The Chinese will settle the disputes over the airport and the building of a container terminal, since these are crucial to Hong Kong's role as China's

main gateway to international trade. The only big threat to the economy in 1995 would be a sudden slump in overvalued property prices, which would undermine financial stability and consumer confidence.

Taiwan is closely watching events in Hong Kong as it tries to determine its future relations with China, an issue that is vital to the island's long-term economic performance. Business favours closer economic co-operation with China, but the government has to contend with growing public support for the pro-independence opposition party. The ruling Kuomintang is straddling the fence on

the China issue, leading to policy confusion. It has unsuccessfully sought United Nations membership in order to appeal to pro-independence supporters. Companies are also being encouraged to shift their investment to South-East Asia to reduce their dependence on the Chinese market. However, Taiwan will still try to expand its economic links with China as demanded by business. That is trying to have it both ways.

A more clear-cut policy favouring improved economic ties with China, including direct transport links across the Taiwan Strait, is likely if the Kuomintang wins, as expected, the December 1994 elections for provincial governor and the mayors of Taipei and Kaohsuing, and the 1995 parliamentary elections. But a surprise victory by the opposition would further muddle policy and lead to a possible political confrontation with China.

Economic factors support closer ties with China, since they would bolster Taiwan's export competitiveness while attracting foreign multinationals that want to use Taiwan as a regional business centre. Although GNP will grow by 6.6% in 1995, this is largely due to domestic demand. Export growth, which is slowing with the move to China of the big textile and footwear industries would be revived with the establishment of direct commercial links. The possible ending in 1995 of Taiwanese flights to Hong Kong, which is Taipei's main entry to China, as a result of Chinese intervention, will only

add pressure on Taipei to open direct routes with China.

South Korea is eagerly embracing China, which has become South Korea's third-largest trading partner and biggest overseas-investment target since diplomatic relations were established in 1992. The attractions of China for South Korea include proximity, its cheap labour and its potential as a huge market for both consumer and industrial goods. Indeed, China is becoming a critical factor in South Korea's industrial strategy. The belief is that China will soak up South Korea's excess production of steel, petrochemicals and cars when demand falls in the West, although this is not of immediate concern.

South Korea's GNP growth of 7.4% in 1995 is based on strong exports benefiting from the weak Korean currency and an expansion of industry at home to meet overseas demand. But South Korea's big conglomerates, or *chaebol*, are already preparing for the next downturn in global demand by increasing their investment in China. Officials in Seoul talk about the creation of an integrated Sino-Korean economic zone encircling the Yellow Sea.

Moreover, the South Korean government needs political co-operation with China to prevent a costly and sudden collapse of North Korea or military adventurism by Pyongyang. Chinese mediation has helped defuse the dispute over North Korea's nuclear programme and Beijing is encouraging the new government of Kim Jong Il to open the country to foreign investment.

The first steps toward economic reform will be taken by the government in 1995—following improved ties with the United States and other western countries.

Singapore is serving as a role model for China, which has admired the city-state's economic success based on close co-operation between state and business and its reputation for strict government. Singapore hopes that the construction of a "mini-Singapore" industrial park in Suzhou will increase its economic and political influence in China and serve as the pioneer for similar model cities in other Chinese regions.

But China remains a less important market for Singapore's exports than the United States, Malaysia, the European Union and Hong Kong. Demand from these countries is expected to keep Singapore's industries busy.

Dragons learning to fly

South Korea 7.4   7.6

Singapore

6.6

Taiwan

GDP growth, %
GDP per capita 1995
Illiteracy rates (age 15+)
Enrolment rates in formal education as a % of those aged 6-23

Hong Kong 3.6

USA 2.9

Source: UN; EIU; Unesco; Taiwanese government

9,600 | 14 | 74   24,900 | 4 | 68   12,620 | 18 | 71   22,840 | 14 | 69   27,400 | 5 | 86

Tiger, tiger, burning bright

Swaminathan S. Anklesaria Aiyar

India's capitalist Raj

Politics will dominate economics in India in 1995. Elections will take place during the year to perhaps five state assemblies, forerunners to the general election due in mid-1996.

When policy issues arise next year, the question the prime minister, P.V. Narasimha Rao, will ask himself will not be, "Is it good for the country?" but, "Will it yield votes within a few months?" Since myopia is rarely the best policy, 1995 may not be a good year for further economic reform.

Yet it will be a good year for economic growth. The task of liberalising the economy is no more than half complete, but Mr Rao has done enough in his first three years of office to spark a temporary boom. By delicensing industries, liberalising imports, cutting tax rates and welcoming foreign investment, he has imparted a new dynamism to the private sector and sent the stockmarkets soaring. This boom will peter out after three or four years in the absence of further reforms, but that is a long time in the life of a politician.

India was on the verge of becoming bankrupt when Mr Rao came to power in 1991, but his reforms led to a sharp rise in exports and foreign-portfolio investment, and so foreign-exchange reserves hit a record $18 billion (Rs560 billion) in September 1994. However, the first step in his reforms was IMF-induced austerity to stabilise an economy living beyond its means. This

Swaminathan S. Anklesaria Aiyar: consulting editor, India's *Economic Times*.

painful squeeze on consumption and capital spending meant that industrial growth was virtually zero in his first two years and no more than 3% in his third year, 1993-94.

Fortunately for him, industrial growth seems to be taking off, and should touch 6-8% in 1994-95. Mr Rao's dream script calls for further industrial acceleration to around 10% in 1995-96, taking voters' minds off issues such as corruption and inflation. However, acceleration is unlikely unless he completes much unfinished business on the reform front, and he does not seem to have the political stomach for that.

Inclusive of the railways, the public sector accounts for almost three-quarters of India's industrial stock, and Mr Rao has refused to privatise it for fear of annoying powerful trade unions.

Nor is Mr Rao willing to amend labour laws that make it virtually impossible to lay off workers. Farmers will continue to get canal water and power at highly subsidised rates, which are bankrupting state governments because nobody has the courage to end these subsidies in a country which is still 73% rural.

But while avoiding major reforms in 1995, Mr Rao will continue to implement some minor ones. Customs duty will be cut further, from the current maximum of 65% to around 50%, and consumer-goods imports will be liberalised. Private investment in telephone services will finally begin. Progress has been slow (and accompanied by allegations of kickbacks) in the award of big power

projects to private-sector companies, and the pace could accelerate.

Private Indian and foreign investment should rise sharply in 1995. With the resumption of economic growth, India's middle class of 200m could double by the end of the century, so foreign investors will spot growing opportunities in automobiles, white goods and consumer electronics. Investments in socially acceptable vices have already been made by R.J. Reynolds, Philip Morris, Seagrams and United Distillers.

Foreign-portfolio investment was $2.5 billion in 1993-94, and will keep rising in 1995. The profits of Indian companies boomed in 1993-94 and will boom further in the coming year, given that demand is up and import duties, corporate tax and interest rates are down.

The Bombay stock exchange has outperformed almost all emerging markets in 1994, and the sharp rise in company earnings is justifying price-earnings ratios which once looked barmy.

Hindu hordes

Few elections in India have been decided by economic issues. The opposition Bharatiya Janata Party (BJP) hopes to attain power on its plank of Hindu nationalism. In 1992 its hordes demolished a disputed mosque in Ayodhya, which it claimed was the birthplace of the Hindu god Ram. However, the BJP lost ground in subsequent state elections (in demolishing the mosque it also demolished its main emotive symbol).

Militants within the BJP argue that the party should regain ground by demanding the demolition of other mosques built on the site of razed Hindu shrines (there are possibly 3,000 such). If they carry the day, next year will witness severe Hindu-Muslim clashes.

That will turn the spotlight on Kashmir, a Muslim-majority region where armed troops are trying in vain to put down an insurrection, and violating human rights in the process.

To take off the international heat, Mr Rao may gamble with a state election in Kashmir in 1995. The militants will almost certainly boycott this, voter turn-out will not exceed 20%, and the discredited National Conference (a local ally of Mr Rao's Congress Party) should win. This election will be denounced by many (including Pakistan) as a fraud. But it will mean that Kashmir is ruled by Kashmiris, not New Delhi, and that will certainly be an improvement.

BANGLADESH
NATURE'S PLAYGROUND

The world's longest unbroken sea beach
The world's largest mangrove forest
Home of the Royal Bengal Tiger
Sparkling rivers
Endless fields of green
Quiet villages
Unspoilt nature at its best.

Even as the 20th century
roars around
there's still a natural retreat!
Biman can take you there!

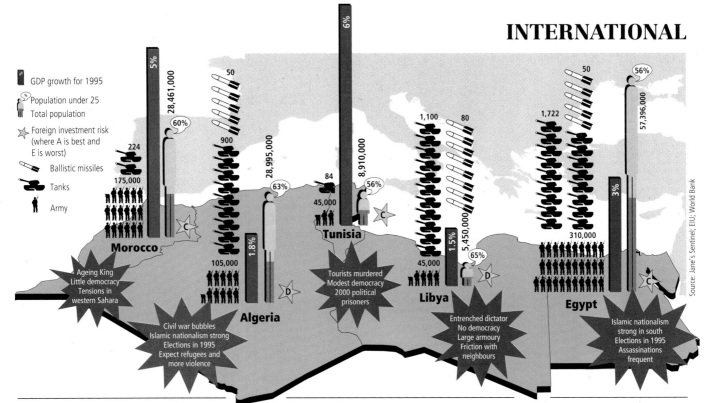

GDP growth for 1995

Population under 25
Total population

Foreign investment risk
(where A is best and
E is worst)

Ballistic missiles

Tanks

Army

Morocco
5%
28,461,000
60%
224
175,000
C

Ageing King
Little democracy
Tensions in
western Sahara

Civil war bubbles
Islamic nationalism strong
Elections in 1995
Expect refugees and
more violence

Algeria
1.8%
50
900
63%
28,995,000
105,000
D

Tunisia
6%
84
45,000
56%
8,910,000
C

Tourists murdered
Modest democracy
2000 political
prisoners

Libya
1.5%
1,100
80
65%
5,450,000
45,000
D

Entrenched dictator
No democracy
Large armoury
Friction with
neighbours

Egypt
3%
50
1,722
56%
57,396,000
310,000
C

Islamic nationalism
strong in south
Elections in 1995
Assassinations
frequent

Source: Jane's Sentinel; EIU; World Bank

North Africa could turn nasty

Dudley Fishburn

The most potentially explosive part of the world in the coming year will be North Africa—that strip of land that runs from Casablanca to Cairo with a burgeoning population of 130m. The five countries in this strip are by no means homogeneous. They have different colonial histories and as wide a variation of cultural traditions as might be found in, say, a slice of Latin America. They have very different economic opportunities.

But it is their similarities that make them dangerous. All are dictatorships; all are overpopulated, with a frighteningly high proportion of the population under 25. None has made its peace with the modern capitalist world. All speak (with different accents) Arabic; all, of course, follow Islam. All of these countries are on Europe's doorstep. And as our map shows, there will be enough flashpoints in each and every one of them to light a political powderkeg in 1995.

Explosions in North Africa will not be isolated bangs. They will affect all of the Middle East, reaching into the heart of the Arab Saudi kingdom in a way that the turmoil in Iran, whose Islamic revolutionaries are not strictly of Arab stock, did not do. Unlike 1994's horrors in Black Africa, any upwards spiral in the

Dudley Fishburn: editor of *The World in 1995*.

bubbling civil war in Algeria, the flood of emigrants from Morocco, the number of murdered tourists in Tunis, will have an immediate impact both in Washington and throughout Europe.

The Mediterranean may be bigger than the Rio Grande, but it is no *cordon sanitaire*. It took Odysseus, leaving Troy in a small boat 4,000 years ago, only a matter of days to reach the land of the lotus eaters in North Africa; wars emanating from Carthage, in what is now Tunisia, were Europe's principal threat under the Roman Empire. It is not to be supposed that, 2,000 years later, a refugee-producing chaos or a militant Islam on the southern shore of the Mediterranean would not have its immediate impact on the political life of its northern shore.

The French understand the stakes. With Algeria and Morocco stamped on recent French history, with huge North African immigrant populations and with Marseilles as a listening-post, France follows the area closely. As ill-luck would have it, Paris, however, has been calling the wrong political shots. That means trouble in 1995.

The most unhappy country is Algeria. The French decision to support the hard-nosed government of Liamine Zeroual in its postponement of elections in 1992

heralded a near-civil war in which some 4,000 people have been killed. The country is under curfew. Political prisoners abound. To cool the cauldron, an election has been pencilled in for 1995. Islamic nationalists get the blame for much of the shooting, the kidnappings and disruption. That is to miss the reason why North Africa is so worrying. The frustrated youths who turn to fundamentalism are, in reality, seeking a government with some kind of legitimacy. They want a coherent way of dealing with—and possibly joining—the West and an economic policy that will create jobs.

An Islamic victory in Algeria, or at least the forced departure of the *Haut Comité d'Etat,* is a betting chance in 1995. It would be a bloody affair, looked upon aghast by its North African neighbours. Tunisia, an Algeria writ small and weak, would feel the immediate blast—perhaps through a collapse of its tourist trade. Morocco, seemingly steady under King Hassan (but with a weak crown prince), is fragile for many of the same reasons as Algeria. It is Egypt, of course, and from there, Saudi Arabia, that have the most to lose. Egypt's Islamic nationalists have repeatedly struck at Cairo's unchanging but not incompetent government. The south of the country is near insurrection: it will get nearer in 1995.

Will Assad hear the whisper of peace?

The lifeline of a Middle East deadline

Roland Dallas

Hatred in the Middle East runs so deep and violence is so endemic that disasters in the peace process are more likely than not. The assassination of a prominent figure could rip it apart, at least for a time. This ever-present risk aside, how-

Roland Dallas: editor of *The Economist*'s Foreign Report.

ever, there will be more good news from the Middle East in 1995.

Apart from **Israel**, the key country will be **Syria**. Once President Hafez Assad starts to negotiate seriously with Israel, other bits of the jigsaw will fit together. Mr Assad has an interest in a settlement: he wants to regain the Golan Heights,

which Israel seized in the 1973 war. The handover would be in stages over several years under international observation and with "confidence-building measures". The price: Syria would agree to full diplomatic and trade relations with Israel.

Mr Assad wants to avoid the fate of **Egypt**'s assassinated president, Anwar Sadat, who signed a separate peace with Israel while there was no settlement between Israel and the Palestinians. Following just such a deal for the Palestinians to administer the Gaza Strip and the West Bank town of Jericho, and one between Israel and Jordan, Mr Assad will negotiate seriously.

That would enable **Lebanon**, now a dependency of Syria, to do so as well. The Lebanese have a strong interest in peace: they would get back the slab of south Lebanon along the Israeli border that the Israelis seized and called their "security zone" in 1978. But Lebanon would have to guarantee that extremists on its territory would desist from attacks on Israel.

Jordan's ultra-cautious King Hussein signed a peace treaty on October 24th 1994 with the Israeli prime minister, Yitzhak Rabin. This opened the way for full diplomatic and trade relations, with the two countries co-operating on tourism, electricity and water. However, Jordan's relations with the Palestinians seem likely to be edgy.

Two important mediators also have a strong interest in an Israel-Syria settlement. Egypt's President Husni Mubarak, who has played host on many occasions to Palestinian and Israeli negotiators,

Will money talk?

Roland Dallas

Iran's clerical rulers are showing signs of wanting to rejoin the real world in 1995. They have some compelling reasons for behaving better. Iran has been living beyond its means. It has rescheduled its debts with half a dozen countries, including Germany. It suffers from high inflation and unemployment, a heavily devalued currency, a large budget deficit and deep cuts in needed imports. Iran's leaders know that they will have more reschedulings to negotiate.

Sporadic riots and simmering unrest are a warning that ordinary Iranians are increasingly fed up with their lot. Army officers who helped to put down a riot in Qazvin in July 1994 told Ayatollah Khamenei, the country's spiritual leader, in a joint letter that it was not their job to "control the internal situation or

strengthen one political faction over another." The danger to clerical politicians is clear. They need a steady government cash-flow to oil the wheels of the economy.

Could it be that in their anxiety not to mess up the debt reschedulings, Iran's leaders have abjured violence? That certainly is the advice they have received, loud and clear, from Germany. The line from Bonn, unlike that from Washington or London, is that Iran may be persuaded to dilute its extremism by a "constructive dialogue".

Iran has committed no acts of violence outside its territory for over a year. This welcome record seemed to be smudged in August 1994 when a bomb was set off in Buenos Aires outside a building used by an Israeli-Argentine association. Argentine officials blamed

Iran. But they said afterwards that they had no evidence of Iranian involvement.

Iran's performance is far from perfect, however. To be declared clubbable, it will be asked first to lift Ayatollah Khomeini's *fatwa*, which sentences Salman Rushdie, author of the controversial "Satanic Verses", to death. Then it will be expected to make a u-turn and support the Middle East peace process. That should include reining in its extremist ally in Lebanon, Hizbullah, which may have been responsible for the Buenos Aires bomb.

President Hashemi Rafsanjani and his foreign minister, Ali Akbar Velayati, are often optimistically described as moderates and pragmatists. Nonetheless, with their economy looking shaky, 1995 should be the year for them to live up to their labels.

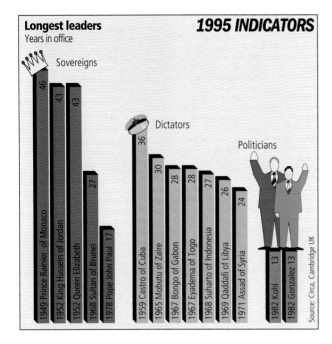

Longest leaders
Years in office

1995 INDICATORS

Sovereigns

46 1949 Prince Rainier of Monaco
43 1952 King Hussein of Jordan
43 1952 Queen Elizabeth
27 1968 Sultan of Brunei
17 1978 Pope John Paul

Dictators

36 1959 Castro of Cuba
30 1965 Mobutu of Zaire
28 1967 Bongo of Gabon
28 1967 Eyadema of Togo
27 1968 Suharto of Indonesia
26 1969 Qaddafi of Libya
24 1971 Assad of Syria

Politicians

13 1982 Kohl
13 1982 Gonzalez

Source: Circa, Cambridge UK

The Gulf 1995

The succession and legitimacy of the unelected leaders in the Gulf will be key issues in 1995. The conservative Crown Prince Abdullah is expected to follow Saudi Arabia's ailing 73-year-old King Fahd. But Abdullah is 71 years old and has heart trouble. In the UAE, the ruler of Abu Dhabi and president of the federation, Sheilch Zayid, is getting on for 80. The question of his successor affects not only the future of Abu Dhabi but future relations among all seven emirates belonging to the UAE.

Don't expect much democracy in 1995. Neither Fahd nor Abdullah is likely to allow Saudi Arabia's infant Consultative Council to play an independent role. Nor will the Kuwaiti National Assembly, elected on a limited franchise, risk any confrontation with its government in 1995: it wants to avoid upsetting the timetable for elections in 1996. The UAE's appointed 40-member Federal National Council, which does no more than review legislation, shows no sign of nascent democracy.

In these circumstances calls for public debate about government policies will mount—but from outside officially recognised bodies. Foreign capitals will provide the loudest platform for opposition groups.

1995 marks the start of Saudi Arabia's sixth five-year development plan. Its renewed emphasis on privatisation is born of the need to bring the government's budget deficit under control. However, a balanced budget will not be achieved.

Spending will be pared through the postponement of infrastructure programmes. The kingdom's massive current-account deficit will persist.

Repayments on Kuwait's commercial foreign debt begin in 1995. They will coincide with the start of two important construction projects at Subiya and Shuaiba, pushing up the import bill and the budget deficit. Kuwait will stay ahead of Saudi Arabia in finding new ways for raising revenue, but still no income tax.

and the lawyerly American secretary of state, Warren Christopher, who wants to retire early in 1995 with an agreement to his credit in the history books.

There are two essential deadlines. One is that Israel holds a general election in 1996, and it is not certain to be won by the ruling Labour Party. The party's leaders, Mr Rabin and Shimon Peres, are strong supporters of peace with the Palestinians; the opposition, led by Benjamin Netanyahu, is sceptical. The second is the American presidential election, also in 1996, which will be preceded by campaigns for primary elections; President Clinton will be paying most attention to his own political survival, not the Middle East's. So it is in everybody's interest to get a wider settlement.

The behaviour of *Iraq*'s Saddam Hussein is unlikely to be any more predictable next year. Nonetheless, he is unlikely to repeat his troop movements that threatened *Kuwait* in October 1994. He is more likely to accept the UN's terms for a settlement. Mr Hussein will demand that this leads to sanctions being lifted and Iraqi oil sold again.

That would cause trouble for oil producers including *Saudi Arabia*, which has been living beyond its ample means. The government borrowed to cover the budget deficit and has been able to raise the money only from domestic banks. Nevertheless, the government has announced multi-billion-dollar contracts to buy airliners and telecommunications equipment. King Fahd's health appears to be frail. For Saudi Arabia 1995 may be a volatile year.

Bad Burma gets better

Roland Dallas

With its rich land, valuable mineral deposits and gentle, intelligent people, Myanmar (formerly Burma) should be prospering economically and serving as a source of Buddhist enlightenment to the world. Instead it will spend the year in economic misery and political despair. As reform and prosperity pervade Asia, Myanmar's 42m people have known only suffering at the hands of a vicious dictatorship. Thirty-two years of misrule by half-baked socialist generals have turned this once well-off country into one of the world's poorest.

In 1995 the plight of this long-suffering people may improve. Some relaxation of the iron grip is in prospect. A return to democracy is even a possibility. Myanmar was once democratic. From independence in 1948 to 1962 it was ruled constitutionally by U Nu, leader of

the main nationalist party. General Ne Win seized power in 1962. Unrest, particularly from students, was savagely repressed.

Hatred of the government became so intense that in 1988 Ne Win stepped down and replaced himself with General Sein Lwin, known widely as "the butcher". He was replaced in turn by a civilian, Maung Maung, who made the great mistake of promising free general elections. He was fired.

Oppression

A free election in 1990 was won by the opposition, led by Aung San Suu Kyi, daughter of a national hero, although she was under house arrest at the time. The opposition gained 392 of the 485 seats, but the generals refused to honour the result. They ruled through the State

KEY INDICATORS

	1993	1994	1995
Saudi GDP growth (% pa)	1.0	-3.0	1.0
Kuwait GDP growth (% pa)	33.0	4.8	3.2
UAE GDP growth (% pa)	-3.0	-0.9	-0.5
Saudi current account ($bn)	-15.3	-14.9	13.4
Kuwait current account ($bn)	4.8	4.4	3.3
UAE current account ($bn)	0.2	-0.1	0.7
EIU COUNTRY AND ANALYSIS FORECASTING			

South Africa 1995

Tensions within the African National Congress-dominated coalition point to a year of weak government in 1995. Unless President Nelson Mandela is able to stamp his authority on the cabinet more effectively, splits in the Government of National Unity will hamper its effectiveness.

Although the former president, F.W. de Klerk, will be reluctant to rock the boat, a growing number of his supporters will press for the National Party's withdrawal from the government. Chief Mangosuthu Buthelezi's Inkatha Freedom Party could leave the coalition over the issue of regional autonomy. This flashpoint is not likely to be reached before 1996.

By taking the job of first deputy-president, Thabo Mbeki is the heir-apparent to Mr Mandela. But his rival, Cyril Ramaphosa, the ANC's secretary-general, will be able to distance himself from unpopular government policies and champion causes favoured by the party's rank-and-file. Unless Mr Mandela's health fails, the succession issue will not come out into the open in 1995. It will, however, be very much there.

The Mandela government faces a tough balancing act in keeping expenditure under control while trying to fulfil its pledge to improve the living standards of the black majority. Three key policy issues will dominate the 1995 budget debate: wage policy, public spending and the exchange rate.

Exchange controls need to be relaxed. The country's two-tier exchange-rate system ought to be scrapped. Expect both in mid-1995. But first South Africa will need to build up its foreign reserves to about three months' import-cover.

The commercial rand will continue to depreciate steadily, adding to inflationary pressures. Given this, interest rates will have to be nudged upwards. Economic expansion will pick up. There will be large inflows of foreign capital. Imports will take off and outstrip export growth, leading to a current-account deficit.

KEY INDICATORS

	1993	1994	1995
GDP growth (%)	1.2	2.7	4.0
Inflation (%)	9.7	8.0	11.0
Prime lending rate (%)	16.2	15.5	16.0
R per $	3.26	3.65	3.98
Current account ($bn)	1.8	0.7	-0.6

EIU COUNTRY AND ANALYSIS FORECASTING

Law and Order Restoration Council—and still do. The generals offered to free Aung San Suu Kyi if she left the country. She refused. It now seems possible that Myanmar's boss, General Khin Myunt, the former head of the secret police, is ready for a deal.

There is much to be sorted out. The currency is over-valued, making it difficult to export goods. The official rate is six kyats to the dollar while the unofficial rate is 100 to the dollar. Lack of foreign currency limits imports of urgently needed spare parts for factory equipment. To pay their meagre way in the world the government is selling off the teak forests. The economy is dominated by 23 state corporations directed by generals or admirals.

To their rescue, critics say, comes China, which promotes a busy cross-border trade in Yunnan province and has sold arms worth about $1 billion to Myanmar for its 286,000-man army.

Myanmar has long been brutal and bizarre. A comedian, Zar Gana, who made jokes about Ne Win, was jailed for four years. Ne Win made the government issue banknotes of 90 and 45 kyats, because his astrologer said nine and multiples of nine were his lucky numbers. The American State Department says Myanmar is one of the few countries that does not co-operate in the international war on drug trafficking.

Burma's jailbird

Will Myanmar's smothered democratic opposition revive? There is a hint of a glimmer of hope. The dictatorship realises that its time is up. Myanmar was allowed, over western protests, to attend the regional forum of the Association of South-East Asian Nations with the association's western "dialogue partners" in Bangkok in July 1994 on the clear understanding that it would not be invited to the next session in 1995 without moves towards freedom and democracy. This has put the generals under pressure to make reforms. Not before time, they look a possibility next year.

Africa's misery

Roland Dallas

On average, Africans are worse off now than they were 30 years ago. Africa's income per head fell by more than 15% in the 1980s and has fallen further since. It will go on falling in 1995. An inconceivable 15 years of uninterrupted growth at 5% a year are needed to recover the income losses of the 1980s.

"Crisis follows crisis," a report for the African Development Bank says. "Civil unrest is rife. So too are poverty, famine and disease. Corruption is widespread. Economies are stagnating. Populations are soaring." The litany of errors and mishaps goes on and on. Food imports are rising and food aid is pouring in, creating dependence on handouts. Recurring famines display Africa's inability to feed itself. Roughly 100m people are malnourished. By 2000 Africa's population will reach 825m, double what it was in 1980. As pressure on the land intensifies, so does over-cultivation, over-grazing and deforestation.

With some exceptions, African politics is, however, more gentle than a decade ago. There are fewer Amins and Bokassas inflicting personal savagery; indeed there have been a number of attempts at democracy recently. Africa's new misery comes not from an evil dictator sitting in a palace but from the overwhelming poverty of the place itself and the brutalism of leaderless, tribal conflict.

Every now and again, as with the events in *Rwanda*, western television together with its props from the United Nations will peer into the continent and be shocked. Expect the next horror story to be in *Liberia*. In *Malawi* one person in ten is HIV-positive; the plight of other coun-

Non-stop every day-U.A.

Uniting London and Los Angeles non-stop every day from Heathrow.

Come fly the airline that's uniting the world. Come fly the friendly skies.

For reservations, see your travel agent or call United on 081 990 9900 (0800 888 555 outside London).

 **UNITED AIRLINES**

"In all mosques, temples, churches I find one shrine alone."

"In all mosques, temples, churches I find one shrine alone." Thus wrote the 13th century Turkish philosopher, Mevlana. He sought to create a climate of universal love, at a time when the world was torn apart by religious strife. A few days in modern Turkey will show you how the tolerance he called for is still alive. Whoever you are, wherever you go in Turkey, you will be greeted by a warm and genuine welcome. You'll feel so at home here, that you'll wonder why you ever thought of going anywhere else.

The Europe you don't know. The Asia you will discover.

TURKEY

1995's new atlas

Roland Dallas

Will any countries disappear in 1995? Look first at the old Soviet Union, where Russia has its beady eye on bits of the tsarist and Soviet empire that have become independent. Many people in Moscow think that these new republics belong under Moscow's wing (much as Lebanon is now a dependency of Syria).

The big one to watch is **Ukraine**, followed closely by **Belarus**. Russians regard Kiev, the Ukrainian capital, as the "mother of Russian cities". Ukraine has always been the vital "bread-basket of Russia". Belarus has been for most of its history part of Russia, and the languages are similar. Both countries have made an appalling job of their recent independence and many of their own citizens want to reunite with Russia. The three could form a "Slavic Union"—a tactful way of returning to Mother Russia's fold. Also this would avoid the huge costs that Russia would face if it attempted to absorb the flagging economies of these countries.

Romanian-speaking **Moldova** could be a candidate for the carving knife. Russia is under pressure to withdraw its 14th army from the Trans-Dniester breakaway area, where it is based against the wishes of the Moldovan government. The Russians promise to leave in three years. But they want a big-brother relationship with Moldova. As if that were not enough,

THE RUSSIAN FEDERATION

UKRAINE

BELARUS

neighbouring Romania would, if given the chance, absorb Moldova tomorrow.

One country that could disappear in 1995—a long shot admittedly—is **North Korea**. Once the decrepit communist regime goes, North Koreans, like the East Germans of old, might beg to be folded in with their richer southern kinsmen.

Next October is the 50th anniversary of the United Nations. In 1995 several countries will be struggling to add their name to the roll of 184 independent member nations. However, don't expect many successful bids.

Taiwan will try some new techniques for gaining recognition. For years after

the communists won the 1949 revolution Taiwan called itself the Republic of China and claimed to represent China as a whole. The mainland People's Republic of China disagreed— and eventually won the argument. Nonetheless, in 1994 Taiwan managed to upgrade its delegation in Washington from the absurdly named Co-ordination Council for North American Affairs to the Taipei Representative Office. In 1995, Taiwan will aim for full diplomatic relations.

The perennial could-be independent country, **Québec**, looks like staying just that. That is despite the provincial election in 1994 which the separatist Parti Québécois won following nine years in opposition. The party won 77 of the 125 seats in the provincial legislature and the federalist Liberals only 47. But the separatists' slim margin in the popular vote (45% to 44%) suggests they may lose the referendum they plan to hold in 1995, when voters would be expected to exercise more caution. Indeed, don't be surprised if the referendum is not held at all.

The old British colonial region of **Somalia** will try to gain recognition next year. It calls itself the Somali Republic, distancing itself from the rest of Somalia which was once under Italian rule. But this nascent republic could die an early death; Somalia is intent on reintegrating the region, by force if necessary.

---

tries is little better and will get worse in 1995.

But not everywhere. The stability in **South Africa** will spread a benign influence throughout the southern part of the continent. Expect continuing improvements in neighbouring **Namibia**, where President Sam Nujoma's multiracial government is doing surprisingly well, financed by a steady income from diamonds, fishing and farming. Another neighbour, **Botswana**, which also does well with diamonds and is one of Africa's few working democracies, will hope to share in the growth. So will **Zimbabwe**, which is in a period of painful economic adjustment under its ex-Marxist president, Robert Mugabe. Zimbabwe will have parliamentary elections in 1995 which will focus on land distribution to the rural poor.

Expect more pain in **Zambia**, where the reformist President Frederick Chiluba has been saddled with a foreign debt

2.5 times bigger than the country's GDP. Mr Chiluba needs to privatise the copper mines and loss-making Zambia Airways if the country is to have a chance.

Devastated by civil wars, **Mozambique** and **Angola** may get an opportunity to pull themselves out of the mire of chaos and hunger if agreements between governments and rebels are implemented. Their record, however, is bad. With its oil, diamonds and coffee, Angola should be one of Africa's richest countries. Its corrupt government has mortgaged the oil to pay for guns. The conflict seems likely to rumble on. Mozambique, also poor but with ample agricultural resources, is closer to stability—but still fragile.

East Africa looks relatively positive. **Kenya**'s economic management has won western plaudits, although President Daniel Arap Moi's autocratic government has not. **Uganda**'s President Yoweri Museveni is also applying IMF reforms with

such success that his one-party government has won international tolerance.

In the Horn of Africa, **Somalia**, **Ethiopia** and **Eritrea** will have their begging bowls out in 1995 because of their huge food shortages. In West Africa, oil-rich **Nigeria**, which suffered a long oil strike in 1994, is becoming dangerously volatile. The country's cocktail of religions and ethnic groups could become explosive. **Ghana** will continue to do well by following World Bank and IMF policies; its GDP is expected to grow by 5.2% in 1995. Former French West Africa will scrape along, with its exporters encouraged by the devaluation of the French-backed CFA franc.

And **Zaire**? By helping with the Rwandan refugees, President Mobutu Sese Seko has regained some of his lost respectability. But Zaire "is reverting to the jungle," says a well-placed diplomat. "It barely exists." And what does exist is Africa at its worst.

Playing games to next year's rules

Matthew Glendinning

Sport, or rather lounge lizards watching sport, is a big industry—and one that will change rapidly in 1995. There are three main trends:
• Cable television companies will become more specific and more demanding: if no one can return a serve at Wimbledon and the audience gets bored, then the rules will have to change.
• Sports federations will have to become less cosy and corrupt. That will mean stronger controls on the use of drugs but a more generous attitude to prize money.
• Stars from ex-communist countries will become ever less successful. The old East-West rivalry in sport will be replaced by a less appealing North-South one. The fastest athletes will increasingly come from the poorest countries. This is bad news for the television companies, whose audiences come from the richest advertising markets.

Prize money and drug use will continue to make the headlines in athletics in 1995. The major event of the year, the World Championships, in Gothenburg, Sweden, will have its share of scandals. The president of the International Amateur Athletics Federation, Primo Nebiolo, will approve prize money for the finalists for the first time. (At the previous World Championships in Stuttgart the winners each received a Mercedes.) The Olympic movement will oppose such a step away from the amateur ideal, but Mr Nebiolo will rightly have his way. The Chinese will emerge from their winter hibernation to win a clutch of long-distance medals: lack of freedom makes people run faster. Expect Kenyan runners to make the biggest impact. Look out, too, for middle-distance

runners from the troubled African state of Burundi: fast runners, but no good for selling advertising space to middle-aged, middle-class whites.

Boxing too will have to struggle for its place on the box. The parole and release from prison in May 1995 of Mike Tyson will overshadow any event that might take place in the ring. Debate will follow on whether he should receive a boxing licence. Cable and network television will bid unprecedented amounts for his opening fights. British heavyweight, Lennox Lewis, will be squeezed out of another championship bid by WBC promoter, Don King. Meanwhile, extraordinary negotiations between "Main Event" promoter, Dan Duva, and Cuban president, Fidel Castro, to promote Cuban fighters like former Olympic heavyweight Felix Savon, in Havana, may founder with Mr Castro's political fortunes. Look out for tough new fighters from the southern states of the old Russian empire, Uzbekistan and Kazakhstan, to make an impact in the ring.

If the characters in boxing are ever less savoury, those in tennis are ever more dull and youthful. The pace and power of the men's game will become an increasing cause for concern. In an attempt to liven things up, the Association of Tennis Professionals has encouraged greater spectator participation in matches and more accessibility to players. It will also try to persuade former players to stop criticising the modern game. Changes in the rules, however, will be resisted until the end of 1995 when new regulations on power-enhancing graphite rackets will be introduced by the International

Tennis Federation.

In the men's game, Pete Sampras will remain in the ascendent. But expect a host of young American stars: Jonathan Stark and Jared Palmer should make the world's top ten. In the women's game, 14-year-old Marina Hingis from Switzerland will be an instant success. But feature story of the year will be the appearance on tour of Venus Williams, a 14-year-old black player from gangland Los Angeles.

There is no sign that horseracing is losing its appeal to the rich. In 1995, more European horses than ever will travel eastwards to contest races in Australia, Japan and Hong Kong. Japan is the big player on the bloodstock scene. However, only five Japanese races a year are open to horses from abroad. Expect the international racing community—and even the occasional summit leader—to complain more about this protectionist policy. Japan has promised to open up 12 races in all by 2000. So much for its free-trade commitment. But with the average prize at over £80,000 ($130,000) and with betting turnover of £25 billion a year, Japan is in no hurry to change. Meanwhile, Hong Kong racing continues to flourish and will remain confident towards 1997.

The Maktoum family will become more self-sufficient and will increase

their operations in Dubai, where 600 horses are already in training. Sheikh Mohammed's "Gadolfin" venture, whereby European horses winter in Dubai and then race in the European spring, will yield success—and less successful imitators. The Maktoums simply have the best horses. In Britain, Sunday racing is to be introduced in line with the rest of the world. But the Derby will shift from a Wednesday to a Saturday.

Matthew Glendinning: *freelance journalist specialising in sport.*

Latin America's great year

William Orme

South Africa will host the rugby World Cup in 1995. The opportunity to show off that nation's new-found respectability will not be lost. The tournament will be a commercial success, with unprecedented sponsorship deals and television rights. The commercial exploitation of rugby, however, will only produce louder calls for the sport to become professional.

The International Rugby Board will announce measures in 1995 to allow players to make more money from the sport. On the field, look out for the big forwards of the Côte d'Ivoire, and possible dark horses in Italy, where the game has developed quickly and the prime minister, Silvio Berlusconi, owns a team. Fears of carnage on the pitch will be countered by tough directives to referees, in the style of the soccer World Cup USA.

As preparations for the 1996 Olympics in Atlanta continue, the Olympic movement will debate how best to maintain its image as the sporting ideal. The International Olympic Committee is keen to appear more accountable.

Meanwhile, the citizens of the state of Georgia will fight against tax hikes to pay for the games. Gloomy forecasts concerning the $1.58 billion needed to stage the games will prove inaccurate, especially after the television-rating success of the Lillehammer Winter Olympics. But one Olympic era will come to an end. Carl Lewis will retire in 1995. He will make a comeback as a commentator in 1996.

Latin America's leaders will preside over an economic rebirth as profound as that begun by East Asia 20 years ago and by Western Europe 20 years before that. But just as things are beginning to go right, political incumbents are losing popularity. A region that only recently pulled itself out of an economic abyss is now worrying about political reform and multilateral security conflicts.

Latin America is also realising that it is essentially on its own. Washington, preoccupied anew by Cuba and Hispaniola, is in no hurry to keep its promises of free trade; the big losers will not be the Brazilians or the Argentinians, who can take care of themselves, but the Guatemalans and Salvadorans, who after decades of war cannot.

Overshadowing all other political events in the region, 1995 will be the year of reckoning for Fidel Castro: either he negotiates a transition to a new order or Cuba implodes into chaos. The former is more likely. With Washington once again focused on the nearby Caribbean, and Mexico merging safely into greater North America, South Americans will concentrate on cementing ties with Europe and Asia—and with one another.

It will objectively be a good year. Latin America will at last grab the grail of sustained real growth. All the major economies, except Venezuela, should expand by 2% or better, the region's best performance since the deficit-financed 1970s. Inflation is largely stabilised or declining. Foreign-portfolio investment is giving way to longer-lasting direct-equity stakes in manufacturing, services and natural-resource industries.

Foreign reserves—earned honestly by selling, not borrowing—will reach record levels in Brazil, Chile, Colombia, Mexico and Peru.

Latin America should be able to maintain this performance for the remainder of the decade. For the first time in a generation Latin leaders can confidently expect continued GDP growth at rates double or treble the rate of population growth. Unlike previous Latin booms, this expansion is built on sound fiscal policies and open markets.

Even more remarkable, this change enjoys such broad political support that it is no longer seen as worthy of chal-

William A. Orme, Jr: director of the Committee to protect Journalists; author of "Continental Shift: Free Trade and the New North America".

lenge. Even leftist opposition parties rule out a return to the days of autarky and expropriation. Neither of the major national elections in 1995—in Argentina and Peru—will force the country to reverse its economic course, whatever the outcome. Private capital, encouraged by this emerging strategic consensus, is at last committing itself to long-term investment, pushing up wages in many industries where salaries had stagnated. This new market ethos is being underpinned by trade and investment pacts.

To that, Latin American voters say, "Terrific, but what have you done for me lately?" Governments are discovering that growth is not enough. Expectations are rising far faster than real incomes, and Latin Americans are increasingly caught up in the mundane concerns of real capitalist life: the quality and cost of schooling and health care; the fear of foreign competition and job security; for the aspiring middle class, the frustrating inability to finance home ownership; for the peasant farmer and urban poor, the pain and anger of observing economic growth as hungry outsiders.

Political parties of the left, right and centre are in rough accord on the need for more trade and investment, but opposition leaders of all stripes are raising concerns about income inequities and under-financed social programmes. Is this backsliding to the bad old days, when Latin policy-makers worried only about the distribution of wealth, not its creation? In most cases, no: even the technocrats are reminding their bosses that the East Asian economic miracles have as much to do with rural electrification and keeping children in secondary school as they do with export strategies.

Latin Americans are sick of authoritarianism, benevolent or otherwise, and of its handmaiden, corruption. These vices are turning voters away from Carlos Menem, who faces Argentina's voters on May 10th 1995, and Alberto Fujimori, who is up for re-election as president of Peru in April. Presidents Menem and Fujimori succeeded in reviving dying economies, but their cronies have got conspicuously rich in the process, and their autocratic habits are tolerated less now that their countries are no longer in crisis. Mr Menem could still survive if his opponent is weak. Mr Fujimori will be beaten—probably by the former secretary-general of the United Nations, Javier

Perez de Cuellar—unless an unexpected resurgence of Shining Path terrorism makes Peruvians yearn for further blows from the iron hand.

In Mexico, Ernesto Zedillo will push the economy into overdrive—he expects 5% growth, and would like 6%—but that still will not be enough. He will be judged chiefly by his commitment to political reform. Here there will be cause for doubt. Yet Mr Zedillo, conventional wisdom notwithstanding, will begin his first year in office in a stronger position than Carlos Salinas did six years ago. He inherits a growing economy, and his 50%-plus-a-whisker victory was much more convincing than the identical win claimed by Mr Salinas in 1988. Mexico's opposition remains fatally divided. The conservative National Action Party will concentrate on regaining ground lost to the eternally governing PRI in its northern-border base. The democratic left will

retreat back into a fractious subculture.

Venezuela's free-market opening, in contrast to Mexico's careful management, was a caricature of 1980s excess. The endemic official corruption that fed popular support for two coup attempts and eventually led to the ousting of President Carlos Andres Perez was mirrored in the private sector by brazen insider trading and the reckless over-reaching of the banking system.

Now, instead of trying to build a constituency for reform, the Venezuelan government is slipping back to 1970s statism, imposing elaborate foreign-exchange controls and expropriating rather than liquidating collapsed local banks.

President Rafael Caldera initially won support for his turn-back-the-clock demagogy, but his popularity will erode in 1995 as capital flees abroad and the economy contracts relentlessly. A drop in oil prices, combined with Mr Caldera's natural crankiness, could provoke a debt-payments crisis.

The most important economic story of 1995 will be the half of Latin America that is Brazil.

More important than Fernando Henrique Cardoso's stunning triumph in the November 1994 presidential election was the consensus reflected by the two candidates' converging views on economic and social policy. Luiz Inacio da Silva (Lula), the quintessential radical populist, and Mr Cardoso, the cosmopolitan candidate of the Sao Paulo business elite, both agreed on the critical importance of attracting foreign investment and competing in the world economy. Lula, like social democrats every-

The shrinking Colossus

William Orme

Latin American leaders start 1995 fresh from a summit meeting in Miami—the first of its kind since the 1967 assembly of western-hemisphere heads of state in Uruguay. Despite Latin America's huge reliance on the American market, American political influence in the region—especially south of the equator—will start to diminish dramatically. Witness the collective Latin refusal to collaborate with American-led military intervention in Haiti, and the increasingly open criticism of the American economic quarantine of Cuba. This trend will accelerate.

With the end of the cold war and the growth of the American budget deficit, the foreign aid that Washington used as leverage in Latin America has dwindled to inconsequential levels. The promise made by George Bush and reiterated by Bill Clinton of NAFTA-like deals for the rest of Latin America was a good diplomatic substitute, but the offer is no longer taken very seriously.

The Americans in 1995 will suggest a token deal to the worthy and distant Chileans, but nobody else. This is intended to symbolise the American commitment to extend free trade from Mexico to Tierra del Fuego. In reality, it will mean that for another year Washington will again ignore almost everything in-between.

where, argued that the victims of foreign competition—like the palm-nut workers who lost jobs after Brazil started importing cheaper Asian cooking oil—deserve special protection from the state.

Mr Cardoso argued that the government should concentrate instead on fostering new private-sector jobs for the unemployed. The former finance minister ultimately won by proving that battling inflation is not just sound economics, but smart politics. For the first time, Brazil was offered rational economic and social-policy choices in a presidential campaign—as well as a choice between two principled and capable politicians.

In its own chaotic way Brazil is preparing to meet the challenge of the outside world. For Brazil, a country that regularly entertains delusions of quasi-continental self-sufficiency, this embrace of reality is historic. It will start to pay dividends in 1995.

Sombrero success
1995 forecasts

Urban population % of total

Inflation %

Economic growth %

Current-account balance $ billion

Source: EIU; Salomon Brothers

Mexico 77.4 / 4.8 / -28 / 28 / 24.3

Colombia 63.8 / 75.2 / 4.5 / -4.9

Venezuela 93.7 / 20 / 205 / 45

Ecuador 2 / -0.8

Peru 75.2 / 5.5 / -2.7

Brazil 80.6 / +0.1 / -1.5 / 2.5 / -8.3

Chile 88.9 / 12 / 5.7 / -1.3

Argentina 88.8 / 4.3 / 3.5 / -11

Western Europe

AUSTRIA

GDP: Sch2.36trn; $199.8bn
GDP per head: $25,010
Population: 7.99m; change 0.5%
GDP growth: 1994 2.4%; 1995 2.6%
Inflation: 1994 3%; 1995 2.8%

• Austria will join the European Union (EU) in 1995. It will be particularly interested in EU policy on agriculture, immigration and the environment.

• A restrictive fiscal policy will be needed once inside the EU. Interest rates will rise in 1995 to protect the schilling.

• The economy will grow by 2.6%. High unemployment and competition from Eastern Europe will help to keep price inflation in check.

To watch
Immigration issues will be heavily exploited by the right-wing Freedom Party.

BELGIUM

Budget deficit
% of GDP

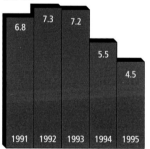

GDP: BFr8.11trn; $231bn
GDP per head: $22,600
Population: 10.2m; change 1%
GDP growth: 1994 1.5%; 1995 2.1%
Inflation: 1994 2.8%; 1995 2.8%

• The coalition government will hold together until the November 1995 general election.

• The budget has been designed to bring the federal government's net financing requirement in 1995 down to 3.6% of GDP, but there will be no new taxes.

• Increases in disposable income will be moderate, given the problems of unemployment and competitiveness.

DENMARK

GDP: DKr994.3bn; $151.8bn
GDP per head: $29,190
Population: 5.20m; change 0.2%
GDP growth: 1994 4.2%; 1995 3.2%
Inflation: 1994 2%; 1995 2.8%

• Despite a significant setback to the centre-left in 1994's election, a rearranged coalition of social democrats and socialists will continue to govern, still led by Nyrup Ramussen.

• Strong economic growth will encourage more restrictive fiscal policies.

• GDP growth will decelerate slightly in 1995, partly as a result of the government's tighter fiscal policy, but private consumption and fixed investment growth will remain buoyant.

FINLAND

GDP: Fmk525.9bn; $104.3bn
GDP per head: $20,410
Population: 5.11m; change 0.8%
GDP growth: 1994 2.5%; 1995 3.8%
Inflation: 1994 1.2%; 1995 2.5%

• Finland will go to the polls in March 1995. The four-party coalition government will be struggling to maintain public support after three years of recession. The opposition Social Democrats will become the largest party in parliament.

• Membership of the EU begins on January 1st, although the entry terms agreed by Finland's negotiators mean that the benefits will be less apparent than had been hoped.

• The economic recovery will gather pace in 1995 as domestic demand finally begins to recover, encouraged by a fall in real-interest rates.

FRANCE

GDP: FFr7.73 trillion; $1.36 trillion
GDP per head: $23,550
Population: 57.9m; change 0.3%
GDP growth: 1994 2.3%; 1995 2.7%
Inflation: 1994 1.7%; 1995 2%

• With the first round of the presidential election due in April, politicians will spend the first few months of 1995 jockeying for position. Expect an acrimonious debate within the neo-Gaullist RPR over its choice of candidate.

• Prior commitments on military spending and civil-service pay mean that the government will face a difficult task in keeping to its five-year public-finance strategy.

• GDP growth will improve but the structural nature of unemployment means that there is unlikely to be a radical fall in the number of jobless.

To watch
Race relations, already damaged by the security clampdown on Arab immigrants, will be further damaged if the immigration card is played by the major parties during the presidential elections.

GERMANY

Current-account deficit
$ billion

GNP: DM3.37 trillion; $2.1 trillion
GNP per head: $26,000
Population: 81.1m; change 0%
GNP growth: 1994 2.4%; 1995 3%
Inflation: 1994 2.9%; 1995 2.1%

• Helmut Kohl's post-election agenda, with French support, is to make the EU more open and democratic in preparation for enlargement and monetary union.

• Tax increases are planned for 1995 to curb the budget deficit but these will not dampen the recovery.

• Inflation is on a downward track, and will be close to the Bundesbank's long-term target of 2% per year by the end of 1995.

GREECE

GDP: Dr25.97trn; $86.0bn
GDP per head: $8,400
Population: 10.3m; change 0.0%
GDP growth: 1994 0.7%; 1995 1.3%
Inflation: 1994 11%; 1995 10%

All figures are 1995 forecasts unless otherwise indicated.

1994 figures are estimates.

Inflation: year-on-year annual average.

Dollar GDPs calculated using 1995 forecasts for dollar exchange rates.

Source:

except where indicated.

The Economist
Intelligence Unit

• Andreas Papandreou will probably relinquish the premiership to stand in the presidential election in May. His most likely successor is the combative Theodoros Pangalos.

• Continuing public expenditure austerity will be supplemented by a major campaign against tax evasion.

• Ambitious targets on reducing the budget deficit and inflation will keep demand in the economy relatively weak. Exports and public investment through EU structural funding will act as the main stimuli for economic growth.

To watch
Greece will look to use EU support to strengthen its foreign policy. Progress on Cyprus may result from UN initiatives.

REPUBLIC OF IRELAND

GDP: I£36.5bn; $53.3bn
GDP per head: $15,100
Population: 3.53m; change 0%
GDP growth: 1994 4.8%; 1995 4%
Inflation: 1994 2.5%; 1995 3%

• The peace process in Ireland will continue. It now looks irrevocable but progress will be slow.

• The Labour-Fianna Fail coalition government is expected to come under strain but remain in office.

• The economy will perform well. Growth should be 4% in 1995. Inflation will remain low and stable.

ITALY

Budget deficit
% of GDP

GDP: L1,785trn; $1.05 trillion
GDP per head: $18,400
Population: 57.1m; change 0.2%
GDP growth: 1994 1.5%; 1995 2.1%
Inflation: 1994 4.2%; 1995 4.3%

• Irreconcilable tensions between neo-fascists and federalists will intensify the instability of Silvio Berlusconi's government.

• Pension reform will be at the heart of the 1995 budget. One aim will be to encourage the under-developed pension-fund sector.

• Economic policy will be essentially short-term in character, at least until a more ideologically homogeneous government can be formed.

• Private consumption will remain subdued, reflecting high unemployment and virtually non-existent real-wage growth.

THE NETHERLANDS

GDP: G600bn; $327bn
GDP per head: $21,300
Population: 15.5m; change 0.6%
GDP growth: 1994 1.8%; 1995 2.3%
Inflation: 1994 2.9%; 1995 3%

• Wim Kok, the Labour Party prime minister, faces a turbulent 1995. Expect trouble from within his own party, including some members of parliament, over the extent of the government's budget cuts.

• Mr Kok's principal coalition partners, the free-market Liberal Party, will attempt to implement their manifesto commitment to reduce the social-security system.

• Exports will be the main engine of GDP growth, with domestic demand constrained by government spending cuts and consumer nervousness in the face of continuing high unemployment.

NORWAY

GDP: NKr830.0bn; $115.6bn
GDP per head: $26,590
Population: 4.35m; change 0.5%
GDP growth: 1994 3.8%; 1995 3.2%
Inflation: 1994 1.3%; 1995 2.2%

• The government has a good chance of remaining in power in 1995 and beyond, whatever the outcome of the referendum on EU membership.

• The government will pursue a strict fiscal policy as long as oil prices remain weak and government revenues are depressed.

• A decline in offshore investments will ensure that economic growth slows in 1995. Inflation will pick up as unemployment declines and wage demands increase.

PORTUGAL

GDP: Esc13.57trn; $68.6bn
GDP per head: $6,900
Population: 9.9m; change 0%
GDP growth: 1994 2%; 1995 2.9%
Inflation: 1994 5.8%; 1995 5.3%

• The ruling Social Democratic Party of Prime Minister Anibal Cavaco Silva is likely to hold on to power in the October 1995 general election.

• Continuing high budget deficits will encourage the government to continue

its high-profile attack on tax evasion, taking on some vested interests along the way.

• GDP growth will be boosted by inflows from the EU, in the energy and transport sectors, including major new road and rail links across the river Tagus at Lisbon.

To watch
Presidential elections are due in January 1996. After ten years in government, Prime Minister Anibal Cavaco Silva will have to decide whether to run.

SPAIN

Gross fixed investment
Real % change

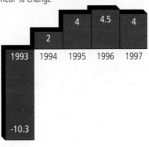

GDP: Ptas68.1trn; $490bn
GDP per head: $12,500
Population: 39.2m; change 0%
GDP growth: 1994 1.5%; 1995 2.5%
Inflation: 1994 4.5%; 1995 4%

• Although embattled, the prime minister, Felipe Gonzalez, is expected to survive a potential leadership challenge.

• Burgeoning social-security and health expenditure will force the government to increase insurance contributions and introduce new levies on tobacco and alcohol.

• A combination of lower interest rates and the beneficial impact of the labour-market reform on employment and business confidence will set domestic demand on the path of moderate growth in 1995. But the current-account balance will deteriorate.

SWEDEN

GDP: SKr1.59 trillion; $205.5bn
GDP per head: $23,270
Population: 8.83m; change 0.6%
GDP growth: 1994 1.8%; 1995 2.3%
Inflation: 1994 2.2%; 1995 3%

• Ingvar Carlsson, the new prime minister, will attempt to lead a minority government into the EU.

• The state of public finances will be the main focus of debate in parliament.

• Capacity constraints in manufacturing mean that inflationary pressures will remain a constant threat.

SWITZERLAND

GDP: SFr373bn; $257bn
GDP per head: $36,430
Population: 7.06m; change 0.4%
GDP growth: 1994 1.7%; 1995 2.2%
Inflation: 1994 1%; 1995 2.6%

• Switzerland's negotiating position with the EU will remain weak because of the country's aversion to integrationist policies.

• The 1995 election will strengthen the conservative parties in parliament. However, the political make-up of the ruling Federal Council is not expected to change.

• Inflation will accelerate in 1995 due to the introduction of value-added tax. The imposition of this tax means that the central bank is likely to be especially vigilant.

• The question of how to pay the state's social security will remain a key issue.

TURKEY

GNP: TL5,730trn; $124bn
GNP per head: $1,990
Population: 62.4m; change 2.1%
GNP growth: 1994 -3%; 1995 2.6%
Inflation: 1994 105%; 1995 58%

• Policy differences between the True Path Party and its coalition partner, the Social Democratic Populist Party, will hamper the prime minister, Tansu Ciller.

• Economic policy will be geared to reducing inflation and stabilising the lira. Privatisation, closure of loss-making state industries and reduction of agricultural subsidies will meet resistance in parliament.

• Insufficient structural reform will keep inflation high, though much reduced from the current level of over 100%. Real GNP will show a return to growth.

To watch
The Islamist Welfare Party is fast becoming a national political force. The next general election (due in 1996) will see the party in a position to influence domestic and foreign policies.

UNITED KINGDOM

GDP: £710bn; $1.11 trillion
GDP per head: $18,950
Population: 58.5m; change 0.3%
GDP growth: 1994 3.4%; 1995 3.6%
Inflation: 1994 2.4%; 1995 2.3%

• Tony Blair, the new leader of a resurgent Labour Party, will worry the ruling Conservative Party, which will

Inflation %

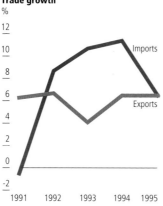

1993	1994	1995	1996	1997
1.6	2.7	3.6	3.7	4.9

find it difficult to identify an issue on which to dent his popularity.

• GDP growth will remain satisfactory, but the risk of a revival of inflation will lead to an increase in interest rates in the early part of the year.

• The government is determined that the move to take the value-added tax on fuel up to 17.5% will go ahead in April. It wants to cut the budget deficit and allow some flexibility for cuts in income tax before the next election. But some Conservative MPS, fearing an electoral backlash from pensioners' groups, will seek to postpone its implementation.

North America

CANADA

GDP: C$791bn; $594bn
GDP per head: $20,800
Population: 28.6m; change1.1%
GDP growth: 1994 3.1%; 1995 3.5%
Inflation: 1994 0.7%; 1995 2.4%

• Despite electing the separatist Parti Québécois in the provisional election in September 1994, a referendum on independence for Québec will be defeated.

• The long overdue recovery is helping to reduce the deficit but a tight fiscal stance will be vital to reassure the financial markets.

• Economic recovery should continue in 1995, though real-interest rates will remain high.

USA

Trade growth
%

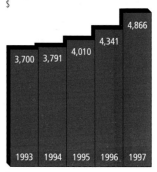

Imports

Exports

1991	1992	1993	1994	1995

GDP: $7.2trn
GDP per head: $27,400
Population: 264m; change 1.1%
GDP growth: 1994 3.7%; 1995 2.9%
Inflation: 1994 2.6%; 1995 3.3%

• Faced with a less conducive Congress, a heavy policy agenda and the dismal poll ratings carried over from 1994, President Bill Clinton's political future will hinge on his ability to score policy successes against the odds.

• Economic growth will slow from the rapid pace of 1994, but inflation will remain subdued though interest rates will have to rise further. Government spending will fall, but private investment will hold up as sustained recovery elsewhere in the G7 boosts exports.

• Wrangling with Japan will continue as the deadline for Super 301 measures closes in; unfinished Uruguay round business will include access to financial markets. Strong trade links with Latin America will be pursued.

Eastern Europe

BALTIC STATES

Estonia
GDP: Kroon37bn; $2.5bn
GDP per head: $1,600
Population: 1.56m; change 0%
GDP growth: 1994 3%; 1995 5%
Inflation: 1994 50%; 1995 20%

Latvia
GDP: Latss2.6bn; $4.8bn
GDP per head: $1,900
Population: 2.50m; change -2%
GDP growth: 1994 -5%; 1995 3%
Inflation: 1994 40%; 1995 10%

Lithuania
GDP: Litas34.8bn; $8.7bn
GDP per head: $2,300
Population: 3.75m; change -0.5%
GDP growth: 1994 2%; 1995 3%
Inflation: 1994 70%; 1995 40%

• The rickety right-of-centre coalition in Estonia is expected to be replaced by a left-wing government during elections in the spring. The new government may devalue the Estonian kroon.

• The current lame-duck administration in Latvia will continue until elections in October 1995. A divided parliament and more weak coalition governments are likely after the elections.

• The indecisive Brazauskas regime in Lithuania will run into trouble with the IMF over its economic policies. A deal with Russia over access to the Russian enclave of Kaliningrad is likely.

BULGARIA

GDP: Lv782bn; $10.4bn
GDP per head: $1,250
Population: 8.36m; change -0.4%
GDP growth: 1994 0%; 1995 1.5%
Inflation: 1994 90%; 1995 75%

• Improved stability should result from a new government. The government will steer a tight path between meeting IMF stabilisation targets and making concessions to the powerful unions. The pace of privatisation will increase.

• 1995 will see an end to recession. Foreign investment will pick up modestly following the debt agreements in 1994. Inflation will stay stubbornly high.

CZECH REPUBLIC AND SLOVAKIA

Czech Republic
GDP: Kc1.18trn; $38.5bn
GDP per head: $3,720
Population: 10.3m; change 0%
GDP growth: 1994 3%; 1995 4%
Inflation: 1994 9.5%; 1995 8%

Slovakia
GDP: Skc425.3bn; $12bn
GDP per head: $2,270
Population: 5.30m; change 0%
GDP growth: 1994 1%; 1995 2.1%
Inflation: 1994 15.0%; 1995 11.0%

• The Czech Republic will remain the most stable former communist country, but tensions in the ruling coalition will surface.

• Radical reforms in the Czech Republic will show first convincing results in 1995, in a second year of GDP growth.

• Despite Vladimir Meciar's victory, extremism should be quelled, but the political scene will still be unstable.

• Slovakia will place a large emphasis on stimulating its sluggish economic growth.

HUNGARY

GDP per head
$

1993	1994	1995	1996	1997
3,700	3,791	4,010	4,341	4,866

GDP: Ft5trn; $41.1bn
GDP per head 1995: $4,010
Population: 10.3m; change 0%
GDP growth: 1994 1%; 1995; 2%
Inflation: 1994 19%; 1995 20%

• The socialist-liberal coalition could strain under the impact of the new round of austerity. The powerful trade unions may become awkward and spurn a social pact.

• Fiscal and external balances are precarious, but devaluation combined with the macroeconomic policy tightening should begin to yield results.

• Although the current-account deficit will decline substantially over the medium term, the deficit itself will still remain large.

• 1995 is likely to confound pessimists. A renewed export surge, efficiency windfalls and the pull of the overall regional recovery should be sufficient to ensure modest growth.

To watch
Privatisation will slow as a result of stiffer employment guarantees, parliamentary oversight and the lack of promising sales prospects.

POLAND

GDP: Zl2,747trn; $100.5bn
GDP per head: $2,610
Population: 38.5m; change 0.2%
GDP growth: 1994 4.3%; 1995 4.5%
Inflation: 1994 30%; 1995 25%

• President Walesa is unlikely to be re-elected in 1995. Tensions in the ruling coalition over economic policy will persist but expect no major upheavals.

• The economy will grow robustly and mass-privatisation will accelerate after years of hesitant progress.

• Direct foreign investment in Poland will accelerate following the completion of the London Club debt-relief agreement in 1994.

ROMANIA

GDP: Lei67.7trn; $31.5bn
GDP per head: $1,380
Population: 22.8m; change 0%
GDP growth: 1994 1%; 1995; 3%
Inflation: 1994 150%; 1995 50%

• Disunity in the dominant Party of Social Democracy in Romania could break out as structural reforms begin to hurt its industrial base.

• The IMF-backed stabilisation and reforms have a much better chance of success than past efforts. An ambitious mass-privatisation plan could break the resistance of entrenched state industrial interests.

• The balance-of-payments constraint is no longer binding as a result of ample foreign funding, increasing reserves and an improving foreign-trade performance.

RUSSIA

GDP growth
Real % change

1993	1994	1995	1996	1997
-12	-10	-2	3	3

GDP: Rb1,350trn; $337bn
GDP per head: $2,270
Population: 148.3m; change 0%
GDP growth: 1994 -10%; 1995 -2%
Inflation: 1994 300%; 1995 150%

• The political scene will be more stable after the severe upheavals of recent years, but campaigning for the 1996 presidential and parliamentary elections will intensify.

• Russia will come to grips with inflation and output decline will be halted by the end of the year.

• Relations with the former Soviet republics will improve. The thaw in relations with Ukraine, following the election of a pro-Moscow president in Kiev, will be a particularly noticeable shift.

UKRAINE

GDP: Kb30,000trn; $30bn
GDP per head: $600
Population: 52.3m; change 0.2%
GDP growth: 1994 -25%; 1995 -10%
Inflation: 1994 2,000%; 1995 1,000%

• Despite a likely IMF agreement, the economy will collapse. The Kuchma government will prove as indecisive as the old Kravchuk administration.

• Relations with Russia may become less tense, and Ukraine may concede Sevastopol to Russia as a naval base. Nuclear disarmament will gather pace in 1995.

• Regional divisions will come to the fore in Ukraine. The extreme right could opt for violence.

• There will be only limited sales opportunities for western goods, due to the continued recession, low incomes and the fact that Ukraine's trade is still heavily oriented towards Russia.

Asia Pacific

AUSTRALIA

Exports
% of total

Others 2.9
Manufactures 22.4
Metals and minerals 45.8
Farm products 28.9

GDP: A$464.5bn; $327.1bn
GDP per head: $18,100
Population: 18.1m; change 1.1%
GDP growth: 1994 3.7%; 1995 3.3%
Inflation: 1994 2.3%; 1995 3%

• The prime minister, Paul Keating, is likely to call a poll in 1995, before underlying economic problems resurface.

• The financial markets may take fright from budget and trade deficits. This may precipitate interest rate rises.

• Economic growth will remain strong in 1995. Investment in machinery and equipment will grow rapidly. Inflation will increase, but remain manageable.

To watch
The deputy prime minister is likely to resign. Those jostling for his position will be first in line to eventually succeed Mr Keating.

CHINA

GNP: Rmb4.29trn; $452bn
GNP per head: $370
Population: 1.21bn; change 0.8%
GNP growth: 1994 10.5%; 1995 8.0%
Inflation: 1994 27%; 1995 30%

• Whether or not Deng Xiaoping dies in 1995, those in the top leadership immediately beneath him will continue to jockey for position. The prime minister, Li Peng, may be an early casualty, replaced by his deputy Zhu Rongji.

• Fiscal policy will remain expansionary, and the central government lacks the means or the power to fine-tune the economy effectively.

• Monetary policy will be erratic and ineffectual, with the People's Bank of China still denied an independent role.

• GNP growth will ease in 1995. Rising wages will push up private consumption, which may be further boosted by bouts of panic buying. The current-account deficit will rise.

HONG KONG

GDP: HK$1.08trn; $139.3bn
GDP per head: $22,840
Population: 6.10m; change 1.3%
GDP growth: 1994 5%; 1995 3.6%
Inflation: 1994 8.4%; 1995 8%

• All of Hong Kong's working population will be able to vote for the 20 directly elected seats in the Legislative Council—a degree of democratisation unsettling to Beijing.

• There will be increasing pressure for the development of social-welfare schemes. The currency will remain pegged to the US dollar.

• Uncertainties over the transition to Chinese rule in 1997 will continue to drag down growth. Increased government spending on infrastructure projects will not compensate for lower private investment, particularly in the construction sector. Inflation will ease only slightly.

To watch
Everything rests on the continuation of stable government in Beijing. Any uncertainty regarding the succession to Deng Xiaoping, and the Hong Kong stockmarket will be hit hard.

INDIA

GDP: Rs8.49trn; $278bn
GDP per head: $300
Population: 923.3m; change 2%
GDP growth: 1994 4.8%; 1995 5%
Inflation: 1994 9.5%; 1995 10%

• The Congress (I) Party will enjoy a strong position, but a general election is unlikely in 1995. Internal security problems will continue in the north-eastern states and Kashmir.

• The economic-reform programme will lose momentum. But gradual trade liberalisation will continue, further financial-sector reform is possible, and inward investment will be encouraged.

• Inflation will remain close to 10%, with monetary policy not restrictive enough. Exports will grow quite rapidly in 1995, and stronger economic growth will result in an upsurge in imports.

INDONESIA

GDP: Rp375.3trn; $166.2bn
GDP per head: $860
Population: 196.6m; change 1.8%
GDP growth: 1994 6.5%; 1995 6.9%
Inflation: 1994 8.2%; 1995 8.5%

• Ultimate political power will rest with President Suharto, provided that he remains in good health. Beneath him, the minister of state for research and technology, B. J. Habibie, is heading an alliance of economic nationalists and Islamic forces, but the military still stands in his way.

• There are fears that the government will rein in the process of political openness launched a few years ago.

• The struggle between Mr Habibie's "technologists" (who want Indonesia to have its own import-substituting high-technology industries, no matter what the cost) and the "technocrats" (who favour developing export-orientated industries) will continue in 1995.

• Hitting government growth targets will require high levels of investment. Exports, particularly of manufactures, should increase.

To watch
President Clinton may try to mend some fences with Jakarta, but continued suppression of the labour movement and the press will not help matters.

JAPAN

Trade surplus
$ billion

141.5	138.1	118.2	112.6	112.2
1993	1994	1995	1996	1997

GDP: ¥485.4trn; $4.71 trillion
GDP per head: $37,580
Population: 125.4m; change 0.2%
GDP growth: 1994 0.6%; 1995 1.7%
Inflation: 1994 0.5%; 1995 0.7%

• There remains a chance that a mass defection of MPs from ruling parties to the opposition will force a general election in 1995. The advent of a new electoral system may encourage the development of fewer, more broadly based parties.

• Government finances will remain under pressure, with continued uncertainty over when and by how much the government will raise indirect taxation. But cuts in income and residential taxes will be extended, and public-works programmes will be expanded.

• The Bank of Japan will try to avoid tightening monetary policy until late 1995. The yen will hang on to most of its gains.

• The modest economic recovery will

gather pace in 1995. After contracting in 1994, corporate spending on investment in plants and equipment will edge up in 1995. Inflation will remain low, and the current-account surplus will contract only slightly.

KAZAKHSTAN

GDP: Tenge1,650trn; $21bn
GDP per head: $1,240
Population: 16.9m; change 0%
GDP growth: 1994 -15%; 1995 -4%
Inflation: 1994 1000%; 1995 200%

• Russian support will keep President Nazarbaev in power. But there will be no economic help from Russia; pleas for economic reintegration will be ignored by Moscow.

• Economic reforms will be slow in response to social unrest. The economy is in a state of near collapse and living standards have plummeted.

• Oil joint ventures will run into government bureaucracy and a lack of export pipeline routes. Kazakhstan will look on nervously as Russia and Turkey limber up for a row over the Straits regime in 1996 when the Montreux Convention is renegotiated.

MALAYSIA

GDP: M$180bn; $70.7bn
GDP per head: $3,520
Population: 20.1m; change 2.3%
GDP growth: 1994 8.4%;1995 7.8%
Inflation: 1994 3.7%; 1995 4.1%

• The ruling UMNO is sure of victory in the next general election, which must be held before the end of 1995. There will be no internal party challenge to the leadership of Dr Mahathir Mohamad.

• Government attempts to combine high growth with low inflation will be complicated by a degree of uncertainty over exchange-and interest-rate policy. A sales and services tax may be introduced after the next election.

• GDP growth will slow slightly due to completion of some major infrastructure projects—the labour market will remain tight. Inflation fears will lead to monetary tightening.

To watch
Reconciling demands for an Islamic way of life with the state's essentially secular aims will remain difficult.

NEW ZEALAND

GDP: NZ$90.5bn; $52.3bn
GDP per head: $14,670
Population: 3.57m; change 1.1%
GDP growth: 1994 4%; 1995 3.8%
Inflation: 1994 1.4%; 1995 2%

GDP growth
%

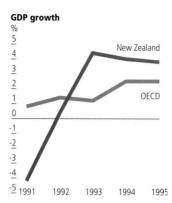

• Once the new proportional representation electoral system is in place, probably in mid-1995, a general election is possible at any time. However, no party is likely to hold an absolute majority in the new parliament.

• While it remains in power, the national government will maintain a tight fiscal stance. Its successor is likely to try to increase spending, particularly on health, but its ability to run up large budget deficits will be hindered by recent parliamentary legislation.

• GDP growth will remain close to 4% in 1995, as demand for New Zealand's export remains buoyant, particularly in the Asia Pacific region. Inflation, however, will remain low although the Reserve Bank will countenance the headline inflation rate briefly rising above 2%.

PAKISTAN

GDP: PRs1.82trn; $56.3bn
GDP per head: $430
Population: 130m; change 3.1%
GDP growth: 1994 3.3%; 1995 5%
Inflation: 1994 10.3%; 1995 9.8%

• The struggle between the ruling Pakistan People's Party and the Pakistan Muslim League will intensify. Pakistan's nuclear capability will complicate relations with India and America.

• Economic policy will emphasise the importance of deregulation and

Private consumption
Real % change

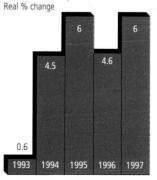

		6		6
	4.5		4.6	
0.6				
1993	1994	1995	1996	1997

privatisation, but political difficulties will make the quick realisation of stated government goals difficult. There will be particular problems with reform of the taxation system.

• Strong export growth should take the pressure off the external accounts, while allowing respectable economic growth. But inflation will remain a problem.

To watch
Political punch-ups, particularly if they lead to protest on the streets, could just force a military coup.

PHILIPPINES

GDP: P1.93trn; $65.4bn
GDP per head: $960
Population: 68.4m; change 2.1%
GDP growth: 1994 3.5%; 1995 4.5%
Inflation: 1994 11%; 1995 8.5%

• Elections for the Senate are due in May 1995, and President Fidel Ramos will encounter opposition from this body. But he should make further progress towards settling the country's two long-standing armed rebellions.

• Top policy priorities will remain the improvement of the country's physical infrastructure (notably power generation and the telephone system), the liberalisation of the economic system and the improvement of government finances.

• GDP growth will accelerate in 1995. Government investment to remove infrastructural bottlenecks should stimulate private-sector fixed capital formation. But a burgeoning trade deficit will put downwards pressure on the peso.

Trade
$ billion

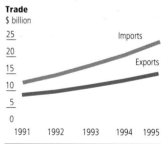

SINGAPORE

GDP: S$111.2bn; $74.1bn
GDP per head: $24,900
Population: 2.98m; change 2.1%
GDP growth: 1994 8.7%; 1995 7.6%
Inflation: 1994 3.7%; 1995 3%

• The ruling People's Action Party will espouse "Asian values", believing that social solidarity will improve the country's long-term prospects. The fledgling Singapore People's Party may attract some support, but the opposition will make no headway.

Foreign reserves per head
US$

Singapore	16,726
Taiwan	3,999
Japan	711
South Korea	458
USA	161

• The government is keen to keep the lid on housing prices, and an adequate supply of new units should ensure this. Interest rates will track those in America and Japan.

• Growth in the electronics sector will ease in 1995, but another substantial current-account surplus will be obtained. Inflation should moderate as the effects of the goods and services tax introduced in 1994 drop out of the calculation.

To watch
More multinational companies will be relocating regional headquarters from Hong Kong to Singapore in advance of the British colony's 1997 handover to China.

SOUTH KOREA

Inflation
%

South Korea	6.6
Hong Kong	8
Taiwan	4.1
Singapore	3

GDP: W340trn; $430bn
GDP per head: $9,600
Population: 44.8m; change 0.9%
GDP growth: 1994 8%; 1995 7.4%
Inflation: 1994 6%; 1995 6.6%

• Seoul may take quite a hard line towards the new leadership in Pyongyang and its South Korean sympathisers.

• American efforts to defuse North Korea's nuclear programme will receive backing from President Kim Young Sam.

• Plans by car and steel makers to increase output will attract government disapproval.

• If the government's commitment to deregulation in the financial-sector is to be believed, it will have to refrain from day-to-day interference in the stock exchange and other financial sector institutions.

• The won will strengthen in 1995, as the current account moves back into surplus. Inflation will subside and gains in real earnings will allow rapid growth in private consumption.

TAIWAN

GDP: NT$6.9trn; $267.8bn
GDP per head: $12,620
Population: 21.2m; change 1%
GDP growth: 1994 6.2%; 1995 6.4%
Inflation: 1994 3.8%; 1995 4.1%

• The ruling Kuomintang will remain in power. Constitutional changes will result in the direct election of the president in 1995. The present incumbent, Lee Teng Hui, is likely to win another term.

• There is unlikely to be any fundamental change in political relations with China, although business links will grow.

• Government spending on public-sector projects will keep the budget deficit high, despite the trimming of current expenditure. Liberalisation of the financial sector will encourage inflows of foreign-portfolio capital.

• Export growth should pick up again in 1995, although this would be jeopardised by any slowdown in China's economy. But growing public-and private-sector investment will be the real force driving GDP growth.

• The official go-ahead for direct air and sea links with China still looks some way off, despite calls from private-sector businesses fed up with having to trade via Hong Kong.

To watch
Victory for the opposition DPP in either the 1995 legislative Yuan elections or the presidential contest would cause a major upset in relations with China.

Real % change 1995

GDP	6.6
Gross fixed investment	9
Exports	7
Imports	8.8

THAILAND

GDP: Bt3.90trn; $156.8bn
GDP per head: $2,600
Population: 60.2m; change 1.3%
GDP growth: 1994 8.2%; 1995 8%
Inflation: 1994 4.8%; 1995 4.5%

• The weak party structure will create political instability. The Thai military's relations with the Khmers Rouges, and some opposition MPs' activities may complicate international relations.

• No major changes in economic policy are expected, and the process of economic liberalisation will continue. The encouragement of economic decentralisation, away from Bangkok, will yield only limited results.

• Economic growth will be robust. Domestic demand, as well as export growth, will be a driving force. Private-sector investment will be directed at higher value-added industries.

VIETNAM

GDP: D165trn; $14.3bn
GDP per head: $190
Population: 73.6m; change 2.1%
GDP growth: 1994 8.2%; 1995 8.5%
Inflation: 1994 9.5%; 1995 12%

• Hanoi will become a full member of ASEAN in 1995. Fears that Vietnam is in no position to integrate economically with the more advanced ASEAN economies will be overridden by the strategic concern to blunt Chinese expansionism in the South China Sea.

• Improved capital mobilisation will keep GDP growing at more than 8% in 1995. However the growth of Vietnamese capitalism may be hindered by rudimentary monetary and fiscal management.

• State-enterprise reform will be achieved by attrition as more loss-making firms go out of business, but key policy issues affecting state enterprises are too contentious to be clearly resolved.

Latin America

ARGENTINA

GDP: PS321.9bn; $309.5bn
GDP per head: $9,030
Population: 34.3m; change 1.2%
GDP growth: 1994 4.5%; 1995 3%
Inflation: 1994 5%; 1995 6%

• Carlos Menem is likely to win the presidential election in May despite growing unease about the impact of his tough reform policies on the working class.

• After the election the government will probably break the fixed exchange-rate system which, since its introduction in April 1991, has been very successful in reducing inflation.

• The economy will slow again in 1995 because of the loss of competitiveness caused by the fixed exchange rate. The large current-account deficit will widen further.

BRAZIL

Real % change 1995

GDP	3.5
Private consumption	3
Government consumption	-2

GDP: R981.9bn; $654.6bn
GDP per head: $4,050
Population: 161.6m; change 1.5%
GDP growth: 1994 2.8%; 1995 3.5%
Inflation: 1994 2,315%; 1995 140%

• Brazil's new president, Fernando Henrique Cardoso, will form a government of centre and right-wing parties and seek a consensus to back economic reform.

• Mr Cardoso will launch a review of the constitution to reorganise government finances, the source of Brazil's inflationary problem. Interest rates will be set high to bear down on inflation.

• The government's anti-inflationary policies will offset the capital inflows and investment attracted by Mr Cardoso's victory. Imports will continue to grow strongly as the economy opens.

To watch
Mr Cardoso offers Brazil its best chance to put its economy in order.

CHILE

GDP: PS22.32trn; $49.6bn
GDP per head: $3,480
Population: 14.2m; change 1.4%
GDP growth: 1994 4.5%; 1995 5%
Inflation: 1994 12%; 1995 10%

Foreign debt

% of GDP

57.3 51.1 49.7 48.1 46.4

17.9
$bn   19.4 20.2 21.5 23

1991 1992 1993 1994 1995

• President Eduardo Frei will face growing tension within the ruling Concertación coalition as the socialists demand greater emphasis on social spending.

• The government will increase expenditure on infrastructure and seek growing private-sector involvement.

• The economy should grow rapidly again in 1995, led by exports and investment. A recovery in copper prices could ease the current-account deficit.

COLOMBIA

GDP: PS78.73trn; $83.4bn
GDP per head: $2,375
Population: 35.1m; change 1.7%
GDP growth: 1994 5.5%; 1995 6.3%
Inflation: 1994 23.7%; 1995 27.3%

• Ernesto Samper, the new president, will aim for a consensus style of government. He will seek to address the problem of violence by increasing social spending and negotiating with guerrilla groups.

• The economy will expand strongly because of supply-side improvements and buoyant demand stimulated by government spending. Inflation will remain stubbornly high.

• Concern for non-oil sectors of the economy will lead the government to look for ways of curbing the real appreciation of the peso which is being driven by foreign investment in the Cusiana oilfield.

MEXICO

GDP: NP1.44trn; $396.2bn
GDP per head: $4,230
Population: 93.7m; change 2.1%
GDP growth: 1994 2.5%; 1995 3%
Inflation: 1994 7.2%; 1995 8.5%

• Ernesto Zedillo, elected in August 1994, faces the problem of meeting opposition demands for greater democracy without losing the support of hardliners within the long-ruling Institutional Revolutionary Party.

• President Zedillo will seek to increase social expenditure while keeping the

government's accounts in balance. Following devaluation of the peso in 1994 monetary policy will aim to reduce inflation.

• With the election out of the way, NAFTA-related investment should rise and exports should perform strongly. But imports, too, will climb and the large current-account deficit will widen yet again.

Gross fixed investment
Real % change

7

6

5

2.5

1.5
1993 1994 1995 1996 1997

VENEZUELA

GDP: Bs15.5trn; $62.3bn
GDP per head: $2,900
Population: 21.5m; change 1.9%
GDP growth: 1994 -5.5%; 1995 -0.5%
Inflation: 1994 70%; 1995 60%

• President Rafael Caldera is likely to lose popularity as the economy continues to struggle. He will try, but may well fail, to privatise the larger state-owned businesses.

• The government will rely on state intervention, maintaining the price and exchange controls imposed in June 1994. It will raise taxes but it will still run a fiscal deficit.

• The economy will shrink again in 1995 as consumer purchasing power continues to be eroded by inflation. The bright spot will be exports, both oil and non-oil.

To watch
Popular unrest is possible if the economic decline is not reversed.

Africa

NIGERIA

GDP: N1.98trn; $66.1bn
GDP per head: $690
Population: 96.1m; change 2.1%
GDP growth: 1994 3%; 1995 3.7%
Inflation: 1994 48%; 1995 40%

• The political crisis facing General Sani Abacha's military regime will rumble on. The military government may impose a new constitution of its own, retaining the federal structure while permitting greater regional autonomy.

• Political parties will be created to contest local and regional elections in the latter half of 1995, but central authority is likely to remain firmly in the hands of the military.

• The lack of common purpose and policy homogeneity within the government will hamper Nigeria's economic performance. Any policy changes in 1995 are more likely to increase direct controls than to promote liberalisation.

• Political uncertainties militate against investment, even in the oil industry. The country's once-large current-account surplus will shrink.

Foreign debt
Total $35 billion

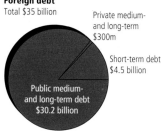

Private medium-
and long-term
$300m

Short-term debt
$4.5 billion

Public medium-
and long-term debt
$30.2 billion

SOUTH AFRICA

GDP: R484.5bn; $121.7bn
GDP per head: $2,940
Population: 41.4m; change 2.5%
GDP growth: 1994 2.7%; 1995 4%
Inflation: 1994 8%; 1995 11%

• Despite relative political calm following the ANC's electoral victory, violence and economic extremes will remain serious threats to a smooth political transition.

• Three key policy issues will dominate in the run-up to the 1995-96 budget: exchange-control and exchange-rate policy, public spending and wage policy.

• The economic recovery should accelerate, but inflation will return to double digits. The value of the rand will slide. With the economy emerging from recession, South Africa's current account will swing into deficit.

• The liberalisation of exchange controls and the abolition of the financial rand will be possible if foreign reserves can be built up to represent the equivalent of at least three months' import cover.

ZIMBABWE

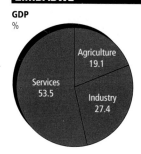

GDP
%

Agriculture
19.1

Services
53.5

Industry
27.4

GDP: Z$53.4bn; $5.63bn
GDP per head: $490
Population: 11.42m; change 3.2%
GDP growth: 1994 4%; 1995 4.7%
Inflation: 1994 23%; 1995 18%

• President Robert Mugabe's ruling Zimbabwe African National Union-Patriotic Front will win the country's presidential and legislative elections at the expense of a fragmented opposition.

• Political stability should prevail, but the government is likely to encounter serious industrial-relations problems as workers' living standards deteriorate under the Economic Structural Adjustment Programme.

To watch
The manufacturing sector will be able to take advantage of the government's trade liberalisation reforms. The government's target to reduce the budget deficit-to-GDP ratio to 5% appears well beyond reach, particularly in an election year.

Middle East

ALGERIA

GNP: AD2.02trn; $43.1bn
GNP per head: $1,510
Population: 28.6m; change 2.9%
GNP growth: 1994 -2%; 1995 3.3%
Inflation: 1994 35%; 1995 30%

• Continued civil strife will increase pressure on the government to pursue dialogue with the militants, but the army may attempt to wipe out the insurrection. A military coup against the president will remain a strong possibility.

• Algeria's political problems mean that the government will be loath to introduce an IMF economic-reform package. Some liberalisation, particularly of exchange rates and monetary transfers, will take place.

• The debt rescheduling of late 1994, along with economic reform and international support, will help the economy to grow in 1995, although the current account will move deeper into deficit.

• Increasingly violent attacks from the Islamist opposition will scare off investors.

EGYPT

GDP: E£190bn; $54.1bn
GDP per head: $910
Population: 59.4m; change 2.1%
GDP growth: 1994 1.5%; 1995 2.5%
Inflation: 1994 7.8%; 1995 7.3%

• The government's prospects of winning the confrontation against the Islamists are good. Meanwhile, there will be no early moves towards substantive democratisation.

• Don't expect much economic reform: the government is too frightened by falling living standards to try anything new.

• Egypt's sound economic performance will continue: inflation will remain in check, the budget deficit will reach no more than 2% of GDP and the current-account surplus will be preserved.

Inflation %

IRAN

GDP growth
%

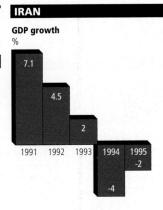

GDP: IR931.2trn; $29.1bn
GDP per head: $440
Population: 66.1m; change 3.4%
GDP growth: 1994 -4%; 1995 -2%
Inflation: 1994 20%; 1995 14.3%

• President Hashemi Rafsanjani will survive, but his authority will be eroded by the majlis, radical Islamic factions and a disgruntled population.

• Economic reform will be pursued erratically, with key policy initiatives postponed or abandoned because of political expediency. Foreign investors will remain wary.

• The economy will contract given Iran's need to reduce imports sharply in order to meet its high debt-servicing costs and because of its limited access to international financing.

To watch
Urban rioting will grow in response to falling living standards and increasing disillusion with the present government.

IRAQ

GDP: ID16.15trn; $19bn*
GDP per head: $870*
Population: 21.5m; change 0.9%
GDP growth: 1994 0%; 1995 0%
Inflation: 1994 300%; 1995 150%
* Calculated using EIU exchange rates

• Saddam Hussein will remain in control in Baghdad; the main threat he faces is from within the regime. He may also be tempted to reassert control over the fractious Kurds. However, it is unlikely that America will agree to a reincorporation of the safe haven into the Iraqi state.

• Economic policy will be geared towards further rehabilitation of the oil sector, in readiness for the resumption of oil sales. Foreign oil companies can be expected increasingly to beat a path to Baghdad.

• Inflation will stay high. The dinar will depreciate. Strict punishments will be meted out to black marketeers and

traders accused of profiteering.

• The government will make overtures to foreign companies, although there is no guarantee that it will honour its commitments once the UN trade embargo is over.

ISRAEL

GDP: NIS251.5bn; $78.6bn
GDP per head: $14,080
Population: 5.50m; change 1.9%
GDP growth: 1994 6.3%; 1995 5.3%
Inflation: 1994 10.0%; 1995 8.5%

• Gradual progress towards the expansion of Palestinian control over the West Bank will force the government to address the question of the status of East Jerusalem.

• Progress is expected in talks with Syria over withdrawal from the Golan Heights which will in turn pave the way for the withdrawal of Israeli troops from Lebanon.

• Reforms of the tax and pensions systems will lead to some political controversy as the power of the Histadrut labour federation is undermined, but neither issue will lead to the downfall of the government.

• Growth will be at 5-6% in 1995, although inflationary pressures may well push consumer price inflation beyond the expected 8.5%.

JORDAN

GDP: JD3.6bn; $5.19bn
GDP per head: $1,330
Population: 3.9m; change 3.5%
GDP growth: 1994 5.5%; 1995 4.8%
Inflation: 1994 5%; 1995 5%

• Domestic opposition to the improvement in Jordanian-Israeli relations is likely to increase as a comprehensive deal approaches. The status of East Jerusalem will prove a particular focus for opponents of an agreement.

• Debt relief offered by the American government as part of the enticement to make peace with Israel will be followed by similar gestures from EU states. Trade with Israel will bring benefits.

• Reform of the tax system in line with IMF requirements will be a politically contentious issue in 1995 but domestic politics will be overshadowed by the peace process.

LEBANON

GDP: $3.38bn
GDP per head: $1,200
Population: 2.8m
GDP growth: 1994 8.5%; 1995 8%
Inflation: 1994 13%; 1995 17%

• If agreement is reached on Israeli withdrawal from the Golan Heights, some progress can be expected on the removal of the Israeli forces from southern Lebanon. Israeli security concerns will, however, require a strong Syrian presence in Lebanon to supervise the activities of the Lebanese Shia militias.

• Investment in the reconstruction of Beirut city centre will begin to filter into the economy in 1995 paving the way for the extension of the reconstruction programme elsewhere in the country. The government's main financing problem will be to improve rates of tax collection.

To watch
Foreign commercial involvement in Lebanon will increase as the reconstruction programme expands. Expect unrest in the south and the Bekaa valley as the Shia population is likely to perceive government policy as biased towards Beirut and the north.

SAUDI ARABIA

Net foreign assets
$ billion

GDP: SR474.0bn; $126.4bn
GDP per head: $6,830
Population: 18.5m; change 3.1%
GDP growth: 1994 -3%; 1995 1%
Inflation: 1994 1.8%; 1995 2.5%

• The conservative religious elements and the liberal opposition will become more vocal, but the ruling family will successfully resist any reduction of its authority.

• Despite worrying budget and current-account deficits, Saudi Arabia will not cut its social welfare programme—which includes free education and health care.

• Steady oil production and firmer oil prices should help ease the kingdom's payments problems, but incremental borrowings and delays on debt repayments will be needed.

General trends

• Completion of the Uruguay round of trade talks will stimulate economic growth in the coming year. GATT gives way to the new World Trade Organisation, which will aim to maintain the pressure for further trade liberalisation. Expect quarrels over the admission of China to this new trade club.

• In 1995 traditional rivals will co-operate. Firms will share the risks of new geographic markets in China, India and Latin America; and new technological markets in interactive multimedia. No major company can afford to be left behind in any of these markets. Few can afford to go it alone.

• There will be a further internationalisation of all markets next year. Electricity will be bought and sold across vast continental networks, car plants will be supplied by huge global sourcing firms and the world's media and entertainments businesses will increasingly compete on a world, rather than a domestic, stage.

Sources: Stockmarket performance figures: Morgan Stanley Capital International. % changes are calculated on the MSCI stockmarket indices adjusted for foreign-exchange fluctuations against the dollar.

S. G. Warburg, Dataquest, BZW, Hoare Govett, Andersen Consulting, Financial Times, DRI-McGraw Hill, Tillinghast, Verdict Research, Kleinwort Benson, Goldman Sachs, A. C. Nielsen, UBS Ltd, Merrill Lynch.

Production

AEROSPACE

Aircraft deliveries
Worldwide

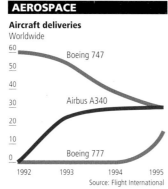

Source: Flight International

Worldwide stockmarket performance (Aerospace and military technology) October 1994

% change from previous year: 14.7
% change from 1.1.94: 2.6
% change from high: -5.8

• In 1995 orders will pick up but there will be a time delay before they feed through into increased production. Over the next 20 years, 12,000 new planes are needed, at least 3,000 of which will supply the rapidly expanding Asian market.

• Competition will focus on the sub-jumbo market. Airbus's A340 and A330 planes were the first of these 200-350 seaters. The Europeans' head start has helped erode Boeing's global dominance in civil aviation. Boeing has spent $4 billion developing its challenger, the 777. McDonnell Douglas won't be missing out on this profitable sector; it has launched its own sub-jumbo, the MD11.

• The race to power these new sub-jumbos will speed up in 1995. General Electric and Rolls-Royce will have difficulty competing with Pratt & Whitney's PW4084.

• Expect a challenge to Boeing's dominance of the aerospace industry by the new Martin Marietta-Lockheed merged firm.

• NASA is poised to invest $1.5 billion in America's aerospace industry. Likely projects include the development of a new supersonic plane. This would be larger and more environmentally friendly than Concorde.

• The rapid expansion of the Asian market will continue. Defence contractors will benefit from increased sales in the Asian region, offsetting the drop in demand from the Middle East.

• The Ariane 5 will make its first space flight. NASA will focus on TV-sized satellites.

To watch
Boeing's all-new 777 will make its first commercial flight. Boeing and Airbus will decide whether to continue collaborating on a superjumbo project. If the decision is no, expect Airbus to take the plunge first.

AGRICULTURE

• Expect disputes over the common agricultural policy (CAP) in the run-up to the European Union's (EU) 1996 inter-governmental conference. Guaranteed prices will come under pressure as the EU moves towards greater use of income maintenance and set-asides.

• The Uruguay round of GATT will be severely tested as countries find it difficult to phase out non-tariff measures. A proliferation of differing national environmental standards could actually increase the number of restrictive measures in 1995.

• An American farm bill planned for 1995 will focus on exports. Critics of the farm export programmes claim that they are skewed towards bulk commodities, where global trade is declining, ignoring the fast-growing trade in processed foods.

Britain's mad cows
Cases of BSE, thousands

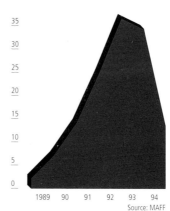

Source: MAFF

• In Britain the old Milk Marketing Board is being abolished. The board, which set prices in the dairy industry, will be replaced by a co-operative of producers, the Milk Marque. Despite hopes of increased competition, the near-monopoly situation of Milk Marque will prevent the creation of a free market in the £3.3 billion ($5.3 billion) milk business.

• 1995 will also see the flotation of Dairy Crest, the dairy-product wing of the old board, which wants to concentrate on its core activities in the face of increased competition from Europe.

• Environmental issues will again be at the fore. In Europe arguments will be put for integrating the CAP with environmental policies. Expect heightened public sensitivity to issues such as biotechnology and gene therapy in food production.

• The European Commission must decide whether to extend the ban on American cattle treated with the hormone BST.

CAR COMPONENTS

• The global car will make a large impact on component makers in 1995. First-tier suppliers aim to win single sourcing contracts with the big producers by following the car makers into Asia Pacific and Latin America.

• General Motors is turning its components department into a separate entity with greater autonomy. The aim is to become the leading global supplier. The new company, ACG Worldwide, will be more than twice the size of its nearest rivals, Bosch and Nippondenso.

• Expansion of the large firms will increase the pressure for consolidation of the industry. By 2000 there could be as few as 300 global suppliers. In Europe 400,000 jobs could go in the next five years. Michelin alone aims to make savings of FFr 3.5 billion ($663m) through redundancies.

To watch
There will be a further exodus towards Asia Pacific. Lucas is planning to manufacture brakes in India, Japanese firms are transplanting manufacturing capacity to south-east Asia.

CHEMICALS

Worldwide stockmarket performance
October 1994

% change from previous year: 20.1
% change from 1.1.94: 19.2
% change from high: -2.8

• Despite an attempt by the European Commission to pool R&D, the European chemical industry will decline. Hoechst and Unilever will restructure, thousands of jobs will go.

• Survival for all companies depends on their ability to invest in low-cost Asian plants. ICI, under the new management of Charles Miller Smith, plans to double the size of its plant in Taiwan, open a new plant in Pakistan and is looking at a potential six sites in China. Western firms need to shift production to Asia in order to supply the Asian market and compete with Asian companies.

• All industrialised countries are supposed to have reduced CFCS to 25% of their 1986 level. From next year use of the ozone-depleting chemical will stop in the EU. An American firm, DuPont, has been permitted to continue CFC production throughout 1995.

• Expect intense lobbying in Brussels as the European Commission plans a new directive on environmental control. The big firms will stress their voluntary achievements. Rhône-Poulenc, the French firm, aims to reduce water, air and solids waste by half in 1995.

Chemical cleaners
Environment spending as % of sales

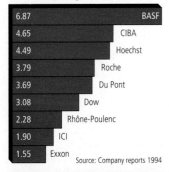

6.87	BASF
4.65	CIBA
4.49	Hoechst
3.79	Roche
3.69	Du Pont
3.08	Dow
2.28	Rhône-Poulenc
1.90	ICI
1.55	Exxon

Source: Company reports 1994

COMPUTERS

Worldwide stockmarket performance (Data processing and reproduction)
October 1994

% change from previous year: 14.8
% change from 1.1.94: 16.1
% change from high: -51.3

• 1995 will herald a revival of the big computer brands and a fall from fortune for the cheaper clones. Compaq is cutting costs and prices. Already the world's largest PC maker, Compaq will undercut IBM and Digital competing in the mainframe and minicomputers sectors. Expect price cuts of up to 20% in 1995.

Computer sales
$ billion

158.92	America
163.48	Europe
64.96	Japan
5.80	Asia's tigers
32.48	Rest of world

Source: European IT Observatory

• Hardware production will be concentrated increasingly in a few large, and mainly American, hands. Apple will push its PowerMac and could increase its world market share from 11% to 20% in 1995.

• There will be many new software programs launched next year to be used on the PowerMac. This PC can run programs compatible with both Apple and IBM. A joint venture between Apple, IBM and a chip-maker, Motorola, aims to counter the dominance of Microsoft operating systems. Microsoft will also come under pressure from Novell, which has expanded by buying WordPerfect. The Seattle-based firm, having put this year's court cases behind it, will retaliate with its Windows NT and Chicago programmes.

• 1995 will be the year in which wireless offices become a reality. Networks of PCS will be connected by radio waves. Wireless technology will also become more popular for tiny palmtop computers.

• The Internet will expand rapidly. Even the president of America now leaves messages on the world's bulletin boards. However, Bill Clinton will come under pressure to drop the National Security Agency plans to develop "Clipper", the encryption code that only Washington officials can decipher.

ELECTRICAL COMPONENTS

Worldwide stockmarket performance
October 1994
% change from previous year: 6.4
% change from 1.1.94: 12.2
% change from high: -4.5

• It will be a year of intense competition between rival chip manufacturers. Motorola has teamed up with IBM, Apple and Hewlett-Packard, to produce the PowerPC. The new chip vastly increases the speed at which computers can work. The PowerPC could win 30% of the market in the next four years. Intel, which currently supplies 80% of the market, is claiming that its new Pentium can outperform any contender. Nonetheless Intel is obviously worried. It aims to develop a new 64-bit chip.

• In Taiwan suppliers of components for American and European firms will start making their own finished products. The same Taiwanese firms will also move into the market for snazzier products such as image scanners and PC add-ons.

• A consortium of nine Japanese silicon-wafer makers will join forces to pool their R&D.

ELECTRICAL CONSUMER GOODS

Europe's electrical appetite
1995, units, m

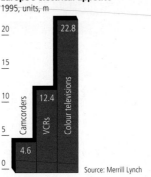

Camcorders	4.6
VCRs	12.4
Colour televisions	22.8

Source: Merrill Lynch

Worldwide stockmarket performance
October 1994

% change from previous year: 11.3
% change from 1.1.94: 6.7
% change from high: -2.1

• The market in electrical goods will be slow in Europe; only cheap microwaves have made steady sales. Hopes for an upturn depend largely on a more buoyant house market. When people move home they tend to replace their old TVs, cookers and refrigerators.

• Japanese producers will stress quality. In a recent poll by Bozell-Gallup Japanese goods were described as good or excellent by 39%. British products scored 22%, Russia came in last with only a 5% rating.

• The long-serving boss of GEC, Lord Weinstock, is due to step down in 1996. Next year he must find a successor. A leading contender is his son, Simon.

To watch
Competition in the TV market continues. Thomson will launch a new range of sets designed by the maverick French designer, Phillipe Starck.

ELECTRICITY

Worldwide stockmarket performance (Electrical and gas utilities)
October 1994

% change from previous year: -10.2
% change from 1.1.94: -10.0
% change from high: -12.8

• Further shake-ups can be expected in Britain. Larger users will persist in demands to be able to buy electricity outside the pool system. Prices are said to be artificially high in the pool

because of subsidies for Nuclear Electric. However, Nuclear Electric says that it will be making a profit next year. It wants to be privatised.

• The British National Grid Company could be privatised in 1995. The company, valued at £4 billion, is jointly owned by the 12 regional electricity companies. The government may also sell off its 40% shares in the two generating companies, National Power and PowerGen. The sale of the government's stake could raise up to £3.7 billion ($6 billion).

• The British government's ban on mergers between the regional electricity companies will be lifted in March 1995. A likely alliance is Eastern Electricity with East Midlands. Companies face a potentially severe price review to take effect from April. Offer, the industry watchdog, could force price reductions of up to 20%.

• Deregulation in the EU will cause further arguments. The Commission wants a single market in electricity supply. Its original plans were to cajole monopoly suppliers into opening up their grid networks to increased competition. Despite privatisation of many of Europe's electricity firms, true competition is still only a very distant goal.

Generating Europe's power
%

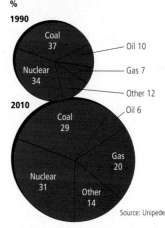

1990
Coal 37
Oil 10
Gas 7
Other 12
Nuclear 34

2010
Coal 29
Oil 6
Gas 20
Other 14
Nuclear 31

Source: Unipede

• 1995 will see an internationalisation of electricity grids. The three European networks are already connected. The aim is to link up with Central Asia, Eastern Europe and North Africa. The free flow of electricity would reduce the need for large reserves.

• China's electricity demand will grow. Beijing has set the target of 300,000MW of installed capacity by 2000. This has created a huge potential for western companies. However the Chinese government has plans to cap the profits that foreign investors can make.

MOTOR VEHICLES

Car sales
1995 m

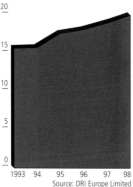

Source: DRI World car industry forecast

Worldwide stockmarket performance
October 1994

% change from previous year: 20.3
% change from 1.1.94: 12.4
% change from high: -6.0

• For European car manufacturers 1995 will be the year many return to profit. The booming American market and the successful revival of the Big Three (Ford, General Motors and Chrysler) will continue. Japanese companies are unlikely to see an end to their dismal fortunes.

• Ford is restructuring into five vehicle programme centres. The aim is to standardise production and cut costs by $2-3 billion a year. Each centre will specialise in the production of one model. Critics say that Ford will have difficulty organising this new structure. The strategy follows on from Ford's $6 billion world car, the Mondeo/Contour. The world car project was heavily criticised but doubters have been silenced by enormous sales figures.

• BMW, will expand production of Rover vehicles in new Asian plants. 1995 could even see Rovers being built in China.

• Attempts to turn Fiat around continue. Integrated factories in southern Italy will be producing up to 18 new models in the next two years. Look out for an all-new Alfa Romeo Spyder.

• Following the failed merger of Volvo with Renault, the Swedish firm will be looking for new partners. Partial privatisation of Renault has now been set in motion, probably before the French presidential elections.

To watch
The executive car will fall in popularity as tastes shift towards multi-purpose, life-style vehicles. 1995 will see the joint development of a city car by Mercedes and Swatch. South Korean cars will sell well but diesel will continue to be controversial.

OIL AND GAS

Worldwide stockmarket performance (Energy sources) October 1994

% change from previous year: 1.2
% change from 1.1.94: 1.1
% change from high:-3.3

• The market for oil will become more bullish in 1995. Oil prices are rising. One reason is the political unrest in Nigeria; another is increasing demand. Asian demand for oil will increase by 50% by 2000. China is potentially the largest market.

• Expect calls for Iraq to be permitted back on to world markets.

• The Caspian region will be the focus of western activity. The region contains the world's third largest supplies of oil. Western firms are already collaborating in Kazakhstan. Expect quarrels over the ownership of Caspian Sea oil. Russia wants joint ownership and it controls the pipelines.

Crude oil prices
Dollars per barrel

Source: DRI Europe Limited

• New oil fields will be explored in Latin America and the South China Sea, where Vietnam and China will argue over ownership.

• British Gas plans to stop subsidising smaller, unprofitable users. Prices will rise for those living farthest from pipelines. Plans to deregulate the domestic gas market by 1998 look likely to be delayed.

• British Gas and an American company, Enron, are set to compete globally as both expand. Global gas consumption will increase 40% in the next ten years.

PHARMACEUTICALS

Worldwide stockmarket performance (Health and personal care) October 1994

% change from previous year: 9.6
% change from 1.1.94: 4.5
% change from high: -8.4

• Drug firms will try to sell their products direct to the consumers

Top ten pharmaceutical companies
Branded drug prescription sales $ billion

Source: Lehman Brothers

creating one-stop health shops. Eli Lilly aims to win contracts to manage whole diseases; it will develop, sell and administer its own products. Firms such as Merck and Pfizer will push their drugs through alliances and acquisitions of pharmacy benefit management companies.

• Consumers will receive information about ailments and the drugs available from computers rather than pharmacists. More choice for the consumer and more advertising potential for the drug makers.

• New rules on trade-related intellectual property decided on by GATT will come into effect. New drugs will be protected by 20-year patent rights. The big firms argue that this is needed to meet R&D costs. Expect protests from poorer nations that will have to pay dearly as prices rise.

• The EU will introduce a centralised body to approve drugs, the European Medicines Evaluation Agency. The agency aims to be self-financing by 1998. Traditional national authorities will continue to operate.

TELECOMS EQUIPMENT

Mobile phones
% of population

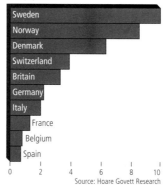

Source: Hoare Govett Research

• Digital mobile-phone networks will rapidly expand. The main European digital standard is called global system

for mobile. European-wide calls will become clearer and easier to make.

• As users switch to digital systems the price of analogue handsets will fall even further. Digital networks will make tariff reductions in an attempt to attract consumers to buy the more expensive digital phones.

• Focus will turn to the local loop that connects houses to the system. A British firm, Ionica, will launch a system based on radio waves. Phones will transmit signals from a small antenna fixed to the house. The waves will then be transmitted into the normal phone network.

TEXTILES AND CLOTHING

Sweatshop salaries
Average $ cost per hour

	Wage	Non-wage costs
USA	8.74	2.87
Japan	14.12	9.53
Germany	9.73	6.76
Britain	8.23	2.04
India	0.41	0.15
Mexico	1.68	1.25
Hong Kong	3.33	0.52

Source: American Textile Manufacturers' Institute

Worldwide stockmarket performance October 1994

% change from previous year: 4.0
% change from 1.1.94: 11.5
% change from high: -20.6

• In 1995 countries must apply the GATT rules to 10% of their textile industry. Governments are likely to incorporate the least sensitive imports first. Don't expect any immediate impact on textile prices.

• China is not a signatory to GATT. Its exports will be covered by bilateral deals. Its silk exports have been tightly restricted in the EU, causing severe shortages of silk shirts.

• European production will decline further as China, India and Pakistan increase the quality of their products.

To watch
Look out for new hi-tech fibres which have a memory, retain heat from the sun and even emit anti-bacteria chemicals.

Services

ADVERTISING

Emerging adspend
Growth in advertising revenue 1995

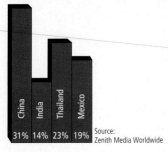

China	India	Thailand	Mexico
31%	14%	23%	19%

Source: Zenith Media Worldwide

• 1995 will bring an upturn in the fortunes of advertising agencies. The recovery will be fuelled by brand ads trying to fight the own-label challengers.

• The huge number of new TV channels will allow advertisers to target niche audiences more accurately.

• Expect interactive adverts. There will be informercials, extended adverts that also provide information, and sponsored programmes. Proctor & Gamble are planning their own game show.

• The big question next year will be whether multinational companies will continue the trend set by IBM to concentrate all its advertising in the hands of one agent.

• The European Commission will publish proposals for an advertising directive.

AIR TRANSPORT

Worldwide stockmarket performance
October 1994

% change from previous year: 11.4
% change from 1.1.94: 6.5
% change from high: -19.3

• Most airlines will still be running at only two-thirds capacity in 1995. Airlines may make profits of $2-3 billion, but $7-8 billion is needed to repair balance sheets and attract investment capital. $850 billion-worth of new planes will be needed over the next 15 years simply to replace old stock.

• United Airlines will come under scrutiny. It has sold a controlling stake to its employees' union in return for cost-saving concessions. Other firms will be watching to see if this tactic can work.

• Expect increased use of codesharing, where firms make agreements to fly each other's passengers, giving the appearance of a seamless service. For example, Delta tickets may take you on Virgin's flights.

• Although 40% of the world market is expected to be in the Pacific region by 2010, the area desperately needs investment in its infrastructure. There are not enough trained pilots, nor runways, to cope with the present growth rate.

BANKING

Worldwide stockmarket performance
October 1994

% change from previous year: -2.6
% change from 1.1.94: 2.0
% change from high: -6.9

• In America, the scrapping of the remaining barriers to nationwide banking will shake up the industry. Mergers are expected. Consumers will gain from the change. They will now be able to bank with different branches of their own bank across all states.

• Telebanking, the use of direct banking over the telephone, will grow. Expect video kiosks, advertising in cash-point machines and a diversification of services on offer.

To watch
The new European Monetary Institute in Frankfurt will begin to flex its muscles in the build-up to the EU 1996 intergovernmental conference.

INSURANCE

Europe's top insurers
Premium income $ billion

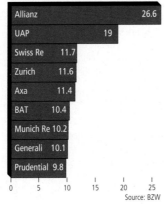

Allianz	26.6
UAP	19
Swiss Re	11.7
Zurich	11.6
Axa	11.4
BAT	10.4
Munich Re	10.2
Generali	10.1
Prudential	9.8

Source: BZW

Worldwide stockmarket performance
October 1994

% change from previous year: -6.2
% change from 1.1.94: -4.6
% change from high: -9.3

• Deregulation in Europe's insurance market will encourage cross-border sales. A simple ten-year life insurance policy can cost up to three times as much in Portugal as in the United Kingdom. Direct telephone sales will be the most successful means of expansion. Direct Line, the leading telesales insurer in Britain, can keep costs as low as 15% of income earned.

• NAFTA will boost the prospects of American firms. Expect expansion of the big insurers into Mexico and Canada.

• Debate will continue over the reform of the American "superfund" law on hazardous waste. Insurers could face lower bills for cleaning polluted sites. All sides want an end to unpredictable liabilities.

• Names at the troubled Lloyd's insurance market will face another difficult year. The three-year accounting system may be replaced so that profits can be brought forward to help finance past losses.

MEDIA

Worldwide stockmarket performance (Broadcasting and publishing)
October 1994

% change from previous year: 10.3
% change from 1.1.94: 0.7
% change from high: -4.3

• The battle of the TV giants will centre on Asia. Murdoch's Star TV has a head start in India and China, but expect things to hot-up as CNN, the BBC/Pearson alliance and the teaming up of NBC and ITN all challenge News Corp's dominance.

• The BBC/Pearson venture will launch two channels in Europe with further stations planned for Asia and the Middle East.

• The BBC will try to justify the renewal of its charter. It will invest £255m ($410m) it has saved through cost-cutting. The BBC's £200m transmitter networks may be privatised.

• ITV stations may begin to consolidate next year. There will be pressure on the government to relax cross-ownership laws.

• QVC, a TV-shopping channel, will expand in Europe. In America the baby bell companies will use their telephone networks for TV. 400,000 British homes will soon be connected to cable; videos-on-demand will become the leading multimedia product.

RETAIL

Worldwide stockmarket performance (Merchandising)
October 1994

% change from previous year: 0.2
% change from 1.1.94: 0.4
% change from high: -4.1

• The trend towards out-of-town superstores will be reversed. Critics of the big malls fear that city centres are being destroyed by creating a two-tier shopping system.

The cost of Nescafé
100g in ecus

Britain	1.77
France	3.19
Germany	4.11
Italy	3.30
Spain	2.21
Switzerland	4.65

Source: A.C. Nielsen

• Expect an increased use of own-label products in America. The big American retailers, Walmart, Shop Rite and Supervalu, will copy European shops where own-labelling is already a substantial sector of the market.

• Electronic tagging will mean the end to queueing in supermarkets and new controllable trolleys will be introduced.

• Cross-border shopping will escalate next year. Even within Europe retail prices vary wildly from one country to another.

TELECOMMUNICATIONS

Worldwide stockmarket performance
October 1994

% change from previous year: 0.1
% change from 1.1.94: -0.6
% change from high: -3.0

• The race to provide the world's 2,000 largest multinational companies with their own telephone networks will intensify. Three alliances dominate the market: AT&T/Unisource, British Telecom/MCI, and Sprint with the French and German Telecoms.

• AT&T will use the acquisition of McCaw Cellular Communication to re-enter the American local markets.

• The British market will become more competitive. There is a new long-distance network, Energis, operated by the National Grid Company. Cable firms will gain a larger share of the local domestic and business markets and AT&T will expand into Britain.

• Deregulation in Europe will continue despite the European Parliament's veto. Companies across Europe have built up an unstoppable momentum in favour of competition. This process will quicken as the remaining European monopolies are privatised.

• Western operators will invest heavily in Asia. Some 200m new phone lines are needed in the next ten years, equivalent to ten BT networks.

Why is France so attractive to international investors ?

France has enjoyed spectacular growth in international direct investment over the last decade. Worth $ 21 billion in 1980, total accumulated levels now stand at a full $111 billion. This fivefold increase, higher than either the U.S.'s or Britain's, ranks France one of the most attractive countries in Europe for international investors.

The world's fourth largest economy has many strengths : a strategic location in the European market, a remarkable choice of sites, and ultra-modern transport and telecommunications networks are but a few of them.

More importantly, France has made significant and continuous efforts to create the kind of pro-business climate sought by international investors everywhere. France's regulatory environment is one of the most liberal for foreign companies. Its labour and energy costs are highly competitive. The corporate tax rate is among the lowest in Europe.

As Ambassador at large for International Investment, I am committed to ensuring that investors receive the highest attention. My team and I will be happy to assist you.

MINISTÈRE DE L'ÉCONOMIE

Ministère de l'Economie
139 rue de Bercy - Teledoc 334
75572 Paris Cedex 12 France
Tel. : (33) 1 44 87 70 21
Fax. : (33) 1 44 87 70 26

Jean-Daniel Tordjman
Ambassador at Large
for International Investment

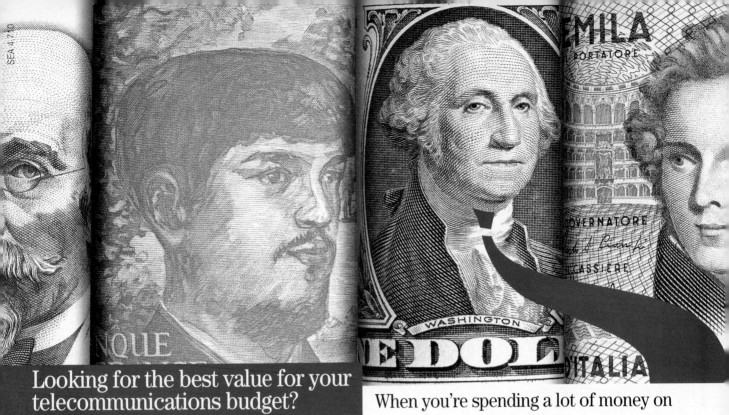

We're all Anglo-American now

Matthew Bishop

In 1995, the economies of Japan and continental Europe will put recession firmly behind them, turning in growth rates of close to 3%. But that good news will be slim consolation to many of the big companies that dominate those economies: in 1995 and beyond, huge changes in global economic conditions will force a profound rethink of the way they do business. Increasingly, they will turn for inspiration to the business practices of America and Britain—practices that thus far they have been more inclined to look down on than up to.

That sniffy attitude is easy to understand. For most of the past 40 years, the rapid growth of the economies of Japan and continental European countries such as Germany and France has made progress in America and Britain look very ordinary. Japanese and Europeans reckon this proves that their brand of capitalism is best. It stresses long-term relations between companies and big investors, such as banks and strategic shareholders, loyalty to managers, and jobs for life for employees. By contrast, they see the Anglo-American variety, in which the stockmarket is king, shares are traded frequently and management change is often effected through hostile takeover, as ridiculously short-termist. They look in horror at the power of the accountant and corporate lawyer, and at the regulation and openness required in Anglo-American business life.

Branding these approaches short- and long-term is misleading. Better labels are "volatile" and "stable". In America and Britain, the stockmarket can force rapid and violent change on a firm or industry. In Japan and continental Europe, change is smoother and more gradual—though, in the end, no less thorough. Indeed, it is arguable that this stable approach to change, which relies on consensus more than fear, was better

Matthew Bishop: economics correspondent for *The Economist*.

in the past at tackling events such as the oil shocks of the 1970s.

The changes ahead will be very different from those of the recent past, however. Technology will allow more companies to disperse their activities easily around the world to wherever is most efficient. The globalisation of capital markets will accelerate as Americans invest more of their money abroad, and more foreign cash pours into emerging markets, so firms can seek out the cheapest source of finance for their investments and capital can go to the most efficient firms. Developing countries will get ever stronger as the World Trade Organisation removes many of the barriers that now keep their products out of developed-world markets.

According to Michael Jensen, an economist at Harvard Business School, such forces will bring about a "modern industrial revolution", at least as far-reaching as the first one 200 years ago. In coping with the changes this will bring, the entrenched stability of Japan-

ese and continental European capitalism will prove more of a hindrance than a help. In the past, restrictions on competition have allowed firms in these countries to adjust slowly without suffering the losses that occur in competitive markets. But in future, if firms respond sluggishly to market forces, deregulation and fewer trade barriers, they will be left behind.

The pain will be felt most acutely by employees, many of whom will no longer have a job for life. As firms' profits tumble, they will have to shed workers (although to soften the blow, they may disguise this by promoting job-sharing and, notably in Japan, lobbying the government for job subsidies). Already, many big Japanese and German firms have cut jobs at home and switched production to countries where workers are cheaper. More will do so. As they do, the consensual approach to running firms will become unworkable. As the priorities of domestic workers differ ever more sharply from those of managers, American-style industrial relations, short-term employment contracts and performance-related pay will become common.

Since 1993, a series of corporate scandals, ranging from the crisis in Germany's Metallgesellschaft, following poorly misunderstood speculation on oil-price movements, to cases of boardroom corruption in Japan, Italy and France, have highlighted the weak accountability of many company bosses to those who hire them. Shareholders and banks will make changing this a top priority. Independent outsiders, including some foreigners, will become commonplace on company boards, replacing the colleagues of the boss. The non-executive "supervisory board" of German firms, which oversees the "management board", will start to meet more often than the present two-to-four times a year.

Awkward shareholders

Managers will start to talk about that American buzzword, "shareholder-value". Dividends, traditionally far below those of Anglo-American firms, will rise. Minority shareholders, who in the past have often suffered at the hands of dominant shareholders and banks, will get better protection as new insider-trading laws start to bite. Managers will consult large shareholders more often before taking strategic decisions. In part, this change will be driven by domestic shareholders, such as insurers and banks, which face increased pressure for higher returns on their shareholdings. But foreign shareholders, especially American pension funds used to corporate-governance activism at home, will wield growing clout as they buy more shares in overseas firms.

Privatisation programmes in Europe will increase the supply of such shares. The necessary legal requirements will ensure that Anglo-American standards are met. European firms, with capital in short supply at home, will get access to new investors by listing themselves on foreign stockmarkets.

One important aspect of Anglo-American capitalism will not be exported soon, however. That is the hostile takeover, a creature to which Japanese and continental European bosses and shareholders alike remain united in their hostility. In America, too, hostile takeovers will be rarer than they were in the 1980s. Then, however, they played a crucial role in the kind of massive corporate restructuring that is now needed in Europe and Japan. Whether these economies can bring about such change without going all the Anglo-American way will become clearer in 1995.

Time's up, partner

Michael Reid

Many people may find it hard to have much sympathy for them. But 1995 might just be the year that one of the six big firms that dominate world accounting—Arthur Andersen, KPMG Peat Marwick, Ernst & Young, Coopers & Lybrand, Deloitte Touche Tohmatsu and Price Waterhouse—goes bust.

And 1995 will certainly see the ancient institution of partnership under further stress: some of the British branches

Cosy then, uncosy now

of the "Big Six" are poised to abandon the partnership model and become limited companies. Already many American law firms are incorporated as "professional corporations": watch for some of the big British law firms to begin doing the same thing.

For centuries, partnership has been the way that professionals in Anglo-Saxon countries have chosen to organise themselves. Apart from favourable tax treatment, the advantages traditionally included self-government, a lifetime career and a share of the profits. These are now breaking down, under the stress of intensified global competition. The flipside of partnership has always been unlimited personal liability for losses. As damages for malpractice mount, professionals are left looking for what Law-

Michael Reid: business correspondent for *The Economist*.

rence Weinbach, the chief executive of Arthur Andersen, calls "a bomb shelter".

The number of lawsuits against professionals is certain to increase in 1995. Mr Weinbach reckons that there are claims worth $30 billion outstanding against American accountants, mostly arising from their work as auditors.

In 1994 legal suits against accountants mounted across the globe, from Italy to Australia. And increasingly, lawyers, who normally do the suing, are being sued themselves: several American law firms have made $40m-plus settlements of malpractice suits arising from their work for failed savings and loan institutions. Architects will find themselves in the firing line as well.

The search for protection from legal claims led the American branches of the Big Six accountants in 1994 to switch to a new juridical format: "the limited liability partnership" (LLP). In an LLP, though the firm as a whole retains unlimited liability, individual partners are no longer liable to have their personal assets seized if legal claims arise from work for which they had no direct responsibility.

The accountants say they are being picked on. Under the legal precept of "joint and several" liability, they can be sued for the whole amount of loss arising from a corporate collapse—even if poor auditing had little to do with it. So accountants want the law changed to allow them to cap their liability (as auditors in Germany can). During 1995 Australia's accountants may make progress towards achieving a system of proportionate liability. But do not expect their counterparts in America and Britain to win their campaign to scrap joint and several liability.

The American accounting firms claim their move to LLP status is a mere technicality. In fact, it is part of a wider flight from partnership that began a decade ago. Then, many surveyors, stockbrokers and advertising agencies decided to incorporate as limited companies in order to raise outside capital.

Neither accountants nor lawyers have yet needed to tap outside sources of capital: Andersen, the world's biggest accountancy firm, with fee income of $6 billion in 1993, invests about $200m a year (mainly on computers and offices) from its own resources. But two other things, apart from liability, are undermining partnerships.

The first is the increasing size and global scope of professional service firms. Today's huge accounting firms are the product of a wave of merger mania in the 1980s. This was partly a reaction to slack growth in the accountants' audit income. But it was also because their clients were going global: the spread of equity capitalism in Asia, the former eastern block and Latin America has opened up huge new markets for American and British accountants and law firms. (In most of continental Europe, accountants and lawyers have never enjoyed the exalted status of their Anglo-Saxon counterparts; many are already incorporated as companies, and some firms of auditors are even owned by banks.)

The result of the mergers is huge, unwieldy firms: in 1993 KPMG, for example, had 6,000 partners (though in 1994 it began sacking some of them). Of the Big Six, only Andersen is set up as a single, worldwide partnership, spreading costs across its 2,600 partners in 72 countries; the others are awkward confederations of regional partnerships, sharing a more-or-less common trading name.

The world lawyer

American and British law firms and, to a lesser extent, those from Australia, Canada and Holland, are growing swiftly too. In 1978, only ten American law firms employed over 200 lawyers; in 1993, 35 did. In 1994, having an office in China was no longer a novelty for the top international law firms; rather, they were opening up in such places as Hanoi, as Clifford Chance and Freshfields, two big London firms, did. But there is still plenty of untapped ground.

So far, lawyers have largely eschewed international mergers. But in 1994 Titmuss, Sainer and Webb, a 147-lawyer London firm, merged with—some cynics said that it was bailed out by—Dechert, Price & Rhoads of Philadelphia. Expect also more link-ups between mid-sized firms on both sides of the Atlantic in 1995, as they battle to compete with the top firms whose reach is global. Others expect American and British law firms simply to continue poaching each other's lawyers. And watch out for previously sleepy continental European law firms branching out abroad, either alone or in loose alliances.

Many big modern partnerships in reality manage themselves as if they were companies: an inner core of partners takes the strategic decisions, leaving the rest to carry on with the business of making money from clients.

That has never been more urgent for professional service firms. Apart from liability and size, the third factor that will undermine partnerships will be increased competition. No longer do clients treat their accountants and lawyers with awe, and pay their bills without question. After rising steeply in the 1980s, professional fees crashed in the recession, and have yet to recover.

Where does your city stand? — **1995 INDICATORS**

	Wages Average hourly wage US$ Gross	Taxes Taxes and social security as % of average gross income	Prices Six-year-old whisky US$	Rents Monthly rent in good residential area for a furnished 4-room apartment US$	Headaches Price per 100 aspirin US$
Athens	6	18.9	11	1,110	3.41
Brussels	13	38.1	15.31	1,144	6.75
Frankfurt			14.70	—	
Geneva	21	26.6		2,013	
Hong Kong	5	15	19.32		7.76
London	11			1,908	6.42
Los Angeles	15	20.8	13.99	2,065	6.90
New York	16	20.2	14.92		10.31
Paris	12	24.6	14.71	2,595	6.75
Tokyo	19	19.3	30.81	8,488	24.52

Source: BICOL; UBS

Television from your telephone company

Jim Chalmers

Just how good is your telephone company? In 1995 you should begin to find out whether it is winning or losing in the new world of multimedia communications. Does it provide television? Have its prices dropped dramatically? Have you been offered access to the Internet? If not, why not?

Next year will show whether there is any truth in the boast made by the world's old-style telephone companies that they are masters of this new interactive universe.

Of all the industries currently converging on the "information superhighway"—computer companies, software developers, media and entertainment moguls, cable TV operators and new pioneers in wireless connectivity—only the telephone companies have the necessary financial clout to take the lead. They have been kept from it so far by regulation. That will change.

The easing of regulation will allow the old monopolies to assert their power in the emerging multimedia market. This process is already well under way in the United States and likely to proceed swiftly in Europe and across large swathes of Asia during 1995.

For the politicians involved there will be some tough decisions. Having intro-

Jim Chalmers: editor of *Public Network Europe*.

duced rafts of regulation to restrain these once-dominant monoliths, most do not favour a U-turn. But they understand that the superhighway age will be seriously delayed unless the old giants are free to go on the rampage. The telephone companies have made it clear that such involvement will take place only on their own terms. Their lobbying efforts will bear fruit in 1995.

So after a decade in which they have remained largely dormant (but ever profitable), telephone companies will emerge anew to dominate a sector upon whose growth many observers now pin the fortunes of advanced economies far into the next century.

They now bear little resemblance to the leviathans of old, following severe reductions in staff levels and commensurate increases in efficiency. They are also rich. Even when corporate flabbiness persists, they will reason that a little surplus fat is never more useful than when a rival needs to be squashed by a combination of cash and muscle. "If you can't beat them, buy them," might prove an appropriate slogan for their strategy as the telecoms business converges with the computer, media and entertainment industries. As one analyst says of these remnants of a monopoly era, "they still possess a 'natural monopoly' on the ability to think big and long-term, and to fund such thinking."

Thus the cross-industry acquisitions that failed to get off the ground in 1994

are likely to be tried again in 1995, successfully this time: the underlying principles remain valid, and the "fighting funds" belonging to the major American operators and Europe's more progressive carriers remain unspent. Talk of new trillion-dollar industries—like multimedia—makes existing billion-dollar companies nervous.

The running will be made in a handful of countries—America, Japan, Britain, Spain, Sweden, Finland, Australia and New Zealand—where significant competition has been introduced. It is bad news for the remainder, including a damningly high percentage of countries in the European Union, which are only now taking deregulation seriously.

Those EU countries may well suffer and, if they do, the European Commission will have to take its share of the blame. Only in 1995 will the liberalisation of the telecoms infrastructure, which will allow competitors to build their own networks, be agreed. Even then, the new rules will not take effect until 1998.

This is sluggish caution in such a dynamic industry. The German and French governments are rightly worried. So high are the stakes in the race to build the networks of tomorrow that companies whose own markets are closed will simply not be allowed to enter the game.

Thus the ever-

deepening alliance between two state-owned monopolies, France Telecom and DBP Telekom of Germany, might yet produce a global company, but only if there is a relaxation of their domestic monopoly strangleholds. The alliance's plans, including the acquisition of equity in a big American carrier, Sprint, due in 1995, will have to include sustained efforts to secure political approval.

Since competition was first introduced in the 1980s, new companies have directed their attention to the long-distance telephone business because of its high margins and economies of scale. Economics at the time dictated that wiring the "last mile" that directly connects customers to the network was not feasible except for the largest corporate users. As a result, traditional operators compensated for squeezed margins in the long-distance business by raising charges in the relatively uncompetitive "local loop", thus maintaining overall profitability.

This fat will be cut away by two new technologies. First, radio will replace the traditional fixed-wire link to subscribers, while offering also some of the mobility associated with today's booming cellular mobile phone networks. Second, optical fibres capable of delivering multichannel TV as well as a telephone service will be coming to your house.

Thus the profitable core of most of today's major telecoms companies is under assault. Nothing will make them fight back harder in 1995.

Trading places

1995 INDICATORS

January 1st 1995: 123 countries will trade in the war-battered, but victorious GATT for the sparkling new World Trade Organisation. Its location? Geneva (home of GATT); its staff? well, unless GATT is your present employer, don't hold your breath.

But continuity is not necessarily a bad omen. The Uruguay round left many issues unresolved. Most importantly the new body must maintain the pressure for liberalisation of trade in services and tackle the growing concerns of environmentalists.

Free trade, worldwide, is the best economic policy. Second best is free trade within a regional group. And the second best is winning. The world's trade clubs range from the entrenched European Union to the more tentative ECOWAS. NAFTA will make an impact in 1995. In Latin America MERCOSUR heads the list of regional agreements. Asia's APEC will intensify competition in this brave new world of large acronymical blocks. Better that they all folded their tents and accepted free trade.

NAFTA $15,807 1994

European Union $21,150 1957

APEC $14,000 1994

MERCOSUR $3,385 1994/5

VISEGRAD $1,603 1994

ECOWAS $438 1975

SEMAC $1,210 1964

G3 $2,570 1994/5

PTA $582 1981

ASEAN $1,680 1967

CACM $1,974 1974

ANDEAN $1,388 1969

UEMOA $449 1994

SADC $1,078 1992

NAME $ 1900

Name of trading block
GNP per head in $
Date of inauguration
Number of members

Source: EIU; World Bank; UN

"We have one golden rule for all meetings. Mobile phones must be switched off."

TRYGVE URDAHL, Senior Executive, Business Development, Ericsson Communications Ltd., New Zealand.
ALFRED LING, Marketing Manager, Ericsson Telecommunications Pte. Ltd., Singapore.

This might seem paradoxical coming from a company known all over the world for its mobile phones and systems. But for us, it's a matter of respect. It's our way of adapting to the new world of telecommunications.

Technology allows us to communicate with anyone, anywhere, anytime. But "anytime" doesn't have to mean that we can't keep in touch while still respecting each other as individuals. Because technology also gives us the freedom to divert calls, or to use an answering service and call back at our own convenience.

Ericsson is a world leader in the development and implementation of cellular systems for mobile phones, serving more than 40 % of the world's cellular subscribers. Ericsson's systems know-how is the foundation of its advanced digital mobile phones and services for GSM, D-AMPS, PCS and DCS-1800.

Ericsson's 75,000 employees are active in more than 100 countries. Their combined expertise in switching, radio and networking makes Ericsson a world leader in telecommunications.

Telefonaktiebolaget LM Ericsson, S-126 25 Stockholm, SWEDEN.

ERICSSON

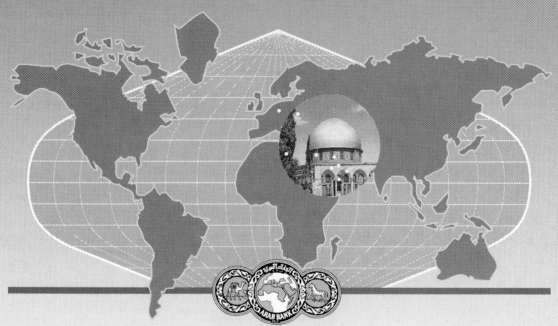

Drug companies do a lot of swallowing

Moira Dower

The oil business after OPEC's shocks; the car manufacturers after Japan's invasion; the computer industry after the felling of IBM—changes that occur perhaps only once in an industry's lifetime.

In 1995 and beyond such a change will come to the world of pharmaceuticals. "Many drug companies will either be out of business or auctioned off at about ten cents to a dollar, leading to perhaps a dozen companies dominating the world pharmaceutical marketplace," according to one recent Wall Street prediction.

A worldwide upheaval is under way. Cost-cutting in Europe, with medicines in the front line of government efforts to curb health budgets, is forcing change. Bill Clinton's failed health-care efforts have jolted things further. But politics alone is not the cause of the change. The industry is having to cater for new customers who take precedence over doctors and patients: "managed care"

Moira Dower: editor of *Scrip World Pharmaceutical News*.

insurer groups, which buy in health care for increasing numbers of Americans. These groups use pharmacy benefit management companies (PBMS). PBMS are middlemen with massive buying power that provide prescription drugs for their insured customers at knockdown prices.

Buyer's market

The world's biggest drug company, Merck, decided that it needed its own middleman and so bought America's biggest PBM, Medco Containment, for $6.7 billion. SmithKline Beecham bought Diversified Pharmaceutical Services for $2.3 billion, and then Eli Lilly offered $4 billion for the McKesson subsidiary, PCS Health Management.

The acquisitions will give these companies much new data on drug utilisation in 1995—data they will use to demonstrate the value of their products. However, what the purchasers have really gained, they hope, is preferential choice for their own products in the

schemes run by PBMS, now administer to almost 100m American patients—or about 40% of the population. This will be a significant benefit in a climate where, for example, the world's leading drug—Glaxo's ulcer treatment, Zantac—could be denied to patients covered by any one of the major American health insurers; for instance, if competitors to Glaxo were to offer insurers better prices for an equivalent to Zantac.

In the face of all this the Clinton proposals for health care—now dead—have been almost a sideshow. Changes in the marketplace have forced drug-price inflation in America down to 1.3%. Next year sales growth (worldwide) will fall to single digits, compared with growth of almost 16% in 1991.

Price cuts are increasingly being demanded by governments (2.5% in the United Kingdom and 10% in Italy, for example). The health services in some countries are refusing to pay at all for a lengthening list of products. The patient himself either has to pay extra or use a cheaper drug.

The drug companies are responding to all this by cutting back hard on their expenses and some 40,000 jobs in the industry have disappeared in 1993 and 1994. There was considerable over-capacity in production facilities and many of these have now been closed, most of

Please cough for the computer

Alexandra Wyke

It began in 1994, it will flourish in 1995. It is do-it-yourself medicine. Patients are taking charge of their own care, partly because they want to. AIDS lobbyists led the way after they became dissatisfied with the service they were getting from the medical establishment. Technology is coming up with all manner of new gadgets to help the consumer doctor help himself. These two trends will help create a multi-billion-dollar market for home doctoring.

So what will the 1995 do-it-yourself doctor be doing? The answer is a lot of what the doctor does now: diagnosis, classifying the nature of a complaint from a hotchpotch of symptoms, prescription and prognosis, predicting prospective health.

For diagnosis, there will be many more books, telephone hotlines and new computer software. Instead of hanging around in waiting rooms, anybody can get on-demand medical information—in

Alexandra Wyke: business and science correspondent for *The Economist*.

the comfort of their own home. Already patients are talking to each other on the Internet. Patients will also be able to get hold of information that used to be available exclusively through doctors. There are new over-the-counter diagnostic kits which alert a person to sickness, be it high blood pressure or whether they test positive for AIDS. The

computer-doctor will also dish out advice about options for medical treatment. As for access to treatment, more potent prescription drugs are becoming available over the counter. The private sector will also profit next year by providing patients with medical care that they cannot get health insurers to pay for.

This consumer health-care movement will, in time, cause a shake-up of the health-care infrastructure: consumers rather than doctors will become its powerbrokers. And the ordinary general physician will slowly have his power and mystery stripped away as, tired and fed-up, he performs less well than an ever-fresh CD-ROM. In many countries doctors have stopped making home visits. In future, some people will stop making visits to the doctor—except to the one blinking and bleeping in the drawing room. Before the century is out, the question will be whether all of this is really a good thing.

them based in Europe.

But the main task for 1995 will be to control the pharmaceutical industry's biggest expense—research and development. It takes an estimated $250m and 10-12 years to bring a new drug to market. The aim is to streamline this process, focus on fewer therapeutic areas and discard those projects that do not immediately look economically viable. Projects that look as if they share the field with too many other companies will be the first to go.

The major beneficiaries of this re-assessment of research and development expenditure are the proliferating "research boutiques". These are small development companies that focus on particular disease areas such as diabetes, strokes and AIDS. The multinationals, having cut back on their in-house research efforts and finally cast off the "not invented here" mentality, are turning to these small outfits for new products and leads. Glaxo, the drug industry's biggest research and development spender, at over £900m ($1.6 billion) a year, has been the leading exponent of this new strategy, with more than a dozen such alliances.

American pharmaceutical companies have also had to look at just how much they depend on their domestic market. These firms still have the lion's share of the top performing drugs. But they have also been the most heavily hit by the drastic shake-ups in their home markets. Many have made moves towards taking on international markets. In particular, American companies are looking for new opportunities in the emerging markets of Eastern Europe, Asia Pacific and South Africa.

One other major headache looks likely to accentuate the problems faced by these research-based companies throughout 1995. Patents on some of their most lucrative products are expiring. By the end of the decade brand-name drugs with annual sales of $30 billion will lose their patent protection in America. When a top-selling drug loses its patent it tends to lose 50% of its sales almost immediately. If a company has no major products to fill the gap, it has serious problems and becomes ripe for takeover.

One-stop health shops

The new giants that are being created will themselves have to become "health conglomerates". This means that they will have to integrate horizontally with each other as well as vertically with other providers in the health system—transforming themselves from compa-

nies that sell pills into organisations that manage total health care.

Taken at its most extreme, this could lead to the industry entering the next century with just three or four huge multinational pharmaceutical firms. One more reasonable forecast is that by 2000 there will be about 15 truly pharmaceutical-based companies each with a turnover of $7 billion or more. This would leave no more than 35 international companies with a turnover of $3 billion-$7 billion; about 50 regional companies with sales of $1 billion-$3 billion;

and about 400 national firms (involved in project development work rather than research) with sales of less than $1 billion.

As a consequence of the upheavals, expect to see American firms hit the hardest. Economic growth elsewhere in the world will probably weaken the American companies to such an extent that their European and Japanese rivals will fill many of the top places by the end of this decade. Don't be surprised to see a Sankyo or Takeda move up the top 20 by way of a takeover in America.

Japan changes

Keith Henry

After three years of recession, the Japanese economy will see a modest recovery in 1995. This will provide Japan with little respite, however, from the pain of the fundamental structural changes that are taking place. The highly valued yen and the prospect of slow economic growth for

Keith Henry: research associate, MIT Japan Programme, Tokyo.

many years are forcing new rules on Japan. How well it can manage this transition will determine Japan's effectiveness in the next century.

Recovery will be seen in several key economic indicators. Capital investment and consumer spending, two traditional engines of Japan's economic growth, will stop shrinking and show a small in-

Japan stakes a claim in Asia

Keith Henry

Exporting manufacturing to Asia not only helps Japan's economy make needed structural adjustments, it also gives corporate Japan a crucial stake in the growth of the emerging markets of the region.

Investment in market structures is the key to success in these new markets. Infrastructure networks will help determine what reaches new Asian customers and how products are sold to them. Competition to create and control these structures in Asia will, therefore, precede the competition to sell products and services.

While western firms still believe that simply peddling exports is the best way to grab a piece of Asia's expanding pie of wealth, Japan's corporate giants are determined actually to control the factories of the region. This policy will bear fruit in 1995.

For example, rather than simply exporting products made in Japan, Japanese car makers are actually exporting their manufacturing know-how and capacity to Asia. Already

Toyota and Nissan have established a matrix of cross-national manufacturing facilities across the ASEAN block. In 1995, expect Honda and Mazda to follow suit.

Next year, Japanese retailers will start by building their own Asia-wide networks of distribution channels and warehouses. A Japanese retailer, Yaohan, will complete construction of 330 stores in China alone.

Japanese banks are also gaining access to Asia's savings. They are becoming partners with local banks, establishing nationwide retail-banking networks. In Indonesia, every Japanese city bank is in a joint venture with a local retail bank. Next year, this process of expansion will spread into China.

Firms that fail to invest similar stakes in the growth of these emerging markets in 1995 will be at a huge competitive disadvantage in the future. Japan's economy may be in a recession today but thoughtful investments will bolster its ability to dominate all of Asia's markets in the coming years.

is corporate Japan's investment in new jobs elsewhere in Asia (an 11.4% increase in new Japanese-created jobs worldwide is planned for next year, the vast proportion of which will be in Asia). Taking advantage of lower costs in Asia, Japanese companies can maintain international competitiveness. Increasingly, a "Made in Asia by Japan" tag will replace the familiar "Made in Japan" label on Japanese products.

Great though the transfer of corporate muscle overseas has been, though, it has scarcely begun. Japan's overseas manufacturing base is, relatively, only one-fifth that of the United States and a quarter that of Germany.

All this will help the economy in 1995. The high yen means that Japan is importing disinflation. Oil, manufactured goods and western knick-knacks for the shops will all be cheaper next year. Although manufactured imports will continue to soar in 1995, the giants of corporate Japan will still call the shots.

Colour TVs are a case in point. Although Japan will be a net importer of colour TVs, few made by non-Japanese companies will find their way into the hands of consumers. Contrast this to the experience of the United States. When America stopped making TVs because it could no longer do so competitively, all its imports were made in Japan by Japanese companies.

Japan remains a manufacturing economy. The country will have a chance to change things in 1995. There will be debate on deregulation in finance, insurance and telecommunications. But despite the recovery progress will be slow.

crease in 1995. Capital spending should increase by 2%. Reflecting confidence in a recovery in consumer spending, electronics manufacturers and retailers will see gains of about 10%.

The challenge for corporate Japan is to reduce its fixed costs. This will mean cutting staff rolls, rationalising manufacturing and selling off assets. Employment costs will be tackled without the massive lay-offs confidently predicted in the West. Because of the bonus system, which makes up one-third of an employee's annual pay, firms can reduce real wages without sacking people. Japan knows how to deal with this: in the 1974 recession the upset was far greater.

Look out for much more co-operation between competitors. Design and production teams that would be deadly competitors in America will increasingly co-operate across companies. Nissan, Fuji and Isuzu recently decided to pool production of crankshafts, for example.

No government will go beyond the list of promises to deregulate made by the Hata cabinet in 1994. Attempts at tax reform will get nowhere in 1995. Political reform, even if successful in producing a two-party system, will not herald in an era of deregulation or increased competition.

Driven by economic incentives, Japanese companies will take a silent leadership role in transforming the econ-

omy. They will want a weakening of the practice by which banks and corporations own each other's shares. There will be less incentive for both simply to hold stock of the companies with which they have close business ties. In 1994 stock sales at 21 major Japanese banks totalled over ¥50 billion ($505m). The figure for 1995 may exceed ¥75 billion.

The most dramatic structural change

Made by Japan, but not in it

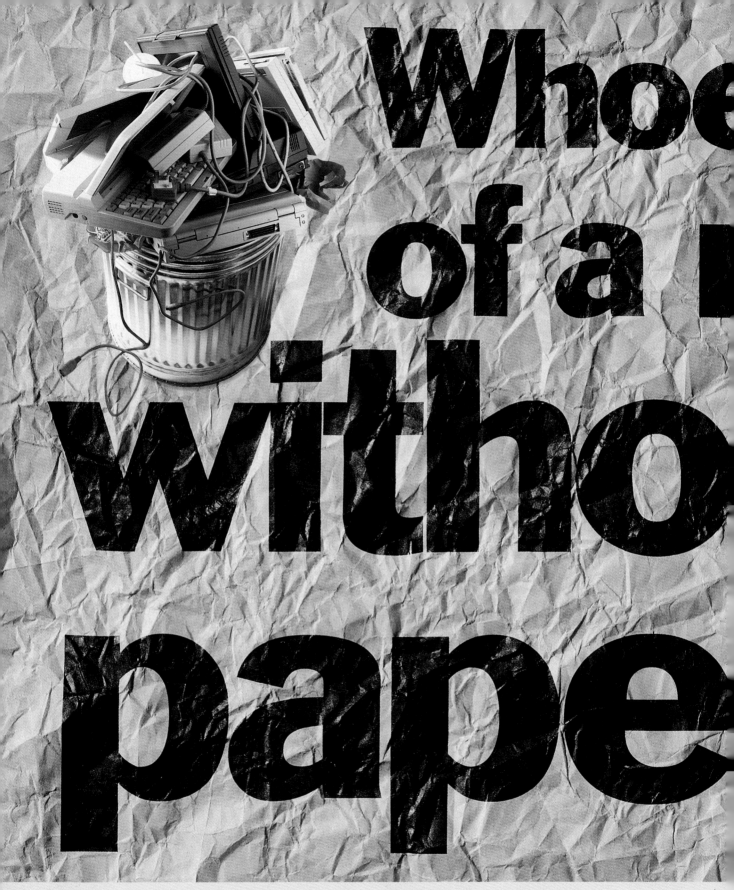

Who of a witho pape

Forgive us for rubbishing the opposition. But they should take a leaf out of our book by providing notebooks with bubble jet printers built-in. Not only does our BN range of notebooks look good on paper, they're practical too. Take the BN32. With its 50MHz 486 processor, super VGA colour screen and full PCMCIA expandability, small wonder it's top of the heap. Commit yourself to paper now, complete the coupon for more information.

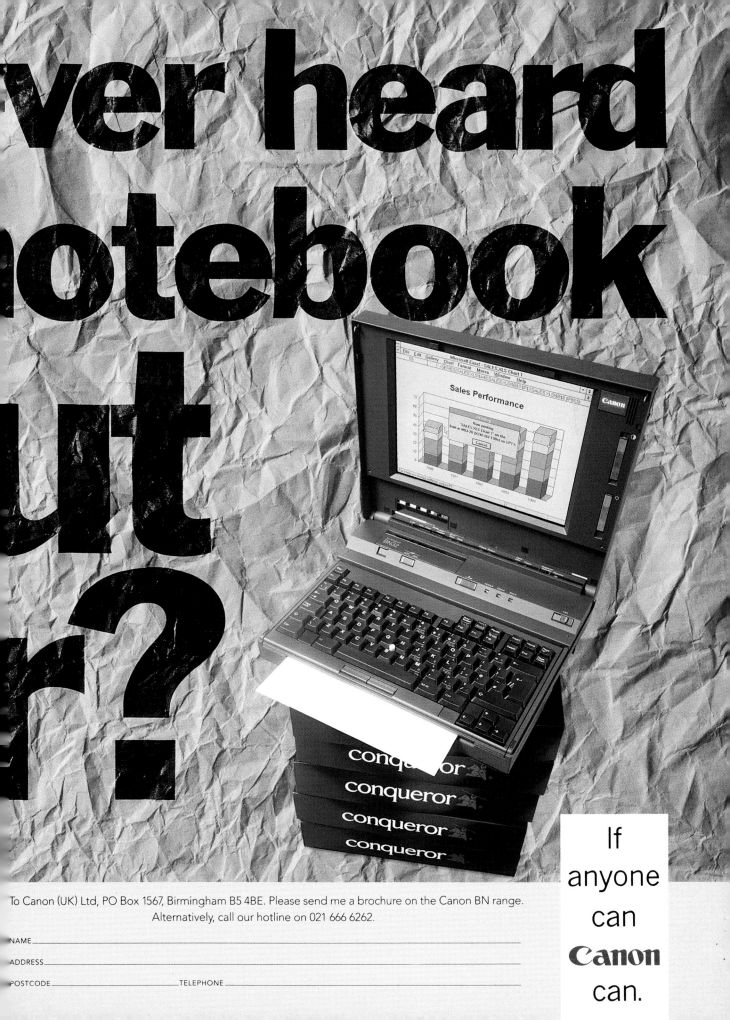

In search of craziness

Tom Peters

A top executive at Toyota admits that, as he drives the streets, even he can't tell which cars are Toyotas. As chairman of Apple Computer, John Sculley complained that the personal-computer industry was just churning out "Rocky IV and Godfather V"—in other words, new models like everybody else's. Even executives at the Big Six accountancy firms lament that their audits are becoming "commodities".

What is going on? In the past decade we've flattened out corporate hierarchies, re-engineered companies to beat the band, emphasised Total Quality Management (TQM) and dramatically reduced product-development time. Yet despite these revolutionary changes, firms, from banks to chemical companies, are offering their customers just look-alike, run-of-the-mill products.

Maybe companies have become so damned efficient that anybody who does anything special today is copied by sunrise tomorrow. A competitive edge in a crowded marketplace marked by "lean and mean" worldwide competition is, perhaps, all but impossible.

A more plausible hypothesis is that the very process of creating the modern corporation has blunted any taste for the offbeat. Bold tries (and concomitant bold failures) are not wanted; so genuine innovation goes by the board. The management revolution of the 1980s has produced a generation of gutless wonders—firms and leaders as insipid as they are efficient.

If so, is there a remedy? Yes. Dullness is not a necessary product of the times. *Fortune* conducts an annual poll of "most admired corporations". IBM won hands down in the early years.

When Big Blue got knocked sideways, a pharmaceutical superstar, Merck, took the top spot. Then in 1994 came a surprise. The winner? Rubbermaid from Wooster, Ohio. This august firm makes rubber and plastic cases for shoes and food and knick-knacks—a lot of them retailing for less than $5 a go. While the financial figures are just fine at the $2-billion-revenue firm, its special skill is innovation.

It is hardly a stretch to say that Rubbermaid has become an innovation machine. And one with taste. An item may well go for $2.15 (the plastic box, called a Keeper's Snap Case, in which I store pens) but Rubbermaid still managed to tie with Microsoft for first place in the number of awards won this

Tom Peters: management guru and author of "The Tom Peters Seminar: Crazy Times Call for Crazy Organisations".

year in America's most prestigious industrial-design competition.

If Rubbermaid can do it, then Toyota and Sony and Apple and KPMG and Procter & Gamble and Unilever ought to stop whining—and get down to work. That means reviving their appetite for adventure. Renault, though hardly a model company, may understand better than Toyota what is needed. Market research suggested that 40% of those exposed to its new Twingo "actively disliked it"; 10% "fell in love" with it. In most companies these days, such numbers would have ended the programme on the spot. But Renault kept its nerve, dismissed the scornful

majority of potential customers and plunged forward. The love affair blossomed and the car quickly became the second-best seller in France.

Take another example. American airlines have been losing billions a year. But not Southwest Airlines. Herb Kelleher, the company's chief executive, insists that flying should be fun. Though his record for safety and efficiency matches anyone's, don't be surprised if a Southwest flight attendant (wearing whatever he or she wishes—there are no uniforms) pops out of an overhead luggage locker to welcome an arriving passenger aboard. Mr Kelleher gets such moderately controlled zaniness by purposefully hunting for would-be employees "who have a sense of humour."

Mr Kelleher or Microsoft's Bill Gates both seek out, by design, adventurous

employees, including those with a screw-up on their CV. Cheryl Womack has turned the seemingly dull business of peddling insurance to independent truckers into an exciting growth company, VCW. The key: people. "We look for passion, flexibility and excitement," Ms Womack asserts. She believes she can teach insurance, but not those three more important intangibles.

Can the average firm, too boring by half, acquire these traits? Maybe. But you need to focus on something far beyond efficiency: namely, spunk, innovation and imagination.

We need a heavy dose of anti-discipline. Canadian researcher Henry Mintzberg, perhaps the world's premier student of management, forecasts the end of strategic planning with his book, "The Rise and Fall of Strategic Planning". Strategic planning has been about reductionism. But business success is about holism: leaps of faith, hunches, and so on. (Does anyone recall Keynes's "animal spirits"?)

Although Mr Mintzberg does not call for anti-discipline, he does point out that the popular "greenhouse" model of innovation (set aside a nook to test new varieties of flowers) is fatally flawed. Greenhouses are the most, not the least, controlled environments. Find your future winners instead, Mr Mintzberg urges, in weed patches, where, from time to time, the most amazing wild flowers bloom.

The time has come to rethink market research, TQM, re-engineering, strategic planning and Draconian cost-reduction-for-cost-reduction's-sake. Tomorrow belongs to the zany.

Flying alliances take off in 1995

Paul Betts

The slow flight back into profit of the airline industry will gather speed next year. After four years in which losses topped $15.6 billion on international services alone, airlines managed a small profit of around $1 billion last year. The worst chapter in the history of civil aviation has closed. What next?

The news is bad: you will be flying in ever-older aircraft. It is also good: the cost of your air-ticket will fall, particularly in Europe. Airlines are not about to shop for new aircraft as they did in the late 1980s. They are still suffering from the hangover of that buying binge, which they financed essentially by borrowing. They are caught with too much capacity. At the same time, increased competition is having a devastating impact on fares and profit margins.

As a result, travellers have become used to low fares. Next year they are likely to go lower still as new, low-cost, regional airlines start up in business. In the United States, still the West's biggest aviation market, these newcomers are forcing the traditional big carriers to set up their own low-cost regional subsidiaries. This trend will spill over into Europe in 1995. Already airlines like British Airways (BA) and Lufthansa have established low-cost airline subsidiaries for regional and intra-European services.

For European flag carriers the competition is coming not only from new airlines barging

Paul Betts: aerospace correspondent for the *Financial Times*.

into their pet routes (especially the big American and Asian carriers), but also from the development of high-speed rail networks and the opening of the Channel Tunnel.

In France, airlines have already lost ground to the French TGV high-speed trains (*trains à grande vitesse*) on some important domestic routes.

The move towards more "open skies" is also making airlines collaborate on a global scale. BA is one of the airlines to have taken the lead in developing a global network with carriers in the United States, Australia and Europe. Many airlines have been reluctant to take the BA route of investing in equity stakes in other carriers. Instead, they have sought to expand their international reach through marketing and commercial agreements. These loose alliances will alter the way we fly next year. Passengers will increasingly be able to buy one ticket covering the whole of even very complex journeys. For example, someone wishing to travel to a minor airport in America from London will be able to book with BA, who fly to the major hub

cities, and then transfer to a USAir flight, all on the same ticket. Agreements such as the one between BA and USAir will proliferate in 1995.

With the industry's centre of gravity continuing to move east, the Asia-Pacific region will grow fastest next year. Air travel in countries like China and India will expand rapidly. International airlines want to form alliances in these fast-growing markets.

Aircraft manufacturers see the Asia-Pacific region as providing the biggest prospect for new business. Boeing and McDonnell Douglas of the United States and the European consortium of Airbus Industrie will use 1995 to forge closer ties with China, India and Vietnam. Asia will absorb a large slice of the $900 billion-worth of new airliners that will be sold during the next 20 years.

The aircraft makers are being told by their customers to supply aircraft with lower operating and acquisition costs. In short, it is no longer what you build, but how you build it that will give an individual manufacturer the edge over its competitors.

The way Boeing has developed the 777, its new twin-engine wide-body airliner, is an example of how manufacturers have adapted their operations. Boeing describes the 777 as a "market driven" airliner. In the past, the world's biggest manufacturer of jetliners felt it knew what was best for its customers. But with the 777, Boeing encouraged airlines, suppliers and sub-contractors to participate actively in the design and planning of the new aircraft.

The 777, which cost $4 billion to develop, will make its service debut with United Airlines in 1995. It will probably be the last all-new airliner programme to be launched this century.

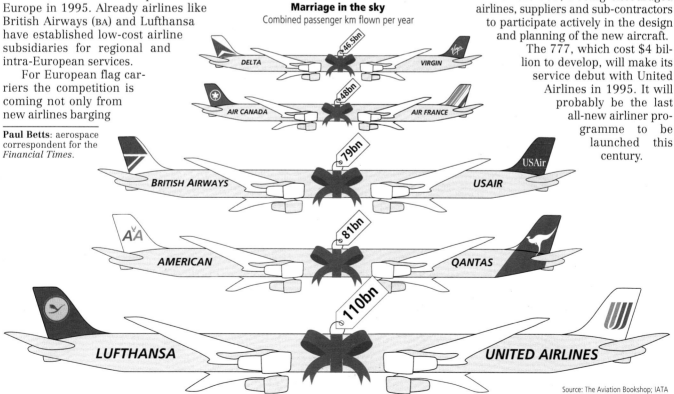

Marriage in the sky
Combined passenger km flown per year

DELTA — 46.5bn — VIRGIN

AIR CANADA — 48bn — AIR FRANCE

BRITISH AIRWAYS — 79bn — USAIR

AMERICAN — 81bn — QANTAS

LUFTHANSA — 110bn — UNITED AIRLINES

Source: The Aviation Bookshop; IATA

WHY
ARE YOU STANDING OUT

NOT SO LONG AGO it was a different kind of person who

stopped to read advertisements about computers. They stood outside

your world. They spoke a different language.

They came from a different place altogether.

Now it seems

that the people who

don't use computers

are the ones

standing on the outside

looking in.

SIDE
THE AMUSEMENT PARK?

We'd like to invite you inside.

Computers are an open opportunity for everybody, and because we're doing things here at Microsoft to make computers easier and more enjoyable to use, we do mean everybody.

That's why we've come up with so many interesting things you can do on your personal computer. You can play golf on a rainy day, learn about music, art and history, fly a plane or even take a walk in space. Software like Microsoft® Creative Writer or Fine Artist helps your children learn to express themselves with words and pictures at a very early age.

As for the business world, the thinking here at Microsoft is to make computers a lot more useful in the office. Because of software like Microsoft® Office, computers can be tools used not just for solitary tasks such as word processing or spreadsheet calculations, but for the broad range of office work and communication.

And since Microsoft® Windows™ makes it so easy to use a personal computer, everybody—and once again, we do mean everybody—can use all these interesting new tools for the office and in the home.

You see, because computers have become more powerful on the inside (and less expensive on the outside), we've been able to create software that makes it incredibly simple for anyone to do something enjoyable or productive with a computer. Right from the moment they switch it on.

So even if you begin using it just for fun, you'll discover each step you take teaches you a little more, and before you know it you'll have climbed a ladder to the top, and your view of the world and its possibilities will be changed forever.

WHERE DO YOU WANT TO GO TODAY?™

Cockpit capitalism

Paul Betts

Will the world's airlines end up owned and run by their pilots and crew? That looks a probability, at least in the United States, the West's biggest aviation market.

Already three American carriers are owned largely by their staff. The employees at United Airlines, the largest, now have 55% of the company. Northwest Airlines is 45% owned by employees; pilots, cabin crew and ground staff control 26% of Trans World Airlines. USAir, the sixth largest American carrier, is also negotiating to give equity stakes to its unions in exchange for labour concessions.

These deals are all seen as ways of salvaging the companies from the growing competition of smaller, low-cost airlines. That requires cutting staff costs and changing work practices. So the heavily unionised airline industry in the United States is becoming stridently capitalist, reducing costs without the strife that has plagued airlines in Europe.

The trend is catching on. In Europe many large national flag carriers are facing exactly the same problems. Air France, for example, is giving shares to its employees in exchange for wage and benefit concessions. And it is not only troubled airlines that are handing out their shares. Staff at profitable British Airways own about 4% of the company's equity and, in 1995, will ask for more.

New ribbons of steel

Paul Markillie

Travelling by train will come back into fashion. A new European rail service starts operating its full timetable in 1995, directly linking London with Paris and Brussels. Passengers boarding the sleek Eurostar train at Waterloo station will travel through the Channel Tunnel and then belt along an arrow-straight track across northern France at up to 300km/h (190mph), arriving in Paris just three hours after leaving London.

State-owned SNCF French railways, one of Eurostar's operators, confidently predicts that high-speed rail will eventually replace air travel as the most glamorous and convenient way to cross Europe. France's pioneering TGV network is linking up with high-speed lines in many other countries. Germany also plans to start running cross-border services with its high-speed Inter City Express (ICE).

Trains are even picking up speed on old, winding tracks. Sweden's X2000 and Italy's Pendolino trains can travel at more than 200km/h because they tilt when going around corners. Unlike a disastrous tilting-train introduced by British Rail in the early 1980s, these trains use computer-controlled tilting mechanisms which do not make passengers feel sick.

France's TGV holds the world's rail-speed record of 515km/h, although commercial services are usually operated at around 300km/h. In 1998, a 350km/h TGV train will be introduced into commercial service. Japan is also tweaking its "bullet trains"; a new generation is being developed which in trials exceeded 400km/h.

Yet the fastest trains will not touch the rails. These are magnetic-levitation (maglev) systems, in which the train hovers on a magnetic field above a monorail. Germany aims to build a DM9 billion ($5.6 billion) magnetic train, Transrapid, between Berlin and Hamburg. It is due to open in 2004 and will rocket along at

Thomas à grande vitesse

some 400km/h.

With its huge, growing cities and expanding economies the most exciting new frontier for railwaymen is Asia. One of the largest high-speed rail networks is being built in South Korea. This is a 432km line between the capital, Seoul, and Pusan. The line is due to be completed by 2001, at a cost of more than $14 billion. It will carry 80m passengers a year and will use France's TGV technology. Taiwan also has plans for a high-speed line to link its capital Taipei with Koashiung, 350km away at the other end of the island. A fast service linking Malaysia's capital, Kuala Lumpur, with Singapore is also planned.

The biggest rail projects, though, will not necessarily be the fastest. China needs to improve its transport network in order to avoid strangling its economic growth. The country has more than 54,000km of railway, but Peregrine Investments, a Hong Kong based securities house, calculates that this works out at 46km of rail per 1m population, compared with 808km per 1m in America. The company estimates that China will spend $46 billion by 2000 modernising its rail network.

The top priority is the 2,370km Beijing to Kowloon railway. A northern part will open in 1995 before being extended south to the special economic zone of Shenzhen, on the border with Hong Kong. When the British colony reverts to China in 1997, the track will be laid to Kowloon. Some 130,000 workers are employed on the project, building more than 500 bridges and 126 tunnels.

Chinese officials are also designing the country's first high-speed line: a 1,320km new track between Beijing and Shanghai. Trains would run at 250km/h on the line, cutting the trip from eight hours to five.

The railroading of America helped to open up that country, but nowadays passenger trains in America are unlikely to chug along much faster than 130km/h, provided they are not stuck behind a freight train.

Yet in 1995 America's Amtrak will select a high-speed train for use on the line between Washington, DC, New York and Boston. Two of the contenders are Sweden's tilting X2000 and Germany's ICE, both of which have been tested on the route.

Paul Markillie: business and finance correspondent for *The Economist* in Hong Kong.

The wired economy

John Browning

Perhaps the world, as cliché would have it, is getting smaller. Or perhaps cyberspace, as techno-visionaries call the world inside computer networks, is getting larger. But in either case new technologies of communication are changing forever the geography of business. If anything, all the hype about tomorrow's "information superhighways" serves only to divert attention from the magnitude of the changes which have already occurred today.

Over half of the computers on American businessmen's desktops are linked to their office mates via local-area networks. The global Internet—a vast network of computer networks, which links many of those office networks to their counterparts around the world—already connects 25m people, and is growing at phenomenal speed. Each month, some 2,000 more businesses join the 20,000 or so that have already set up virtual shop on the Internet.

Business on the Internet merits study—not because it is big (it isn't), but because the Internet represents the extrapolation of trends happening in technology generally. As computers and networks become widespread, the electronic delivery of goods and services becomes commonplace. No longer does a proprietary computer network with a link to customers confer competitive advantage, because everybody is already connected. Instead proprietary networks become a disadvantage, because they force the builder to bear all costs—without taking advantage of the investments made by others.

Big companies are cautiously venturing forth on to the new electronic commons. Reuters, for one, which has traditionally

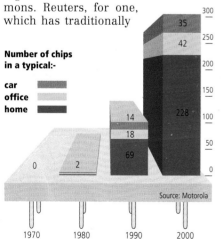

Number of chips in a typical:-

car
office
home

Source: Motorola

1970   1980   1990   2000

sold its news and financial information through its own proprietary network, recently created a subsidiary called Reuters New Media to explore the technological opportunities both in the distribution of existing products and the creation of new ones. But it is small firms that most clearly display the opportunities and challenges of the new world.

Take for example Chris Cooper, a Silicon Valley entrepreneur, who in the summer of 1994 became a partial competitor of Reuters when he began selling financial information over the Internet through his new company, QuoteCom. QuoteCom sells financial information to small investors for as little as $10 a

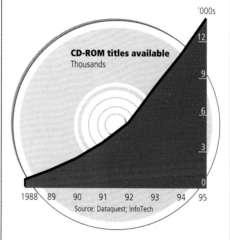

'000s

CD-ROM titles available
Thousands

12
9
6
3
0

1988 89 90 91 92 93 94 95

Source: Dataquest; InfoTech

month. For Mr Cooper to have set up his own electronic networks would have cost millions of dollars—and made his product prohibitively expensive. By plugging into the Internet, Mr Cooper held start-up costs to a few hundred thousand dollars. Within three months of setting up shop, Mr Cooper had signed up 3,500 subscribers, and he hopes eventually to sign up over 100,000.

Mr Cooper is not alone. Other small firms have used the Internet to reach customers they could not otherwise afford to serve. The Future Fantasy Bookstore in Palo Alto, California, put its catalogue on the Internet and suddenly became a global firm. Roswell Computer Books flourishes in Halifax, Nova Scotia—thanks to customers elsewhere, reached via the Internet.

Instead of reaching new customers, other firms use the new economics of networks to cut prices. An example is the

John Browning: writer and consultant on technology, based in London.

Internet Shopping Network—a sort of electronic mail-order firm for computers and software, which was recently purchased by the larger, richer and nearly eponymous Home Shopping Network, a leader in home shopping via television. Because the Internet Shopping Network's customers "browse" by connecting their computer directly to the firm's database, the company can eliminate the expense of printing and mailing catalogues. Customers send their orders into the Network's computers, eliminating the need to employ rows of people to answer telephones. The result is prices markedly lower than traditional mail-order rivals.

Such networked entrepreneurs put big, established firms on the horns of a dilemma. Even the most successful of the network newcomers is still a tiny business—and many, if not most, will be unsuccessful. The technology is fast-changing and confusing. Most big firms would prefer to wait until the business gets more remunerative and the technology more settled. But, equally, they fear waiting too long.

The obvious worry is that while the big boys wait the little ones will become big themselves. But a more subtle and more powerful fear is that even little firms can steal away the hearts and minds of customers.

Bill Smart, a vice-president for advanced technology at Bank of America, points out that some customers—albeit today only a small minority—have a stronger loyalty to the personal-computer software that balances their cheque book than they do to the bank that provides the cheques. Although they still need banks' services when they use, say, Quicken, a personal-finance software recently purchased by Microsoft in a bid to enter electronic finance, the bank sits in the background, a behind-the-screens provider of commodity services such as money transfers. That is not a position that many retail banks would like to be in. In a quiet way, Bank of America has offered electronic home-

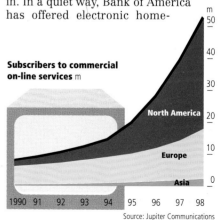

m
50
40
30
20
10
0

Subscribers to commercial on-line services m

North America

Europe

Asia

1990 91 92 93 94 95 96 97 98

Source: Jupiter Communications

There *is* a
difference

Client/Server computing is good for your people because it gives them easier access to more information. It's good for your business because it removes barriers between existing systems, giving you new flexibility to reorganise and to reengineer.

Client/Server from IBM. Because a solution has to take the pressure from both the inside and the outside world.

So the question is not whether to explore Client/Server, it's what to look for in the people who help you. Here's a suggestion : if they don't have a long list of references in multi-platform, multivendor integration, and a solid knowledge of your kind of business, call someone who has; someone like IBM.

We keep careful track of everything we learn, because although each Client/Server solution is unique, we'll compare your situation with ones we've faced before to give you the direct benefit of real-world experience. What's more, we can help you at any stage : from initial consulting to implementation.

So if you want a solution that can take the pressure, call us first. Simply contact your local IBM representative.

banking for years, and it has always lost money. It plans more electronic services, using newer technology and higher capacity networks from cable television and digital telephone lines. But after years of losses on home-banking, the bank is far from confident that it can find the magic combination that will unlock big new electronic markets.

Jostling for market position is growing more intense. When Microsoft announced a deal in October 1994 to pay $1.5 billion for Intuit, maker of Quicken, it appointed Scott Cook, Intuit's founder, head of a new division for "electronic commerce". Rupert Murdoch's News Corporation bought Delphi, a provider of on-line services and Internet connections for home users, to ensure that News Corp—rather than a separate network-service provider—would control the electronic presentation of its newspapers and magazines as it began republishing them on-line. To help sell its financial information to mass markets, Reuters New Media has created both technical and marketing links with Wealth Builder, a popular brand of portfolio-management software for personal computers.

Meanwhile, executives at British Telecom (BT) enthuse that new network services could enable BT to become an electronic retailer of digital goods and services—instead of merely an information haulier—so gaining direct relationships with customers who would otherwise take BT for granted. The additional factor that could make this jostling for position explode into bloody battle, however, is the rapid growth of big companies' internal networks.

While most big companies have been baffled by the question of what their customers might want from networks, they know all too well what information their employees need—and they have been hustling to use networks to provide it. At Britain's First Direct, a retail bank which does most of its business over the telephone, tellers' terminals are linked to marketing databases, which statistically predict what products should most appeal to the customer they are serving—and prompt the tellers to sell accordingly. Bankers at Manufacturers Hanover, together with consultants at Coopers & Lybrand and a variety of other white-collar workers, use information-sharing software called Lotus Notes to keep each other abreast of the information needed to serve clients.

Where things get interesting, and potentially bloody, is the point at which internal and external networks meet. Technically this is happening at great speed. Already Lotus, developer of Notes,

the most commonly used product for sharing information within companies, has announced technology that will make it easier to link Notes to the Internet, which is probably the most widely used medium for sharing information between companies. But commercially the consequences are both potentially vast and as yet unpredictable.

Given that many internal networks are being built to supply information to customers, one question to ask is whether customers would prefer to get the answers for themselves, direct from the network. Employees who earn their living from customer service—which includes almost everybody who makes a living from talking on the telephone—

have reason to be nervous about the answers. But they are not the only ones.

What happens to the sales department when customers can collect bills and send out orders over the network—as America's Departments of Defence and Energy are already starting to do?

What happens to the factory when designers can send plans electronically straight to the automated production line of a freelance manufacturer—as both clothiers and semiconductor makers are starting to do?

As they enable just about anyone to plug into just about anything, networks effectively break companies down to basic components. So how should they be put back together?

The world of work

Graham Mather

Who's competitive?

👍 Best 👎 Worst

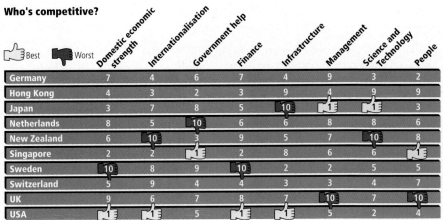

	Domestic economic strength	Internationalisation	Government help	Finance	Infrastructure	Management	Science and Technology	People
Germany	7	4	6	7	4	9	3	2
Hong Kong	4	3	2	3	9	4	9	9
Japan	3	7	8	5	10	1	1	3
Netherlands	8	5	10	6	6	8	8	6
New Zealand	6	10	3	9	5	7	10	8
Singapore	2	2	1	2	8	6	6	
Sweden	10	8	9	10	2	2	5	5
Switzerland	5	9	4	4	3	3	4	7
UK	9	6	7	8	7	10	7	10
USA	1	1	5	1	1	5	2	4

Source: The World Competitiveness Report

The star job-creators, America and Japan, will take very different routes in 1995. In America the economy favours a high labour-content. So even where growth is slow, jobs will multiply—especially in the service sector.

In areas like personal health care, the Bureau of Labour Statistics predicts a wave of new jobs in 1995 and beyond. Japan, in stark contrast, creates employment by high growth with relatively few people: in other words, by a productivity miracle.

Europe does neither. It has created few jobs in the private sector in the past two decades. Most have been in the public sector, which is exactly where they will be lost in the years ahead. In the EU's sluggish national bureaucracies and its state-owned enterprises, hundreds of

thousands of jobs will come to an end with increased competition. As open procurement, competitive tendering and market-opening arrive, so the massive hidden unemployment of these workers, who do not really have all that much to do, will become painfully clear.

However much the EU may hope to see more jobs in manufacturing, the European Commission's thorough research into employment in Europe recognises that "industry cannot be regarded as a major direct source of employment growth in future years."

Europe's leaders talk proudly of the distinctive European model. "Social Europe" seeks to guarantee its citizens' welfare on a generous scale. Can the price—taxes and social-security contributions that account for 40% of the Union's GDP—be reduced?

A single male European worker may

Graham Mather: president, European Policy Forum; MEP, Hampshire North & Oxford.

take home less than 55% of what it costs his company to employ him. This cannot last. Taxes will increasingly be raised on things like petrol and less on labour. But even so there is little chance that the EU target of 15m new jobs by the end of the decade will be met.

Some politicians will simply want to redistribute the jobs. People in Europe work too long, they argue. In Britain, for 55% of men the normal working week is over 40 hours. Some work unsocial hours: over 40% of men say they sometimes work on Saturdays. So some politicians in Europe say, therefore, that more jobs would be created if, by law, people worked fewer hours.

The issue comes to a head over part-time work. Is it a means of allowing workers—especially women—to choose a job which suits their preferences? Or could such "atypical" work be brought more firmly within a regulated labour market and its terms and conditions approximated to those of full-time employees? Should they be levelled up until they meet the full-timers working shorter hours, or left alone lest the consequence of upgrading is fewer jobs overall?

These rhetorical questions bump into some jagged realities. One reality is that in the 1970s and 1980s, in the European Community, EFTA and Japan, all of the net new jobs came in services. And in the United States it was also in services that the overwhelming majority of net new jobs arose.

Another reality is that real opportunities are arising in private health and social care. Although state-provided systems may be encountering the need to ration services, there is no sign that customers or their families want to cut spending. But these jobs will only come about if governments allow part-time work with flexible hours and low add-on costs to flourish. If so, expect a useful economic dividend: more spending, and more jobs, in the caring sector—financed voluntarily through the market system.

At all levels skills count. Highly skilled professional and technical jobs demonstrably survive recessions better than less qualified posts. Although low-skilled employment picks up in periods of economic growth, aptitudes, competence and quality of service are inseparable from customer satisfaction, profits—and jobs.

So the prizes will go to those with the best education and training. More choices for parents, more incentives for teachers, more credible systems of examination: all are widely recognised as desirable, but few economies can yet feel satisfied that they are in place.

The world car

Daniel Pearl

In 1995 Toyota's car plant in Turkey will use Welsh-made engines, BMW will build a Rover factory in Asia, and Citroën will join forces with Malaysia's Proton. The world car will have arrived. Out in front will be Ford which, on January 1st, merges Ford Europe and Ford North America to become the first truly multi-continental car company. Its world car, the Mondeo, will sell strongly throughout 1995. Indeed the car industry, Japan apart, which was so near bankruptcy three years ago, will have a record-breaking year.

In the process of reinventing itself, Ford will divide its American and European sides into five centres. Small and medium-sized cars, which account for 90% of the European market, will be the sole responsibility of Ford's European centre, divided between Dunton in Britain and Merkenich in Germany.

Ford's challenge is to reorganise without harming the booming American market. American cars are even making inroads into the Japanese home market. Despite enormous losses for all three American giants as recently as 1991, profits are now breaking records. Ford's third-quarter results in 1994 showed that profits had reached a record high of

Daniel Pearl: deputy editor, *The World in 1995*.

$1.1 billion; General Motors' profits, though less dramatic, are also good.

The battle against the Japanese giants is being won largely on the back of a very strong yen which keeps Japanese-made cars expensive. But the most important factor behind this renaissance has been massive corporate restructuring. Chrysler has been so successful at cutting costs that it is now the leanest, most efficient producer in America. Chrysler's elegant new models are a breakthrough in the car industry. Each Chrysler car now brings in after-tax profits of $1,360.

Chrysler has halved the cost of developing new products by moving to tightly managed, team-based projects that focus design and development in one centre. This is the goal of Ford's restructuring, aiming to make savings of $3 billion over the next few years. Cost cutting will also be crucial for the recovery in Europe. British-made cars will gain most. Britain's car production in 1995 will reach a 21-year high.

But the race to supply China's insatiable demand will come to a standstill. Beijing is putting a freeze on new firms building in China until 1996. This will help those like Volkswagen (VW) who already have plants on the mainland. Chinese demand will reach 2m cars in 2000; 1.8m of these cars will be built locally.

Changing tastes will also fuel the recovery. With demand for executive cars in Europe falling by 20% over the next five years, manufacturers are staking their bets on new models. Ford and VW's Minivan will challenge Renault's Espace in Europe. Land Rover's Discovery will remain the most sought-after of the all-purpose vehicles. Who would have predicted that Europe, with its small suburban families, would have such a thirst, in 1995, for family buses or rough off-the-road cars?

Fiat will try to revitalise its fortunes by launching 18 new models by 1996. But, in the short-term Fiat will be satisfied simply to remain independent. A potential stalker is Volvo, still reeling from its failed merger with Renault.

German Rover's American winner

ISSUERS

INVESTORS

To bring together those who have money to invest with those who seek to raise it is a simple fundamental of international investment banking.

To do so in primary and secondary markets with skill and strength, in a way and at a price that leaves both sides well satisfied, is a simple fundamental of BZW.

INVESTMENT BANKING. FROM **A** TO

Rising interest rates, then rising prosperity

Hamish McRae

1995 will be a year of rising interest rates as governments around the world tighten monetary policy in the face of rising inflation. This is always a tough period in the financial cycle. But this time the cyclical rise will be set against a background of what is surely a secure long-term trend of falling inflation. The task for the markets will be to look through the peak of interest rates in 1995 (and doubtless some unsettling news on inflation) and make a cool, sensible judgment about the underlying value of financial securities and currencies in the years beyond. If the markets allow themselves to be panicked by inflationary fears and take the view that the long-term downward trend is not secure, then they face a difficult year.

The world's bond markets are the principal stage on which this play will be performed. The collapse of bond prices in 1994 was predictable (and predicted in *The World in 1994*) but the ferocity of the movement took even some bears by surprise. By the third quarter of 1994 most markets offered reasonable long-term value: even allowing for some upswing in inflation, most offered a real

Hamish McRae: associate editor of the *Independent*; author of "The World in 2020".

yield of 3-5%, and some offered more. But the scars left by the collapse are deep, and investors will be extremely cautious through 1995. In particular they will demand proof from countries around the world that their governments will continue to lean against inflation and that they will be adequately disciplined in the control of fiscal deficits.

The sheer volume of debt issued by governments over the past five years has helped lead to an important long-term shift in power in the markets, a shift which only became fully evident when the bond-market cycle turned. Total bond issues in 1993 were some $1.6 trillion, a massive 10% addition to the stock in issuance. Analysts talk of a global shortage of savings, which naturally gives savers more power. But maybe it is clearer to see the imbalance in terms of excessive demand for such savings, principally from governments of the developed world.

At some stage, probably during the course of 1995, it will become accepted that most governments have done enough tightening, and conditions for a bond-market recovery will be in place. The turning-point will vary from country to country: rationally, the United States

should turn first, given the position of the American economy as the leader in this economic cycle. This turn in the bond market will precede the turn in interest rates, which will continue to rise through 1995.

What will be the peak of the United States bond-yield cycle? The most likely single period would be around May 1995 when the 30-year benchmark yield on dollar bonds may be as high as 8.5%. That would suggest long-dated D-mark bonds at a similar level and the long-dated sterling securities close to 10%, though this may be too high. But the more important strategic issue is not to call the turn of the bond market precisely (and be wrong) but rather to judge whether the bull market in world bonds is ready to run at some stage during 1995. The overwhelming balance of probability is that it will be. The boom will be less euphoric than the market of 1993, but ultimately more sustainable. A solid United States bull market in bonds would inevitably lead to a recovery in virtually all other markets. The "virtually" is there because there is some danger that countries with unacceptably high deficits (Italy and Sweden are two favourite candidates) might see a collapse of their markets before they establish corrective measures.

The world's equities are inevitably a more diversified bunch than its bonds. The common point for all major markets (with the exception of Japan, which is a rather special case) is that they had, at least during the first three quarters of 1994, avoided the savage rerating experienced by bonds. They were able to maintain that performance because of the support given by the prospect of future earnings growth.

At some stage in each country, as the recovery matures (and it is already very mature in the United States), it will no longer be credible to look forward to continued solid growth, and markets will start to focus on the nature of the next downswing.

Around goes the cycle

So 1995 will be a difficult year for equities worldwide, and most difficult for countries (like the United States) at the head of the cycle. Some markets will experience sharp adjustments; others will at best move sideways; in the special case of Japan, much will depend on the currency, with a reasonable performance in equities requiring some weakening of the yen. A new general upward swing on the world equity markets will not be established until it is evident that bonds are set to recover, and that will not be clear until well into 1995.

For currencies the outlook is calm. There is some prospect of a dollar recovery, supported by higher interest rates, but this will be muted against European currencies.

The single most likely surprise would be a sharp fall in the yen, perhaps to the ¥115-120 region against the dollar, triggered by a resumption of capital outflows and a narrowing of the current-account deficit. While the long-term secular trend of the yen is still upwards against the dollar, a cyclical reversal is in prospect.

European currencies will remain within narrow ranges, leading to further suggestions of a partial rebuilding of the exchange-rate mechanism. Sterling will move upwards against other European Union currencies, helped by low inflation and a surprise return to current-account balance during the course of 1994. But it will not participate in any attempt to relink the EU currencies.

Beyond 1995 there is another positive period for financial markets as it becomes clear that non-inflationary growth will continue. But whether that period starts before the end of 1995 depends on both policy-makers and markets keeping their nerve.

Bursting bourses

Christopher Wood

All too predictably, the emerging-market bubble of 1993 burst in 1994. But the crash in prices, most notable in the debt markets, was just a correction in a secular trend which is established for the 1990s. Developing countries will enjoy faster rates of economic growth than most of their OECD counterparts. They will, therefore, be a necessary and growing part of most investors' portfolios.

1995 will see more money piling into emerging markets. That is a near certainty. What will change will be the markets themselves. If Asia and Latin America have been the focus of emerging investors' efforts in the early 1990s, there will henceforth be more concentration on Eastern Europe and the former Soviet Union. After numerous false starts in the cold-war era these countries are now showing huge promise for stockmarket investors, especially as South-East Asia and Latin America are, by comparison, so well discovered.

Clearly, the most dramatic opportunity in terms of

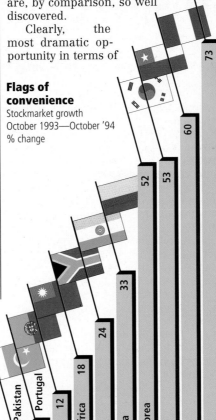

Flags of convenience
Stockmarket growth
October 1993—October '94
% change

Country	%
Pakistan	5
Portugal	7
Taiwan	12
South Africa	18
India	24
Colombia	33
South Korea	52
Chile	53
Peru	60
Brazil	73

Source: Baring Securities

cheap assets is presented by Russia. That country's largely unheralded but hugely successful privatisation effort produced what can only be described as the sale of the century in terms of the bargain prices paid. This episode will prove to have marked the beginning of what is likely to be the biggest bull market of the 1990s. For Russia is a hugely rich country in terms of natural resources which is at the initial stages of building a capitalist society from the ground up.

Opportunities

This anomalous situation means fantastic opportunities for those investors with the expertise to know what to look for, in terms of analysing companies, and the historical imagination to understand the opportunity presented. Russia today could be compared with America after the Civil War. After all, America was an emerging market then.

True, investing in Russia is fraught with risk. There is, for example, still no central-settlement system in place for the transfer of title to shares. Instead, each company keeps its own register of shares. Still, more than $1 billion of mostly private foreign money was invested in Russian equities in the first nine months of 1994, an inflow of capital which caused share prices to soar.

Russia is but the largest of the new East European markets. Poland is so far the greatest success. But within five years there is no reason not to expect functioning bourses with active foreign investment in most countries of the region, be it Romania, Ukraine or Uzbekistan. For the lesson of recent years is that it is wrong to dismiss completely any country as a potential candidate for stockmarket investment. Less than ten years ago conventional wisdom in the fund-management world would have dismissed out of hand the prospect of investing in countries like Argentina or Peru. Yet both countries saw major bull markets in the early 1990s.

Likewise, those who today dismiss the idea of investing in Russia and the former Soviet republics may prove to be similarly lacking in foresight. In fact it is interesting to note that most pundits still view China as the fashionable emerging market of the future, even though that country still has a communist regime

Christopher Wood: equity strategist for emerging markets at London-based Morgan Grenfell.

LARGEST VOUCHER INVESTMENT

Recently, the stories about JSC MMM received wide coverage in western media. Analysis of the publications revealed that they do not distinguish between JSC MMM and MMM-Invest. In most newspaper articles JSC MMM is referred to as "investment fund", whereas MMM-Invest is classed as a voucher investment fund. The present report is aimed to put the record straight.

The voucher investment fund mmm-invest was established in December 1992 to participate in the privatisation process and is the largest in Russia. The voucher investment fund obtained the license from the State Property Committee of the Russian Federation, numbered 58 and dated January 29, 1993. Fund authorized stock was registered by the State Property Committee on February 1 and September 1 1993. Paid up share capital amounts to Rbl. 42.167 bn or USD 15,954 m at the rate available on October 3, 1994 the number of shareholders is estimated at approximately 2.4 mln.

An efficient investment strategy provided to fund assets has been sourced from the shares of privatised enterprises and, qualified as highly liquid assets, their market value is continuously growing. The figures below illustrate the growth of market value of highly liquid fund assets during recent months.

Date	Liquid assets value ("000USD)	Asset value per single placed share ($/share 1000rbl. par value)
01.08.94	43 453	1,03
07.08.94	45 696	1,08
15.08.94	54 501	1,26
21.08.94	61 359	1,45
30.08.94	74 086	1,75
07.09.94	100 268	2,37
15.09.94	117 479	2,78
21.09.94	121 694	2,88
30.09.94	126 476	2,99

A major shareholding (3% to 24.4% of ownership capital) of the privatised enterprises gives the right to participate in the decision making processes of the management of the enterprises. The fund's representatives are on the Boards of Directors of some of the largest Russian enterprises.

Profit for the first quarter amounted to USD 12,308 m. A profit tax amounting to USD 4,308m. was contributed to the State. Out of all the voucher funds operating beneath equal conditions, MMM-Invest was the only one to make a major profit. By decision of the shareholders taken at the general meeting, May 10, 1994 this profit gained from the fund activities was allocated in dividends.

The Fund is represented by a team of highly skilled professionals. Some of the top managers are doctors of economics and many have gained qualifications in securities dealing from the Finance Ministry of Russia.

The voucher investment fund MMM-Invest is financially and legally fully independent from the companies incorporated in the MMM Association, and, from JSC MMM, which has been the subject of great discussion in recent months in both Russian and Western media.

FUND IN RUSSIA

LIST OF INVESTMENTS
Voucher investment fund "MMM Invest"
In excess of 3% ownership capital:

Name in alphabetical order	% from ownership capital	Description of activity	Location
AVTOVAZ	8,18	Car Production	Samarskaya dist.
ANGARGSKNEFTEORGSYNTHES	11,30	Oil refinery	Irkutskaya dist.
BEREOZKA IN LUZHNIKI	19,43	Trade	Moscow
VAREGANEFTEGAZ	3,04	Oil and gas extraction	Tyumenskaya dist.
MIL HELICOPTER PLANT	7,55	Design and production of helicopters	Moscow
HOUSING CONSTRUCTION CENTER N.9	3,06	Construction	Moscow
LENINGRAD OPTICS AND MECHANICAL PLANT (LOMO)	4,80	Precision Manufacturing	St. Petersburg
MOSCOW JEWELLERY PLANT	24,48	Jewellery making	Moscow
RYAZAN OIL PROCESSING PLANT	6,86	Oil Refinery	Ryazan
TOMSK OIL AND CHEMICAL PLANT	18,58	Oil Refinery	Tomsk
TOURCENTER SUZDAL	11,65	Tourist industry	Vladimir dist.
UAZ	17,02	Car production	Uliynovsk
TSUM	5,50	Trade	Moscow
JAVA TOBACCO	4,02	Cigarette making	Moscow

Up to 3% ownership capital:

"On Tverskaya" (hotel "Minsk", Moscow); Ostankino meat processing plant (Moscow); Hotel complex "Kosmos" (Moscow); "Red October" (confectionary, Moscow); "MIKROMASHINA" (MIKMA, consumer appliances, Moscow); PURNEFTEGAZ (oil and gas extraction, Tyumen dist.); NOJABRSKNEFTEGAS (oil and gas extraction, Tyumen dist.); KONDPETROLEUM (oil and gas extraction, Tyumen dist.); SAKHALINMORNEFTEGAS (oil and gas extraction, Sakhalin dist.); NORILSK NICKEL (ferrous metallurgy, Krasnojarsk region); MEGIONNEFTEGAS (oil and gas extraction, Tyumen dist.); KIRISHINEFTEORGSYNTHEZ (oil refinery, Leningrad dist.); NIZHNEVARTOVSKNEFTEGAS (oil and gas extraction, Tyumen dist.).

MMM – Invest is currently seeking foreign companies wishing to participate in the privatization process in Russia. MMM – Invest offers business consulting services and joint operations in securities in the Russian market.

Tel: (7095) 201 3908 Fax: (7095) 201 3746

Banking the world

Peter Middleton

1995 will be good for banks. The United States will remain profitable. So will the United Kingdom. Europe will recover. And banks in the Pacific rim will do well.

Banks are prone to relax when things look good. They will not do so this time. They are having to cope with forces that will alter the very nature of banking. In retrospect, 1995 will be an important turning point.

Two great forces that have driven banking in the past will continue to shape the future: technology and regulation. But they will do so against a changing world.

For there are major swings in the flow of funds. Levels of national debt throughout the world are at unprecedented heights. However, the corporate sector in most countries has moved into surplus. If companies are net savers, not only do they need less from banks, they can begin to compete with them by dealing directly with each other. Large companies frequently have better credit ratings than the banks.

At the same time the geographic flow of savings has changed. Developing economies are amassing huge reserves—about two-thirds of the world's reserves are in these countries. They are much the most important supply of credit and will become more so. Successful banks need to be able to get at these savings and direct them to the markets where they are needed.

All wired-up

The new demands of customers and the sophistication of the international market place is driven by technology. Technology has resulted in the multinationalisation of finance reducing costs and increasing competition. The changes have taken place largely irrespective of governments. Wise governments have recognised what is happening and taken advantage of it. Unwise ones have tried to resist and have suffered.

In banking, there was a phase of automation in the 1970s which involved back offices, usually in a domestic context. In the 1980s there has been an explosion of front-office activity based on powerful information systems. The secret for 1995 and beyond is to use these systems ever more imaginatively and internationally.

Investment banking—the provision of specialised financial services to large corporate, institutional and public-sector

Sir Peter Middleton: chairman of Barclays de Zoete Wedd.

clients—is developing a completely new range of products. Partly they complement traditional banking services. Increasingly they replace them. Companies insist on products which fit their precise requirements at home and overseas—and minimise their tax liability at the same time.

Traditional lending products have become low-margin loss-leaders in this market. For example, the attractions of bond finance syndicated and distributed to investors in many markets, swapped into any number of currencies, are infinitely greater to a multinational business than a primitive bank loan.

The modern investment bank is light years away from the merchant banks which earlier dominated much of London's international business. To succeed in the big league they have to be truly global in their product and currency range, and in their ability to take risk. This development cannot be stopped. We shall see large, successful, investment banks grow stronger—selling products and supported by systems that many will barely understand.

Governments, staggering along in the wake of these changes, have become part of the competitive process. An unfavourable tax change, the injection of uncertainty into the legal system or increased regulation can cause whole sections of the business to migrate elsewhere.

The world of international banking is at present like three huge interlocking wheels, with London, New York and Tokyo at the centres. Business can move with great speed down the spokes or into another wheel. London, which is not supported by a huge domestic market, is particularly vulnerable in this regard.

Wherever the centres might be, they are becoming more closely linked by derivatives—simply defined as instruments derived from other products. IT systems search out small differences in products in different markets. And bankers make money by ironing out the differences.

Some regard derivatives almost as witchcraft. In reality they are a means of separating out risk, reducing it, and increasing the perfection of worldwide markets. There will be more controls

exercised by monetary authorities, but we shall see an increasing profusion of derivatives based on smaller and smaller discontinuities in markets, as the markets themselves become more efficient.

Domestic banks are going through a similar revolution. Indeed, some have ceased to be domestic at all. Private banking—the provision of personal financial services to rich people—is offered as a separate service on a

So solid outside, so liquid inside

worldwide basis.

Other banking products that tend to be taken for granted—transmitting money, looking after documents, securities registration and so on—are either provided on an international scale or contracted out to banks that have developed these expensive, system-based services into global—and potentially very profitable—businesses.

Perhaps most significant of all, consumer pull and technology push are exerting a huge influence on retail banking—where huge volumes of retail products are sold to large numbers of individuals.

These services have long since ceased to be the simple depositing of money and lending to business on a short-term basis. Banking is now a series of businesses related to finance. But that is only a stage along a path which is increasingly relating banking to retail services in general.

Banks are already competing with other retailers and retailers are certainly competing with the banks. They use similar delivery channels and spread the costs by increasing the range of products and services on offer. The common thread is that the consumer is king. This is crystallising the market into more specialised services, suited to particular client groups—each of which will be a potentially huge market. Banks must decide which clients to target.

A key issue is whether retail banking services—or indeed retailing in general—will remain primarily domestic. As the market splits into segments and the number of delivery channels increases, there is certainly scope for internationalisation. Moreover, regulatory barriers have eased. But it has not yet proved possible to market successfully these volume services, even in a segmenting market, without a substantial domestic presence.

The likelihood is that people will never lose their taste for shopping, regardless of how easy it is to sit in a chair and buy things by television. So, equally, people will wish to feel part of a bank branch and buy financial services face to face.

Those premises need to be attractive, to be in the right place and offer the right products. We are only at the start of the process of reshaping branch banking. But that is what it will be. A reshaping, not a demise. People will still want a bank in the high street in the next century.

Regulation will be a headache for regulators and regulated alike. More products and more countries mean more regulators. Big institutions can have a dozen or so regulators in major markets—and soon they will have even more. But it is well-nigh impossible to regulate global phenomena such as credit. So regulation will increasingly set minimum standards of competence, and bankers must adjust to this new form of control. It is not a control we have thought of in the past.

and almost no functioning banking system. The surprise might be that, despite all the negative media hype directed at the country, it is Russia not China which proves to have the more exciting investment arena in the next five years.

If Eastern Europe is still rich in investment opportunities, in terms of the availability of cheap assets in embryonic capitalist societies, Africa and the Middle East provide two other regions where the opportunities for portfolio investment have barely begun to be picked over. Africa holds natural appeal for any contrarian. It is hard to see how matters could get much worse. Stockmarkets which are already attracting foreign investors include, aside from South Africa, Botswana, Zimbabwe and Ghana. Kenya will soon open up to foreigners.

As for the Middle East, there are some unlikely areas of appeal. One example is the Lebanon, which is returning to a semblance of normality and where the commercial spirit is strong—but where so far there is only one company quoted. Another is Iran. Unbeknown to most professional investors, the Iranian stockmarket was reopened in 1991, having been closed since 1979. Even more extraordinarily perhaps, foreigners are allowed to invest. The combined capitalisation of the 124 companies quoted on the Tehran stock exchange was only $1.3 billion at the beginning of 1994. This is clearly minimal in terms of the potential of the country.

The point is that no country is off limits in the emerging-market game. For the developing world is engaged in a huge game of catch-up, which means tremendous opportunities for those companies of the developed world doing business in these regions. It is truly a virtuous circle.

Why your pension won't be paid

Jonathan Hoffman

One racing certainty of 1995 is that governments will try to beat an honourable retreat from impossibly generous pension commitments. A second is that they will fail. Mouth the single word "pensions" and normally eloquent finance ministers are lost for words. They have long known that because of the combination of greater longevity and lower fertility, unfunded public-sector pension liabilities have reached colossal proportions. But (with the honourable exception of New Zealand) they have been too scared to admit the sheer size of these hidden debts.

Hidden costs

Thanks to work done at the Dutch civil-service pension fund, the value of unfunded pension liabilities in Europe can be estimated. The calculations show that with the exception of Belgium, Ireland and Britain, the ratio of "true" debt to GDP is more than double the ratio as conventionally measured. True debt includes the pension liabilities ignored by calculations of conventional debt.

In 1994 the political hazards of pulling back from pension commitments were vividly demonstrated in Italy (where in 1993 deaths outnumbered births for the first time this century, barring the years of the first world war). The

Jonathan Hoffman: director of economics, CS First Boston, London.

pensions issue is now at the top of Silvio Berlusconi's agenda. The treasury minister (and former central-bank governor), Lamberto Dini, argues that action can no longer be avoided. But other coalition members feel that the political risks are too great.

Another country where grey power is on the rise is the Netherlands; there the Pensioners' Party won six seats in May's elections. And in Germany the ever-vigilant Bundesbank, worried lest it might be forced by a future populist government to fund Germany's pension liabilities by resorting to the printing presses, has begun to take a close interest in quantifying the government's unfunded liabilities.

The pensions problem is confined neither to Europe nor to the public sector. The unfunded liabilities of the Japanese public-pension system are only slightly lower in relation to GDP than those in Germany. In the United States, however, the ratio of unfunded debt to GDP is little more than half the German level, thanks to low pension levels and more even demographics.

Things are not much better in the private sector. Even in the United States there has been a sharp rise in the incidence of underfunding within company pension funds. In Germany private schemes are usually of the defined benefit type and more than 60% of priva

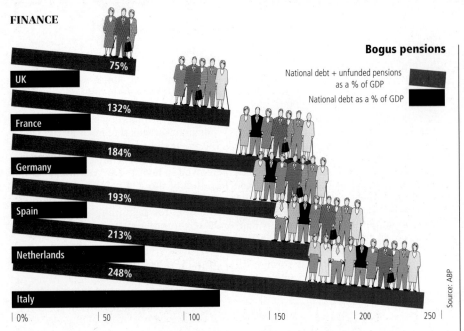

Bogus pensions

National debt + unfunded pensions
as a % of GDP

National debt as a % of GDP

UK 75%

France 132%

Germany 184%

Spain 193%

Netherlands 213%

Italy 248%

0%   50   100   150   200   250

Source: ABP

pension obligations are held within company balance sheets. But separate pension funds will increase under pressure from redundancies, volatile bond yields and the need for separate funds for employee contributions.

Forced saving is probably not feasible (though note that in Chile 10% of wages must be committed to private-pension funds). But governments do need to admit the existence of the problem in order to encourage voluntary evasive action, in the form of higher savings. In some countries people have long suspected that pension commitments would not be honoured (how else, for example, can one explain Italy's perpetually high

savings ratio?) but in others the message has yet to get through.

Second, pensions need to become less generous over time, either by raising retirement ages (as in Britain, where the 1993 budget announced a phased rise in the pension age for women from 60 to 65) or by a progressive cut in the value of the pension.

However there are obvious limits to this process; in Britain, where the pension is linked to prices rather than wages, a politician, Frank Field, has pointed out that by 2045 the pension will fall to a derisory 8% of average earnings.

Third, there needs to be greater availability of private-sector pension

funds. For an Anglo-Saxon observer this sounds obvious but in some countries there is deep-rooted resistance; in France the general secretary of a trade-union organisation recently asserted that "private pensions are theft."

Finally, if there is to be greater reliance on private, funded schemes, the managers of those schemes must be free (within minimal prudential guidelines) to invest across asset classes and across borders. An attempt to liberalise pension-fund investment across the European Union collapsed in disagreement earlier in 1994.

Even countries that claim to have abolished all controls on the movement of capital retain Draconian restrictions on foreign investment by pension funds. German funds, for example, can invest no more than 4% of their assets abroad. The Dutch civil-service pension fund (the world's second largest, with assets of over $90 billion) can invest no more than 10% abroad, and that only in selected OECD markets, although further liberalisation is due in 1996.

Such restrictions are nakedly protectionist. They may allow governments to fund themselves more cheaply but they certainly do no favours to future pensioners, whose assets are being poorly invested, with no exposure to the fastest-growing regions of the world. Memo to the new secretary-general of the OECD: add to your duties the task of policing investment restrictions; in the long run they can be every bit as harmful for the world economy as trade barriers.

Coming to America

Matthew Bishop

The New York Stock Exchange (NYSE) is the holy of holies of American capitalism. In 1995 it will be hailed as the most potent symbol of American economic success. Foreign firms, at last, will be rushing to list their shares on the American exchanges. So far, for example, only one German firm has its shares traded on the NYSE. Several more will follow soon.

The one German firm already there is Daimler-Benz, which listed in 1993. Its experience has so far deterred other foreign companies from following in its path. In order to win approval from the Securities and Exchange Commission (SEC), America's stockmarket regulator, Daimler-Benz had to agree to issue accounts conforming to American ~~standards~~. These are very different from ~~~~ ones, indeed, although ~~~~ German accounts ~~~~thy profit, its American

accounts revealed a hefty loss.

However, the SEC's attitude to foreign accounts appears to be softening, re-awakening the interest of other European firms. The next German

company to seek a listing may well be Veba, an energy conglomerate that has already adopted an unusually Anglo-American pro-shareholder stance. It plans to list next year.

Equities abroad foreign companies listed

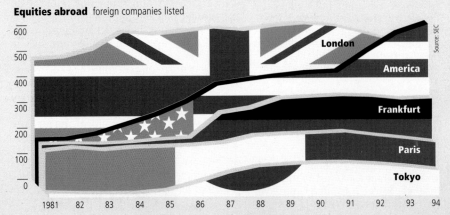

600
500
400
300
200
100
0

London
America
Frankfurt
Paris
Tokyo

Source: SEC

1981 82 83 84 85 86 87 88 89 90 91 92 93 94

"If this is your view of global futures markets you're missing a world of opportunities"

MIKE STONE, MANAGING DIRECTOR, HSBC FUTURES: *"When using futures and options, our clients have very high standards in terms of liquidity and security. MATIF meets these standards".*

MATIF, the Marché À Terme International de France, has become one of the world's leading futures exchanges not only through the success of its contracts - such as the Notional, Pibor and CAC 40 Index, which can be traded around the clock on GLOBEX®, and the recently introduced currency options - but also through tight security control. MATIF, time and again, meets the demanding requirements of its international clients.

FOR FURTHER INFORMATION PLEASE CONTACT MATIF AT (33 1) 40 28 81 81

M A K E   T H E   M O S T   O F   Y O U R   F U T U R E

Uncle Sam sees the light

The World in 1995 asked **Arthur Levitt**, chairman of the Securities and Exchange Commission, to put the case for America's predominance in the international markets

During the 1932 presidential campaign, Franklin D. Roosevelt challenged Herbert Hoover to "Let in the light!" on securities issues by compelling corporations to disclose more information to investors. When he gained the White House, Roosevelt took steps not only to let in the light, but also to build a lighthouse. The Securities and Exchange Commission (SEC) has been a beacon for investors ever since.

Sixty years later, America's marketplace is in good order. In 1934, businesses raised $641m in the capital markets; in 1984, $126 billion; and last year that figure was comfortably the other side of the $1 trillion mark. Total turnover on our stockmarkets was over $3.5 trillion (the next largest market, Japan, was just under $1 trillion). Mutual funds have become a cornerstone of American investment. In 1980, one in sixteen American households owned mutual funds; in 1995, it will be one in four. For the first time in history investment-company assets now exceed the total deposits of the commercial banking system. What is behind this vote of confidence by investors? In a word, transparency.

Transparency is what happens to a market when you let in the light. People can see what they are investing in, kick the tyres, find out how it has performed in the past. Regulators can more easily discover unethical behaviour. Nothing breeds confidence quite like it.

I hope that the state of our marketplace will provide support for those in foreign markets who champion transparency. Capital follows opportunity and security, though not necessarily in that order. As the competition for international investment heats up, all other things being equal, capital will favour the most transparent, honest markets.

The SEC is working to eliminate the practice of "pay-to-play" in our municipal bond markets by severing the link between political-campaign contributions and the awarding of bond business. Investors can be confident that the force that drives our bond market is an invisible hand, not a greased palm.

The SEC will also move against rogue brokers. A joint study we did with the exchanges in 1994 showed that only a small fraction of industry professionals were dishonest. Others might have sighed with relief at this result; for us it was a call to arms. In an industry which relies so heavily on investor confidence, there can be no compromise on ethics. One bad broker is one too many.

Full disclosure is fundamental to market integrity. We recently cast our

"Investors can be confident that the force that drives our bond market is an invisible hand, not a greased palm."

beam into mutual fund prospectuses and found them wanting. George Orwell blamed the demise of the English language on politics, but anyone who has ever read a prospectus knows there is plenty of blame to go around. Dense prose often rules, with poetry reserved for claims about performance. The SEC will simplify and standardise prospectuses so that they are not only comprehensive, but also comprehensible.

Enhanced disclosure and better accounting should go a long way towards addressing concerns about derivatives. These enigmatic instruments can provide valuable risk-management tools, when properly used and understood. But their complexity, illiquidity and volatility can introduce significant risks. These characteristics should keep some of the more unpredictable derivatives out of such traditionally conservative investments as money-market funds.

For the SEC, 1995 will also be the year of the individual investor. In 1937, one of my predecessors, later Supreme

Court Justice William O. Douglas, interpreted the agency's mandate in this way: "We have got brokers' advocates; we have got exchange advocates; we have got investment-banker advocates; and we are the investor's advocate." In recent years, our clientele has expanded enormously as inexperienced investors left the safety of bank certificates of deposit to try out the market. Our mission is not to see that they win or lose the game, but rather to help them understand the rules and to ensure that the field on which they play is fair. In 1995, for the first time, we shall be taking our case directly to individual investors through brochures, speeches, television and radio; we shall even institute our own electronic bulletin board accessible through the Internet.

At a time when cross-border listings in other major markets have either hit a plateau or declined, foreign participation in the American markets has grown dramatically in the 1990s: more than 370 foreign companies have entered the American public market for the first time, bringing the number of foreign listings to 637.

The SEC wants to internationalise our markets. We signed a Memorandum of Understanding with the People's Republic of China in April 1994, the 15th country with whose regulators we now have agreements. We shall reduce costs for foreign companies entering the American market while maintaining the high disclosure standards that American citizens expect. First-time entrants now have to reconcile only two years, rather than five years, of historical financial information; threshold levels for requiring reconciliations for acquired businesses have been raised and the reconciliation, if required, is simpler; pro rata consolidation is now permitted for joint ventures; cash-flow statements prepared in accordance with International Accounting Standard 7 need not be reconciled; six financial schedules have been eliminated.

In the year ahead the SEC will explore ways to reduce costs for all issuers, foreign and domestic, large and small, who seek to raise capital in the American market. But we shall never lose sight of one underlying reality: our markets are the deepest and most liquid in the world not because of this fee or that piece of paperwork, but because of their transparency and integrity.

Unstoppable derivatives

Marjorie Deane

Paranoia about financial derivatives will not go away. But 1995 will see new uses for, and new users of, ever-more complex and sophisticated instruments designed to provide flexibility and manage risk in money transactions. There will be trickle-down too; individuals and small businesses will increasingly get in on the act. Expect some intriguing new ideas to become commonplace in 1995: American hurricane futures, "Acts of God" bonds and option contracts on natural catastrophes.

The setback after some mutual funds and some big companies, such as Procter & Gamble, burnt their fingers dabbling in derivatives was no more than a hiccup in the progress of an industry that dates back ten years and more. Ironically, legislators created the very things they now fear. Forwards, futures, swaps, options, securities embodying options—all are an outgrowth of deregulation.

Take down the barricades around specialised markets, remove exchange controls, reduce geography to insignificance, and inevitably creative minds will turn to dissecting the risks that drive asset values in a global marketplace which is marked by high volatility.

Immensely helped by advanced technology, innovators make an art of unbundling and repackaging risks, dazzling clients with displays of how to shed unwanted ones or take on new ones that suit particular portfolios.

Derivatives have enhanced economic efficiency, says Alan Greenspan, chairman of the Federal Reserve. Hold on, though. Wasn't that said about petrodollar loans to the third world in the 1970s before the debt crisis erupted? The paradox about derivatives is that they have the potential to create risk as well as contain it. Ingenuously used, you can lose your shirt on them. And the usual markers are missing when the most sophisticated contracts never see an exchange, existing only in a computer. Much of the trading—particularly of equity derivatives—is for speculative rather

than hedging purposes. Yet speculators are needed; even with them, trading in some derivatives is so thin that sustaining market liquidity is a problem.

Ignorance among end-users will bring more calamities in 1995. Ignorance among congressmen will bring

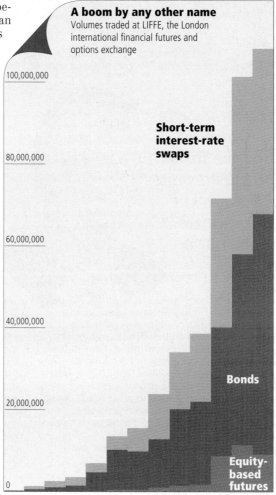

A boom by any other name
Volumes traded at LIFFE, the London international financial futures and options exchange

Short-term interest-rate swaps

Bonds

Equity-based futures

more over-reaction. Yet the odds are that no substantial legislation, such as would restrict banks to dealing in derivatives only through separately capitalised subsidiaries, will be passed in the United States in 1995.

This is largely because American banks have greatly improved the credit quality of their assets and are now strongly capitalised. And though unregulated participants in derivatives are cause for regulatory concern, they are as yet small players; both in New York and

London, more than three-quarters of the huge business in swaps and options is conducted by a small handful of large, authorised financial firms. This concentration leads some central bankers to worry about systemic risk from potential interbank failure. But others stress the implied degree of sophistication and expertise behind the business.

So regulators like Mr Greenspan, who think remedial legislation would do more harm than good, should have a chance to test their own approach in 1995. There will be a drive for improvements in statistics, public disclosure, regulatory reporting and accounting. There will be efforts to get supervisors of banks and securities firms to talk the same book. There will be attempts to iron out international differences in tax and accounting treatment, in settlement and legal requirements. Most important of all, having acknowledged they cannot do the job themselves, supervisors will have to satisfy themselves, the legislators and the public that the industry is practising self-regulation.

That will be no pushover. The supervisory onslaught will bring disappointments. Disclosure sounds admirable, but what will people read into it? The market value of a financial firm's risk exposure changes from one day to the next; a single figure can be dangerously misleading.

The guidelines designed to promote "sound" internal risk management by everyone involved in derivatives, including end-users, may also raise more questions than answers. Can the measured risk really be translated into language understandable by board directors and senior staff who are told they must control exposures? It is not blindingly obvious that good management requires skills in higher mathematics and physics—yes, physics, since diffusion theories underpin financial-risk assessment.

The Basle Committee on Banking Supervision, which draws up international standards, will decide by 1995 how to assess the amount of capital banks must set aside against trading risks. Almost certainly banks will have won their battle to use their own internal value-at-risk "models" for assessment, which will dictate lower capital requirements than the standard formula the Basle committee first proposed. However, supervisors will

Marjorie Deane: private consultant and writer on international finance; co-author with Robert Pringle of "The Central Banks" (Hamish Hamilton, Viking Penguin).

have to "recognise" each bank's model (rather than "approve" it, which might lead to liability if things go wrong). For the Bank of England, unused to on-site examinations of banks and with at most a handful of people with the necessary skills, the task could be a nightmare. At best it will be somewhat artificial; every model depends on out-of-date assumptions.

So the derivatives business will lose little of its opaqueness in 1995. To hard-liners in Congress, the cave-in to banks over "own models" will smack of hocus-pocus. And throughout the year derivatives will be sprouting new growths.

Japanese banks will become bigger players in derivatives as restrictions on their use at home are lifted. In the third world, the dynamic Asian economies will similarly make some leaps forward. Fund managers will see increasing scope for hedging securities positions.

As more trustees allow them to do so, pension funds will become active users. So, too, will life insurers. New strategies will be worked out for lenders of fixed-rate mortgages to protect themselves against prepayments and other eventualities. And repackaging of industrial and commercial credit risks will take off.

There will also be continuing development of yesterday's exotic derivatives that seem almost commonplace today. Interest-rate swaps of perhaps no more than £100,000 ($160,000) will be offered to individuals to hedge portfolios. Small banks and non-banks will join in. If big firms wanting fixed-rate dollars find it cheaper to borrow flexible-rate sterling and then swap, small businesses will seek the benefit too. It may be risky to get into derivatives, but it will be riskier to stay out.

A neural network is watching you

Matt Ridley

The year ahead promises to be a bad one for crooks on the financial markets. To the surprise of many in the computer business, one of the first things that "intelligent" computer programs called neural networks are proving good at is the detection of credit-card fraud, insider trading and other forms of cheating. Such machine detection will soon begin to make itself felt.

The amount lost by Visa to credit-card fraud fell for the first time in 1993 (from $679m to $655m). Among the reasons was a new neural-network program called Falcon, developed by HNC, a small computer company in San Diego. Neural networks are pattern-recognising devices that improve themselves by trial and error. They derive their name from a largely fanciful notion that they use the same principles as parts of the human brain.

Falcon, uniquely, looks at every single transaction by a credit card and judges whether it is likely to be fraudulent or not. It can compare the time, place and type of purchase with the normal history of a card. So, for instance, if an old woman's card not normally used outside her own suburb suddenly asks for authorisation to buy a Ferrari in Mexico, bells ring.

A human being could make the same judgment, but not in four seconds and not for 88m accounts at over 30 banking organisations. Every quarter Falcon tests itself on all the previous quarter's credit-card transactions sent in by a consortium of banks, compares its success rate with the known fraud rate, adjusts itself and tries again until it is as good as it can get. Falcon is consistently 20-30% better than human beings at both detecting fraudulent transactions and not annoying customers by falsely accusing them of fraud. It is also faster. On average, a stolen card runs up $1,800 before Falcon stops it, compared with $2,500 for a human fraud detector.

At the other end of the scale, computers are also hard at work on insider dealing. SearchSpace, a small company founded by a group of academics at University College London, has been contracted by the London Stock Exchange to look for patterns that imply insider trading. Using a combination of neural networks, conventional statistics and "genetic algorithms" (programs that evolve by unnatural selection rather than learn by trial and error), SearchSpace designed a program that will be remarkably good at spotting different share-dealing accounts that worked in concert.

With over 40,000 bargains settled each day on the exchange, each of which has about 100 different kinds of information available about it (name of account, time of deal, history of account, etc), the problem is astronomically beyond human competence. This makes it extremely easy to camouflage an insider deal among the dense foliage of activity on the market.

The program is expected to go live in 1995. If it does, London will have the most advanced system in the world for detecting insider dealing. So far the market for neural networks is dominated by small companies. Some financial firms have in-house teams working on them. IBM has purchased a neural-network technology from Nestor, one of the first neural-network companies founded by researchers from Brown University in Providence.

Criminals, no doubt, will eventually find neural networks useful as well. If they can be used for detecting crime, they will also be good at disguising it.

Matt Ridley: formerly with *The Economist*; columnist for the *Sunday Telegraph*; author of "The Red Queen: sex and the evolution of human nature" (Viking Penguin).

Why some very old questions will need new answers in 1995

John Maddox

Scientific enterprise everywhere is under increasing pressure to deliver marketable goods. It is therefore piquantly ironic that 1994 ended with two discoveries likely, in the year ahead, to enliven researchers' interests in fields that are almost ostentatiously separate from wealth creation. One bears on the origin of human beings, the other on the origin of the universe.

The outlines of human evolution have been reasonably well worked out in the past three decades. The ancestors of human beings were also relatives of the ancestors of the great apes, the chimpanzee, gorilla and orangutan. Hominid fossils from 2m-3m years ago and assigned to the species called by the generic name *Australopithecus* reveal an unsurprising pattern of evolution: the brain-case gets bigger, the physical frame more erect and the competence of the emergent animal more evident from the inspection of the fossil bones. All that happened in Africa.

The new development, in September 1994, was the discovery (by Tim White of the University of California at Berkeley) in a long-buried river valley in central Ethiopia of fossil parts of several early hominids living within 100,000 years or so of 4.5m years ago. The species from which the fossils come has even been given a name: *Australopithecus ramidus*.

These discoveries must change and refine our view of human evolution. First, they carry it back in time, by more than a million years. Second, they span the time-gap between the previously oldest hominid fossils and the divergence of the human line from the great apes of perhaps 6m years ago. Darwinists scorn the phrase "missing link", but these fossils are it. And human beings' closest relative is confirmed as the chimpanzee, not the gorilla.

The new date is earlier than the

Dr White...

...and his ancestor

onset of the Pleistocene ice ages, although not much. The landscape of central Ethiopia 4.5m years ago was wooded savannah, neither desert (as it is now) nor tropical forest (where chimpanzees have settled down). That means that the newly discovered fossils are incompatible with the belief that human evolution was triggered by the onset of the Ice Age.

There are more subtle questions to be decided, many of which will be fiercely argued in 1995. Insect species apart, *Homo sapiens* is probably the youngest identifiable species on the surface of the earth. Molecular geneticists have been able to work that out by using the natural rate of genetic change as a kind of clock. That fixes the antiquity of *H. sapiens* at about 200,000 years, or less than 5% of the age of the fossils now found.

The first questions to be argued will be about what happened in the remaining 95% of the time between *A. ramidus* and the emergence of human beings. The immediate predecessor of human

beings is known as *Homo erectus* and goes back perhaps a million years. Before that are several species of hominids labelled australopithecenes and including *Australopithecus africanus* (discovered by Raymond Dart 70 years ago) and the older *Australopithecus afarensis* from northern Ethiopia. Now there may be enough material to reconstruct the course of hominid evolution as far as *H. erectus*, suggesting what changes in the environment of Africa gave that process impetus.

That will be a heart-rending process, unassisted by fossil DNA of the kind that allowed Steven Spielberg's film-makers to reconstruct the dinosaurs for "Jurassic Park". Probably, it will emerge that there were many unsuccessful evolutionary lunges in the direction of *H. sapiens* of the kind represented by the European Neanderthals of 100,000 years ago. Already, the early contemporary of *H. erectus* called *Homo habilis* seems vulnerable as a member of the evolutionary line. Beyond that is the question of where *Pan*,

John Maddox: editor of *Nature*.

Virgo will question big bang

the chimpanzee, came from. We may learn more after Mr White returns from this winter's season in Ethiopia.

What's 10 billion years?

Meanwhile, cosmology will spring into life again, largely because of measurements of the distance to the Virgo cluster of galaxies reported at the end of 1994. For many years, the proper description of the universe has been hampered by uncertainty about its rate of expansion. On the standard assumption that the universe began as a Big Bang at some stage in the past, the expansion rate determines when that happened; the faster the expansion, the younger the universe must be.

For some decades, cosmologists have been unable to decide on the expansion rate, meaning that the age of the universe might be anywhere between 10 billion and 20 billion years (in round numbers). The possibility that the true age of the universe might be only 10 billion years has been an uncomfortable thought: there are many stars in our own galaxy older than that.

The new measurements will magnify this discomfort—except among the small band of people (Sir Fred Hoyle the most prominent among them) who have always been sceptical of the Big Bang. But the argument is a long way from being decided.

It is not quite the scandal it may seem that, since the early 1960s, cosmology has lived with such an essential doubt about the age of the universe. The problem is not so much one of measuring the speed of distant galaxies (which can be done accurately enough by measurements of their spectra) but of telling how far away they are.

Since the Hubble Space Telescope was first designed (early in the 1970s), one of its goals has been the refinement of the yardsticks used to estimate distance, and therefore time, in the universe. The designers realised that the telescope would make it possible to pick out, in distant galaxies, stars known in our galaxy as "Cepheid variables", which vary rhythmically in light output on a schedule determined by their intrinsic brightness. Thus they should make good "standard candles", as astronomers say.

That is what has now been done. Cepheid variables have been picked out in two separate galaxies of the Virgo cluster, and yield essentially the same rate of expansion for the universe, whose age is placed at the low end of the permissible range, 10 billion years or so.

The first outcome will be meticulous argument about the interpretation of the measurements. The Virgo cluster of galaxies (to which our galaxy may or may not belong) includes hundreds of nearby galaxies apparently being drawn together by their gravitational attraction for each other.

The interpretation of the measurements may be contaminated by this collective motion of the galaxies in the Virgo cluster, although that seems improbable. That, and the almost certain antiquity of known stars in the globular clusters of our own galaxy, is likely to downgrade the Big Bang from a "theory" to a "hypothesis" before 1995 is out.

Among astronomers, there will be ironical rejoicing that in the search for Cepheid variables in Virgo, the Hubble Space Telescope (even as restored to something near its design performance by a crew of astronauts) was beaten to the result by a ground-based telescope in Hawaii, which yielded the first successful measurement.

That does not prove that ground-based astronomy is best, but rather is a sign of how much better a space telescope could be built with the techniques now being used.

More generally, the likelihood that 1995 will be enlivened by arguments about the origin of the universe and of human beings will not, in itself, lift the pressure on scientists to do useful things.

But these two reminders that science also has things to say about the philosophical question of where we came from may lift the spirits of people who might otherwise harbour suspicions of being undervalued.

That damn'd explosive Internet

John Browning

By the middle of 1994, the Internet connected over 2.2m computers, serving 25m people. Just one part of the network (albeit a high-volume part) carried over 12 trillion bytes of data—the equivalent of about 40m books. And for all that the network is still doubling in size and volume each year.

All of this raises two fundamental questions. First, why should so many people want to throw themselves into an electronic world created by nerds, for nerds? And given that they do, how can the network sustain its pace of growth?

Part of the answer to the first question is simple fashion. Young people today embrace technology for some of the same reasons that their parents embraced rock and roll. It's new; it's exciting; and it makes the old folks nervous. But a more fundamental reason is that the nerds who built the Internet have found new ways of meeting a basic human need: the desire to communicate with other people.

Underlying the Internet are three basic means of communication. E-mail sends electronic messages from one person to another—like letters, but capable of crossing the Atlantic in 15 minutes or so. File transfers move bulk data from one computer to another. And so-called telnet services enable someone to connect to a computer miles away, and, network speed permitting, use its services as if it were sitting on his desktop.

In their original form, such services were next to impossible for those without a degree in computer science. But in the past two years, new software has hidden most of the Internet's complexity, and made it as easy to use as pointing a mouse at the appropriate picture on the screen, and click—the world's databases are at your fingertips.

With these capabilities, the Internet becomes post office, printing press and meeting place all in one. Some use the Internet to exchange letters with loved ones. Others connect to remote computers to play games, or to do research. Others join groups to discuss sex or semiconductors. America's Securities and Exchange Commission is using the network to distrib-

Make mine a modem, please

ute reports on corporate finance. NASA distributes photographs from space. And farmers can wallow in a database called "Not Just Cows".

Technically, the reason that the Internet can cope with such helter-skelter

growth is that it was conceived originally by America's Defence Department, way back in the late 1960s, as a prototype of a network that could withstand a nuclear strike. This means that the Internet has no central authority and no central switching facilities which could be wiped out by pre-emptive strike, or choked by unexpected growth.

Instead, the Internet is a network of networks, linked together by a collection of voluntarily agreed technical standards (notably TCP/IP, if you must know the jargon). Each company, university or organisation is responsible for communications among its own computers, and all co-operate in communication between networks—with much duplication and re-routing.

Two sound management maxims underpin the Internet's rapid international growth. First, the Internet is a sort of barter economy, in which the services each network provides are repaid in kind by its counterparts. Second, the Internet's organisation naturally pushes responsibility for any given problem down to the lowest level at which it might be solved—which is something all managers might learn from to help cope with the fast-changing complexity which the Internet helps to create.

Denizens of the Net

John Browning

At some point, most networks sink under their own complexity. Any personal-computer user will know how hard it is to keep track of all the information on his hard disk, and to remember how to make his word processor, spreadsheet and other software work together. With networks, that complexity grows exponentially. Two technologies that can help tame the mess are "objects" and "agents".

An object, or object-oriented software, to use the full name, is information that knows what can be done with itself. To edit a conventional electronic document, for example, a person must find the appropriate word processor, start it up and set to work. But with an object, the person sends the object a message to find its own word processor, start it up and get ready to be edited.

This may not sound like much, but

amid the complexity of large networks and compound documents (which contain, say, spreadsheets which must be updated as well as text to be edited) even a little help can enable people to do a lot more work. So all of the big computer companies—including Microsoft, Apple and IBM—are working on the standards that will enable objects to communicate with each other in simple ways to help tame networks.

One of the more ambitious applications of objects comes from Lloyd's of London, an international insurance market. The forms that need to be filled out to buy or sell insurance are a nightmare. They must cover highly specialised risks ranging from a sinking boat to burning buildings, and they must meet different regulations in just about every market they are sold in. About a third are typically filled in wrong. So Lloyd's IT staff is working to

build objects that can automatically check to see that the right information has been entered for whatever risk is being insured.

Agents are objects that don't wait to be told what to do. They have their own goals, and wander about networks, hopping from machine to machine, working on behalf of their masters, who are off doing other jobs.

One exemplary agent is being created by John Evans of News Data Corporation, part of the News Corp empire. Mr Evans hopes eventually to sell an agent, named Oliver after his dog. This intelligent agent knows enough about travel and travel databases to retrieve automatically, for example, a list of all flights from London to San Francisco on July 31st—so doing the simplest, and most time-consuming part of the job that a human travel agent does.

Gene therapy

The World in 1995 asked Daniel Cohen, director of the Centre d'Etude du Polymorphisme Humain in Paris and the man responsible for first mapping the human genome, to predict where this research will lead

There is a tacit contract between science and society to make life better. Science is also asked to answer fundamental questions on the nature of the universe.These two contracts come together in the research on the human genome map. Genetics will, in all probability, open a new era for humanity, with a dramatic improvement in the way we treat disease. The human genome is being decrypted—with equally dramatic increases in our volume of scientific knowledge. The genome can be compared to a magnetic band enclosed in each of our cells which contains all the information required for living organisms to function and to adapt to their environment. All of the cells contain the same program that has been inherited from our parents from the time the first cell is created by the fusion of the sperm and the egg. This strand of information comprises three billion characters. But there are only four variants: A,T,C,G linearly assembled (...ATATCTGCATCGTGTACA...).

Within this sequence some segments determine the make-up of individual cells. These segments are called "genes". They can be compared to words, although they are 10 to 50,000 characters long instead of five to 15 in our human language. And, as in a dictionary, these genetic words make up the collective human genome of 100,000-200,000 genes.

A given gene can have several slightly different spellings varying among individuals; this is called "polymorphism" and is responsible for the charm of humanity. What a nightmare life would be if everyone were identical. Unfortunately, certain spellings cause disease. Most human diseases are linked to gene spelling. In some cases it is a real misspelling: the gene is wrong and inevitably induces disease in the carrier. Such diseases are called monofactorial diseases; there are about 3,000 such genetic diseases, mostly apparent from childhood. In other cases, the spelling is not singularly ~nonsible for the disease, but causes ~when combined with ~l factors. Most of these ~adults. They are called ~eases. These include, ~diovascular diseases,

diabetes, asthma, obesity, cancer, nervous-system disorders: most diseases have a genetic component.

The race has been on, therefore, to read the genome. This is called "mapping and sequencing". The first effort has concentrated on the identification of the genes involved in human disease. Many of these genes have been identified, but it will probably take 15 years for us to track all of them. This "mapping" is essential if we are to

"The inhuman use of genetics will occur only if society itself becomes inhuman."

treat genetic disorders. Until it is completed, there is no possibility of understanding the mechanism underlying these diseases.

When the genes are found they help not only to understand the intimate mechanism of the disease, they also offer a clue to the development of a cure. Indeed, in most cases until now, medicine was not able to cure a disease but only to treat its symptoms. Understanding the exact make-up of the genes now offers the possibility of a targeted approach to robust therapeutic cures. It should be possible to compensate for a misspelt gene by grafting a good one into patients.

This is possible through a new body of techniques called "gene therapy". To do this, as always, scientists try to mimic nature, which usually uses a virus. A virus has a tiny genome with perhaps 10,000 characters containing a few genes. Viruses are able to penetrate cells and reproduce themselves at the expense of the living cell, which is killed. It is possible to modify the virus genome to retain its aptitude to enter cells, but without damaging them. It is

also possible to integrate new genes in such modified viruses. Such inoffensive and gene-grafted viruses could enter the cell without altering it, and express the correctly spelled gene, compensating for the badly spelt gene present in the patient.

Successful results have been obtained in some children with diseases such as inherited immunodeficiency or haemophilia. In these cases, the good gene was grafted externally to the patient in cells that were extracted and then re-implanted. Unsuccessful trials were done for cystic fibrosis, one of the most frequent monofactorial disorders. In this case, patients were inoculated with the modified viruses. It is believed that the patients reject the virus using their immunological defence. It is therefore intended to create a stealth virus, invisible to this natural defence mechanism.

Potentially, gene therapy will be able to cure cancer. Cancer cells can be easily killed when they express a gene known to sensitise them to certain chemical agents. Such genes can be grafted into tumour cells.

This is of enormous consequence for cancer therapy. 1995 will probably be full of news about this approach to cancer. But it is unknown if gene therapy will have a permanent impact on genetic disease. A lot of effort is being devoted to compensate for the ill effects of the wrong genes by imitating the good gene effects with small molecules which can be created by modern engineering. These beneficial agents could be created at a cost low enough to make them available on a large scale, to the general population.

This therapeutic research is the final goal of most genetic study and justifies significant investment. It is essential to keep this kind of genetic research going. I am convinced that the inhuman use of genetics will occur only if society itself becomes inhuman. In that case, the consequences of genetic research would be negligible.

Therefore, the most important point is to fight not only disease, but the dogmatism which is at the root of most inhuman behaviour. We must also remember that the benefits of science should not only apply to the quarter of humanity that lives in the northern hemisphere, but to the entire world. This should also be implied in the contract between science and society.

Who needs steel?

Matt Bacon

Some little pigs' houses may be made out of straw but next year smart pigs will choose materials developed for the aerospace business. Stuff that worked well on the B-2 bomber might work very nicely in the building of more urbane structures, such as bridges and office blocks.

Composites combine the best properties of several components—glass fibres, resin, carbon—into a single super-material, greater than the sum of its parts.

Two things are bringing advanced composites to the building business. First, there is not much money in aerospace these days. Second, companies have figured out how to make glass fibres better and cheaper than ever before. Glass is a surprisingly strong and tough material, but engineers have tended to ignore it because, compared with carbon fibre, it is heavy. New techniques have now revolutionised glass-fibre composites. Soon, for example, large structural parts of your car may be made from woven, shaped glass fibre.

Already, there are all-composite bridges in Britain and America. Using a process called pultrusion, in which glass fibres are pulled through a plastic resin bath, and then through a shaped die in which the resin hardens, it is possible to make long beams with complex shapes out of glass-reinforced plastic composite. These beams can be locked together in various ways, to form the deck of a bridge, or the floor of a building. And although each beam is more expensive than its steel equivalent, it is much lighter, easy to assemble quickly—and of course, it will never rust.

One British company, Maunsell Structural Plastics, has gone as far as to develop a small family of standard glass reinforced plastic parts, like grown-up Meccano, which can be joined to create everything from bridges to the company's own headquarters at the River Severn crossing. Maunsell has also recently completed Britain's first all-composite road bridge, in Gloucester, using the system. The light weight of the material was the crucial factor in keeping the cost and construction time to a minimum.

In 1995 Maunsell will build a bridge incorporating an underlying steel structure beneath a composite cladding. Upgrading the bridge to prolong its life, or change its capabilities, will be a simple matter of replacing the cladding alone, rather than the whole thing.

In Germany, a chemical company, BASF, has turned to aerospace-grade carbon fibre for bridge-building. BASF replaces the steel cables of suspension bridges with resin tie-rods reinforced with pultruded carbon fibre. Again, they are far lighter and stronger than a steel cable, allowing bridges to be longer and assembled more quickly—even flown to the site in one piece by helicopter.

But it is in Japan that carbon fibre is really making progress as a construction material. Already, seven bridges in the sea-coast province of Ishikawa have been built using carbon fibre reinforcing bars, which are invulnerable to salt sea-spray. The Florida Department of Transportation is collaborating on carbon reinforced bridges like those in Ishikawa. In California, carbon fibre is being used as a cladding on buildings to protect against earthquakes.

Architects will use these advanced materials to achieve dramatic visual effects impossible with traditional materials. Glass-fibre textiles, coated in muck-and-water-shedding Teflon, provide an astounding tent-like roof for the new Denver International Airport. At Llangollen, Welsh bards will declaim beneath the drum-taut PVC and glass roof of a new Eisteddfod Centre.

Home, straw home

Of course, not all composites have to be high-tech. A form of building that will be growing in popularity in 1995 uses the oldest composite material of them all—mud and straw. In the United States a company called Out on Bale specialises in the construction of straw houses. The bales of straw are piled into walls, like huge bricks, and carefully coated with cement or stucco. In the dry south-western states, the walls are soon baked to a waterproof render by the sun. Inside, the house is cool, protected by the excellent insulation of feet-thick straw walls. Expect to see many more straw-house dwellers in 1995, unafraid of any huffing wolf.

Not too many babies, just too many oldies

Norman Macrae

For the past 40 years we have been told that the world is breeding too many babies. The forecast figures of disaster have proved dramatically untrue, as did the previous wails in the 1930s that the world was producing too few. The detailed forecasts of huge future births by the 1994 world population conference at Cairo will also prove wrong, but don't be too cheerful. The world is on course to preserve too many old people instead.

The peak of nonsense was talked at a previous UN world population conference, inappropriately held in Ceausescu's Romania in 1974. Experts then talked of a desperate need to check a birth rate which they said was about to propel the annual growth of world population above 3.5% a year. Actually, so far as can be told from still inadequate statistics, the top percentage rise in population ever known was probably just over 2.1% at the tail end of rich countries' post-war baby boom, circa 1971.

Since then the annual percentage rise has been slowly declining. The 1994 Cairo conference was told (probably inaccurately) that the world's total population was now 5.7 billion, and it was hyped that last year's rise of 86m was the highest absolute figure ever. Note that 86m is only a smidgen above a rise

Matt Bacon: science and technology editor of *Focus* magazine.

Norman Macrae: columnist for the *Sunday Times*, formerly with *The Economist*.

of 1.5%. That is below 1971's probable 2.1%, and way below the 3.5% about which the Bucharest conference agonised. This continuing drop in percentage growth of population means that the absolute figure of growth will start to drop within about three years; and we will then move, more quickly than the pressure groups and "experts" at Cairo thought, to the stage where birth rates themselves are no longer bringing a net increase in world population. This stage is naturally reached after the average woman has started to have less than two children during her life. She is already down to, or below, two in North America, Western Europe, ex-communist Europe and the "dragon" en-richening countries of East Asia.

We have now reached the stage where the average number of children per woman is falling fast in most of the world. The rate has come down sharply, with increasing prosperity, even in Catholic Latin America. It has come down (for different reasons) in China, India and Bangladesh. The high rates of six or seven children per woman now only exist in Africa and some parts of the Islamic world. The sharpest fall occurs when most girls are at school at the time of their first menstruation. A World Bank study finds that in areas where there are no girls in secondary school, the average woman has seven children; when even 40% of girls go to secondary education, the average drops to three children.

The education of women in poor countries is going to rise enormously, aided by cheap two-way computer-assisted learning. The girl in a remote area will respond to a question put to her by a computer sited continents away. The computer will work out her learning pattern from her answer, and decide which question to put next.

Poor peasant countries, with 75% of their workforce in labour-intensive agriculture, breed more children to do useful work in the fields; with modern agricultural techniques, countries can feed themselves with only 3% of workers on the land, and the days of 75% peasant countries are ending. The new sorts of jobs becoming available tend to offer more employment to women than to men, so motherhood gives way to money-making.

The poor countries that grow richer will be those that follow the free market and freer-trading route to efficiency. This has a provenly bigger

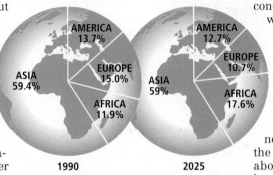

Who lives where...

1990 — AMERICA 13.7%, EUROPE 15.0%, ASIA 59.4%, AFRICA 11.9%

2025 — AMERICA 12.7%, EUROPE 10.7%, ASIA 59%, AFRICA 17.6%

effect on birth control than do do-gooders trying to distribute condoms free. Because of import barriers and inept distribution, condoms cost about 25 times as much in once-rubber-producing Brazil as in freer market lands.

If we continue with UN population conferences every ten years (1974, 1984, 1994), the conference in 2024 will produce the opposite panic to today's—that

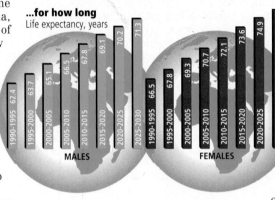

...for how long
Life expectancy, years

MALES: 1990-1995 62.4, 1995-2000 63.7, 2000-2005 65.1, 2005-2010 66.5, 2010-2015 67.8, 2015-2020 69.1, 2020-2025 70.2, 2025-2030 71.3

FEMALES: 1990-1995 66.5, 1995-2000 67.8, 2000-2005 69.3, 2005-2010 70.7, 2010-2015 72.1, 2015-2020 73.6, 2020-2025 74.9, 2025-2030 76

we are breeding too few babies. But we will by then have made the awful discovery that we are keeping alive too many of the world's old people. Thanks to the computer, microsurgery and the revolution in genetic knowledge, we are going to advance in the next few decades to making nearly all diseases (including cancer, AIDS and heart trouble) rather

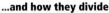

...and how they divide

1990 — 75+, 70-74, 65-69, 55-64, 45-54, 35-44, 25-34, 15-24, 0-14, 0-9

2025 — 75+, 70-74, 65-69, 55-64, 45-54, 35-44, 30-34, 20-29, 10-19, 0-9

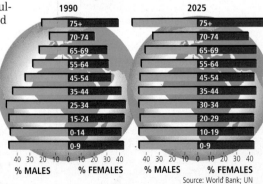

40 30 20 10 0 10 20 30 40 — % MALES / % FEMALES

40 30 20 10 0 10 20 30 40 — % MALES / % FEMALES

Source: World Bank; UN

easily curable. This revolution will not conquer most of the process of ageing—with luck, we will become enlightened enough to stop it doing any such terrible thing. But most citizens in rich countries probably will start to live through until whatever becomes a man's or a woman's natural term (about 95 years?). Some of us will live through to some age like 115.

The largest single block of people now in rich countries are those born in the post-war baby boom from 1946 to about 1970. If these people start living longer, there will be a huge number of 80-to-95-year-olds in the advanced lands from 2026 to 2065. This will be happening when we have not even begun to put systems in place to deal with them.

State pension finances in all welfare democracies are heading for bankrupt chaos. We have made medical care a universal right, free at the point of delivery for the old, thus rendering demand infinite from hypochondriacs. Old people demand several times more medical care than fit younger ones. We have abandoned the culture whereby granny lives with the family, at just the wrong moment.

The age bulge in poorer countries will come later. Their population surge (the one that pressure groups at Cairo panicked about) came with the marvellous improvements in curbing infant mortality in about 1965-95. That will give them an impossible surge in 80-to-95-year-olds in about 2045 to 2090. They won't feel able to finance them, and changes in morality will occur.

The "too many babies" scare has already changed morality about abortion and contraception in a scary way. In the past 40 years "liberals", especially the most aggressive members of what used to be called the gentler sex, have taken to the idea of killing (aborting) inconvenient unborn babies in the womb; they now regard this as an inalienable women's right, where 40 years ago everybody regarded it with horror. In the next 40 years there will be the same move to regard as "moral" euthanasia for many of you when you become great-granny or great-grandpa. State-aided pensions will probably become fixed-term annuities; you will have to pay more if you choose a later euthanasia date than 90 or so. Increasingly, medical practitioners will be told not to keep "hopeless case" old people officiously alive.